Through the Looking Glass

Observations in the Early Childhood Classroom

SECOND EDITION

Sheryl Nicolson
Saddleback College

Susan G. Shipstead
California State University, Fullerton

Merrill, an imprint of
Prentice Hall
Upper Saddle River, New Jersey   Columbus, Ohio

Library of Congress Cataloging-in-Publication Data

Nicolson, Sheryl.
   Through the looking glass : observations in the early childhood
classroom / Sheryl Nicolson, Susan G. Shipstead. — 2nd ed.
     p. cm.
   Includes bibliographical references (p.   ) and index.
   ISBN 0-13-651993-8 (alk. paper)
    1. Observation (Educational method)   2. Early childhood education.
  3. Child development.   I. Shipstead, Susan G. II. Title.
LB1027.28.N53   1998
372.21'072—dc21   97-16725
                                                            CIP

Cover photo: Susan G. Shipstead
Editor: Ann Castel Davis
Production Editor: Linda Hillis Bayma
Production Coordination: Spectrum Publisher Services, Inc.
Design Coordinator: Julia Zonneveld Van Hook
Cover Designer: Russ Maselli
Production Manager: Patricia A. Tonneman
Illustrations: Jane Lopez
Director of Marketing: Kevin Flanagan
Marketing Manager: Suzanne Stanton
Advertising/Marketing Coordinator: Julie Shough

This book was set in New Baskerville by TCSystems and was printed and bound by Quebecor Printing/Book Press. The cover was printed by Phoenix Color Corp.

© 1998 by Prentice-Hall, Inc.
Simon & Schuster/A Viacom Company
Upper Saddle River, New Jersey 07458

Earlier edition © 1994 by Macmillan Publishing Company.

Photo credits: All photos copyrighted by individuals or companies listed. Brian Cummings, pp. 12, 104, 126, 164; Susan G. Shipstead, pp. 2, 8, 14, 16, 25, 32, 37, 55, 58, 61, 62, 69, 80, 88, 92, 94, 100, 108, 112, 117, 128, 134, 139, 144, 148, 152, 154, 160, 172, 179, 186, 192, 203, 210, 213, 222, 231, 240, 246, 254, 263, 270, 273, 274, 290, 294, 296, 304, 311, 312, 317, 322, 328, 333.

Printed in the United States of America

10 9 8 7

ISBN 0-13-651993-8

Prentice-Hall International (UK) Limited, *London*
Prentice-Hall of Australia Pty. Limited, *Sydney*
Prentice-Hall Canada Inc., *Toronto*
Prentice-Hall Hispanomericana, S. A., *Mexico*
Prentice-Hall of India Private Limited, *New Delhi*
Prentice-Hall of Japan, Inc., *Tokyo*
Simon & Schuster Asia Pte, Ltd., *Singapore*
Editora Prentice-Hall do Brasil, Ltda., *Rio de Janeiro*

Dedication

For my husband, Norm, whose gentle love and constant support made this book and so much more possible. For my Mom and Dad, each with special gifts that I've woven into my life. And for all children, especially those who are close to me—Christopher, Ryan, and Garrett. May your lives be enriched by teachers who see clearly through the looking glass.—S. N.

In my life I am blessed with a great love, Patrick,
Two treasured children, Matthew and Maggie,
And the rich memories of my parents.
To you five, I dedicate this work.   S. G. S.

Preface

In the fall of 1988 we taught a course on observation in the early childhood classroom, and therein we sowed the seeds of the first edition of *Through the Looking Glass*. The second edition you hold in your hands is the product of our continued commitment to write a book on observation that unites solid methodological instruction with a broad understanding of children's development. We have found that learning *how* to observe while also paying close attention to *what* to observe encourages educational practitioners in using their skills to full potential. This book maintains a close relationship between observing, understanding what one observes, and improving the educational curriculum and environment.

New to This Edition

Because our goal in *Through the Looking Glass* is to integrate observation and child development within a professional context, we have included several new, helpful features in this edition. Chapters 2 through 13 present an ethic from the National Association for the Education of Young Children's "Code of Ethical Conduct" and a concrete application to connect our daily work with our professional values as early childhood educators. Chapters 2 and 3, describing highlights of development during the preschool and primary grade years, serve to establish a common ground of information for both knowledgeable and novice readers in the field of child development. Our revised "Growth Indicators" of child development are concrete guides for *what* to observe and are now reprinted in Appendix B for easy access. In each chapter presenting an observational method, we offer two detailed examples, one from preschool and one from a primary grade, to model how educators effectively study issues in classrooms, interpret the data, and initiate follow-through plans; several are new to the second edition. Brief vignettes at the beginning of each chapter ask the reader to examine a question or problem that anticipates the chapter's content. Practice Activities and Action Projects provide the reader abundant opportunities to acquire expertise in the observational process, and we hope our readers will integrate information into their personal storehouses of knowledge as they ponder the final section of each chapter, Take a Moment to Reflect.

Upon completion of the original manuscript, we flipped a coin to determine the first author's name. We hope our readers remember that the order was set by chance and is a fair reflection of the teamwork that produced *Through the Looking Glass.*

Contents

PART III

Observing Children, Teachers, Interactions, and Environments

CHAPTER 10

Observing Children and Teachers at Work by Using Tally Event Sampling

CHAPTER 11

Observing Children and Teachers at Work by Using Time Sampling

Special Acknowledgments

This work builds on many years of memorable and invaluable experiences in the field of early childhood education. From my beginning college days and continuing into the present, my life has been touched by numerous caring and committed professionals. I especially want to thank my sister, Linda Crosswhite, for her wise counsel and thoughtful suggestions; the Cooperative Urban Teacher Education Program sponsored by the University of Missouri at Kansas City for teaching me to recognize, respect, and appreciate varied cultural perspectives; Janece Kline for facilitating my transition from elementary to preschool teaching; Jonathan Knaupp at Arizona State University for excellent mentoring; Roberta Berns for her inspiration and encouragement to write; Susan Shipstead, co-author, for her incredible emotional strength and ability always to be her best; and the many children and college students with whom I have had the privilege of working—they have been my true teachers!

—Sheryl Nicolson

Many of my contributions to *Through the Looking Glass* have direct threads running to significant people of my past. I send global appreciation to the many children, teachers, directors, and students with whom I have had the good fortune to work. I am indebted to Courtney Cazden for a masterful class on observation at Harvard. My work at High/Scope Educational Research Foundation was enhanced by experiences with Dave Weikart, Clay Shouse, Carole Thomson, Joanna Phinney, Mary Hohmann, Linda Rogers, and Bernie Banet; I salute one and all. I thank my Stanford heroes, John Flavell and Dick Snow, for their exemplary instruction, guidance, and fine human nature. The professional and wise leadership of Judy Ramirez has graced my years in Child and Adolescent Studies at California State University, Fullerton.

The contract for the second edition of this book coincided with my dear father's terminal illness and death. As I look back at nine months as his primary caregiver, I'm not sure how I managed to get my work done, but I am certain I could not have done so without the unwavering love and support of my family; my friends, Mary Terry and Bev DeNicola; and my partner, Sherry Nicolson. My gratitude knows no bounds.

—Susan G. Shipstead

Collective Acknowledgments

We wish to thank our students, friends, and colleagues who offered valuable suggestions for our second edition, especially the students in observation classes at Saddleback College and the students in practicums at California State University, Fullerton. We extend our gratitude to the many friends and educators who contributed ideas or welcomed us into their schools and classrooms: Ingrid Andrews, Judy Austerman, Gayle Bendeck, Sheri Bentley, Cal Burt, Pauline Dinger, Heather Eazell, Tarry Goeden, Tannis Gibson, Ellen Grangaard, Dillon Henry, Peter Hernandez, Jennifer Jourdan, Michael Kohler, Joann Kronick, Martie Lubetkin, Bonnie Maxey, Julie Maxwell, Kate Nicolson, Terry Petersen, Jody Prichard, Pat Reisch, Shannon Rhodes, David Rover, Jeff Schiller, Georgie Tiernan, and Bev Vargish. The writing of this revision was assisted by the helpful research done by Mitzi Fletcher and Kathy Shepard; we acknowledge you both. The library staffs at Saddleback College and California State University, Fullerton, offered time-saving help, and they, too, have our thanks.

Revising the manuscript for the second edition is only half the tremendous task of creating a new book. We would like to express our appreciation to those who have carried out the publishing half. We thank the fine staff at Merrill, in particular Ann Davis, Editor; Pat Grogg, Editorial Assistant; Linda Bayma, Production Editor; Carol Sykes, Developmental Editor; Anthony Magnacca, Photo Researcher; and Kevin Flanagan, Director of Marketing. Our book moved smoothly and rapidly through production thanks to Kelly Ricci, Production Manager at Spectrum Publisher Services.

The reviewers of our second edition have offered important suggestions, insights, and information. Their various regional perspectives, backgrounds, and experiences were beneficial to us as we worked to make revisions that meet the needs of all observers. Your contributions were most helpful, and we thank you! Our reviewers included Teresa T. Harris, James Madison University; Kathy Nolan, University of Alabama; Colleen K. Randel, University of Texas at Tyler; and Pauline Davey Zeece, University of Nebraska, Lincoln.

Preparing the Looking Glass

Welcome to *Through the Looking Glass!* In Part I, "Preparing the Looking Glass," you will build your foundation for effective observations of children, teachers, interactions, and environments. Your observations will be sabotaged from the beginning if you do not first discover the value and role of observation in the early childhood classroom and understand at least the highlights of child development. These are the *why* and *what* keys of observation.

Part I contains three chapters. The first, "Toward an Educational Approach," begins your journey to sound observation by exploring reasons for observing, appropriate topics to observe, general guidelines for classroom observation, and observers' subjectivity.

The next two chapters, "Highlights of Development During the Preschool Years" and "Highlights of Development During the Primary Grade Years," are included because seeing a child's behavior is not necessarily the same as understanding it. An observer might see a child engage in a certain activity, but unless the observer understands the behavior within the context of child development, he or she is severely limited in planning appropriate and supportive experiences. Therefore, in order to establish a common ground of information for knowledgeable and novice readers in the field of child development, Chapters 2 and 3 describe highlights of development during the preschool and primary grade years. Given the bulk of information to cover in even condensed form, two chapters are devoted to this goal; recognize, however, that development is gradual and individual differences abound. The break between the preschool and primary years is not abrupt; for example, a 4-year-old child in preschool may be more advanced in some areas than a 5-year-old child in kindergarten. In these two chapters you will study what to observe, as well as Growth Indicators that summarize the key points and provide specific reminders.

In subsequent chapters you learn the methodology of classroom observation, the *how* keys, but for your initial foray into the field in Part I, you focus on the foundations of why you should observe and what you will see.

1

Toward an Educational Approach

Imagine you are an early childhood educator in a preschool classroom. This morning, you are standing outside near the swings. As you turn your head, you catch a glimpse of Annie whisking the red tractor away from Tajima.

- What are your initial thoughts?
- What details do your senses absorb?
- Do you smell the first hints of lunch about to be served, which might have reminded the youngster of a fleeting opportunity to get the treasured toy?
- What do you see the child do?
- What do you hear the child say?
- Did the child have the toy first and simply reclaim it?
- Or had the child been wandering around the play yard when she grabbed the toy in an unprovoked act?

Even in an ordinary situation such as this, you may accurately or inaccurately appraise the situation and respond appropriately or inappropriately. Your skills as an observer make a difference in your guidance and education of this young child.

Continuing on this flight of fantasy, consider what you might know about the child and this behavior.

- Is this the first time you have seen this child grab a toy from another, or has this deed been a frequent classroom concern?
- Have you noticed a pattern of preceding events that predictably prompt this act, such as rejection by other children?
- What circumstances or expectations outside of school might have promoted this seizure? For example, is the child dreadfully lonely now that a beloved sibling has gone off to college? Or is grabbing ignored in the home so that it has become the child's common strategy to procure a desired object?

Stop and think for a moment about what else you want to know about this child and the episode before you decide how to respond. What major piece of this puzzle is not yet in place? What information is crucial to your thoughtful and appropriate response?

Your understanding of the child's developmental level is essential to the selection of a supportive response. If the child is a young 2-year-old whose energies have advanced gross motor skills more than language, you would evaluate the event and respond differently than if the child is a 5- or 6-year-old with well-developed language skills. One of your jobs as an educator of young children is to understand child development in enough detail so that your responses are individually based and ensure future growth.

For those who have studied child development and early childhood curriculum, the classroom provides opportunities to apply useful information. By understanding the milestones of physical, cognitive, psychosocial, and creative development and by applying a variety of observational methods, novices can enter the field of early childhood education equipped with the ability to plan activities, experiences, and environments that enhance children's growth. With experience, well-trained teachers can select materials that challenge individual children at opportune moments. They can suggest and organize activities that encourage children to think differently about familiar experiences. They can respond to problem behaviors with flexible strategies. They can view children's similarities and differences with a broad perspective. They can improve their own teaching effectiveness. They can guide children's social growth. The list goes on and on.

You can be a good early childhood educator if you provide developmentally appropriate materials and experiences for children; *developmentally appropriate* means that the selection is based on the age, stage, cultural, and individual needs of the children in the program (Bredekamp & Copple, 1997). Set your sights higher. You can be a remarkable teacher if you understand child development and are able to provide materials and experiences that optimize each child's total development. The key is observation.

Ambitions of This Book

In the beginning of this chapter, you imagined a preschool scenario and engaged your mind in thoughtful considerations. Learning is not passive. One of your jobs as a reader is to stop and think about the points, examples, and questions raised in this book. Make the information your own by thinking about how it relates to your unique store of knowledge and experience. Expect to answer questions in the book and raise more of your own. To enhance this process, each chapter begins with a classroom vignette and ends with an invitation to reflect on pertinent topics.

Beyond working as an active reader, you will be asked to participate in practice activities and apply what you have learned in each chapter. Search for additional opportunities to explore topics and ideas new to you. Look, listen, and watch the young children around you—in grocery stores, in shopping malls, and in your own and friends' homes. Plan field trips to observe model early childhood education centers. Integrate your new knowledge with your own experience base. How does it fit? What questions do you have? Are there inconsistencies? Explore these ideas.

The purpose of this book on observation for early childhood educators is to teach the application of an array of observational methods within a child-development framework. A strong foundation in child development is a must for observation. Therefore, the beginning chapters of this book highlight the general physical, cognitive, psychosocial, and creative growth patterns of preschool (ages 2½ to 5) and primary grade (ages 5 to 8) children, drawing on developmental theory and research. Continued emphasis on the comprehensive development of preschool and primary grade children is intertwined throughout the examples, applications, and interpretations of observations in each chapter.

Early childhood educators receive professional guidance, support, and stimulation from the National Association for the Education of Young Children (NAEYC), founded in 1926. The organization prepared a Code of Ethical Conduct for its members in 1992 (see Appendix A), and *Through the Looking Glass* aims to connect this code to the classroom by including an ethic and application in Chapters 2 through 13. Ethics are not lofty dreams; they are values brought to life through action on a daily basis.

Throughout this book, the goal is to present the methodological tools to tackle specific questions and concerns in early childhood classrooms with skill. Competence is gained in observational skills by studying each method's definition, appropriate applications, strengths, and limitations and by practicing the construction and use of each. *Through the Looking Glass* guides you in achieving this competence so that you will be able to approach your own classroom concerns with confidence.

The book emphasizes that one observational method is not inherently superior to another. Understanding observational methodology allows the educational practitioner to select a method based on its appropriateness to a particular situation. Further, developing an ability to use a variety of methods promotes a view of the subject (child, teacher, or interactions) through different windows. Just as the appreciation and understanding of a statue is limited if you stand only in front of it or to the side, so the grasp of people and their relationships is confined by relying on a single method of study.

The organization of this book addresses this importance of keeping the subject (child, teacher, interactions), not the method, as the focus of observations. This book begins by presenting highlights of child development and introducing observational methods appropriate to the study of individual children and related topics. Then the looking glass expands to include teachers and teacher–child interactions. The integration of child-development theory and the application of observational skills in working with young children are stressed; a multitude of examples helps you keep real classrooms and real people in mind. Learning how to apply observational methods increases the joys of teaching and furthers your progress in becoming a remarkable teacher.

On the Road to Sound Observation

Now the journey of this book begins. In the first step on the road to sound observation you examine the reasons for observing and exploring topics suitable for classroom study. Next, you review guidelines for effective and unobtrusive observation in the early childhood classroom. Finally, you learn how to minimize subjectivity in observation and gain practice developing observational skills that are more objective than subjective. Let us begin.

Reasons for Observing

"Assessment of children's development, learning, and interests should be an integral part of all early childhood programs" (Schweinhart & McNair, 1991, p. 4). In the vibrant classroom, the teacher frequently has a pen and pad in hand as observational notes are written; the process occurs daily and is the foundation for rich learning experiences. Box 1.1 lists eight important reasons for classroom observation:

Box 1.1
Reasons for Observing in the Early Childhood Classroom

- Chart developmental growth (physical, cognitive, psychosocial, and creative) for each child.
- Evaluate each child's strengths and limitations from a realistic perspective.
- Analyze specific problems.
- Plan appropriate curriculum, materials, responses, strategies, and interactions based on individual needs.
- Plan responsive environments indoors and outdoors.
- Maintain records for study teams, conferences, and ongoing feedback to parents.
- Arrive at a comprehensive understanding of each child or a teacher through the application of several observational methods.
- Appraise teacher practices, and design staff development.

Framer (1994) emphasized the importance of the teacher's role in the process of observing:

Good teachers are keen observers. Crucial to teaching is the ability to observe and listen to children. It is through this process that teachers can discover students' skills, interests, and needs. Good teachers are able to use the information they gather to augment the learning environment so that it can both nourish children and grow from them. (p. 31)

On a daily basis, teachers document small developmental steps in children and plan supportive experiences. Weekly, they supplement the curriculum and learning environment according to the appraised needs of individual children. They also use their observational skills to choose appropriate responses to behavioral difficulties, such as a preschool child grabbing a toy from another child or a primary grade child using fists to solve a playground problem. Teachers use the well-drawn details gleaned from classroom observations to measure and record each child's developmental growth over the entire year in an individual portfolio. (A *portfolio* is a collection of observational records and work samples for one child, usually kept for a period of 1 year.) This wealth of information is used to communicate with parents during conferences. From daily to weekly to monthly to yearly, the observational process is a cycle of recording, evaluating, planning, and communicating repeated over and over (see diagram). In the diagram note that the base of the triangle inside the circle represents shared family/teacher support for the center of the observational process, which is the child.

Note that the child is usually the focus of observation; on occasion, observations may be used to evaluate a teacher's proficiency or classroom environments (see Parts III and IV).

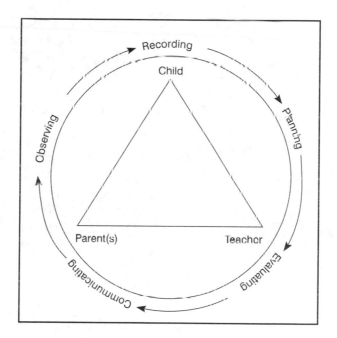

What to Observe

Look at the four photos on page 8 of a classroom filled with busy children. Examine what the teacher and children are doing. What materials are they using? What activities are in progress? How are the children interacting?

The early childhood classroom provides diverse and abundant opportunities for observation.

Now stop for a moment and write down ideas about what might be observed in this classroom; list the topics in Practice Activity 1.1. You may want to add other ideas not suggested by the photos. Think about examples of children's developmental growth, environmental influences, developmentally appropriate practices, family concerns, children with special needs, cultural awareness, and teaching strategies.

Practice Activity 1.1 _____
Topics of Observation

List topics to observe in an early childhood classroom.

Examples:

- Children's separation from family
- Types of roles enacted in the dramatic play area
- Frequency of on task behaviors

1.

2.

3.

4.

5.

6.

_____

The following is a typical list of observational topics brainstormed by teachers-in-training interested in preschool and primary grade classrooms. It is based on their own experiences.

Topics of Observation

1. Listening and learning
2. Frequency of aggressive behavior on the playground
3. Classification skills
4. Personality
5. Block building
6. Types of teacher questions
7. Clarity of speech
8. Motor skills
9. Maturity
10. Kindergarten readiness
11. Active role of teacher
12. Frequency and context of family involvement in school
13. Evidence of anti-bias curriculum

Look at Practice Activity 1.1 and compare your ideas with the preceding list. Are there similarities? Did you think of items not on this list? Now study both lists carefully while thinking about how each topic could be observed in a classroom.

All the items in the Topics of Observation are concerns teachers may have, but not all are directly observable. Some are too general and some too vague; being specific and knowing what area of a large topic we want to observe are crucial. Observation is most useful when we can pinpoint exactly what it is we are looking for and what it is we want to see. For example, "frequency of aggressive behavior on the playground" could be categorized and accurately observed, but "listening and learning" is too complex to specify exactly what behaviors we would be looking for. Thus "listening and learning" is too general and too vague. Narrowing the topic to state a specific act of listening, such as listening during story time, suggests a manageable focus for the teacher.

Let's try one more. How would you classify the topic "personality"? Can you see that it is also too vague and general? Personality is multifaceted, making it difficult to observe. We need to know what aspect of personality we are to observe in order for this topic to be appropriate. Now turn your attention to Practice Activity 1.2 to evaluate topics to observe.

Practice Activity 1.2
Evaluation of Topics of Observation

Using your list from Practice Activity 1.1 and the Topics of Observation list, consider each item carefully, and determine if it is an appropriate topic for observation or if it is too general and vague. Place each item in the proper column below.

Appropriate Topic	**Too General/Too Vague**
Example: Frequency of aggressive behavior on the playground	Example: Listening and learning

You are on the road to sound observation when you can identify topics that are specific and observable. If you found that in Practice Activity 1.1 you listed some vague or general items, see if you can now revise them to be more explicit or delete them if they are not workable.

As a teacher, you will conduct a variety of observations on many different topics. Continue to practice selecting appropriate behaviors to observe; use all available opportunities.

Guidelines for Observation

In learning to be a competent observer, you will be spending time in classrooms practicing various methods. Reasonable preparations for a classroom observation will help you get off to a good start and maximize the amount of information you will be able to gather. The following helpful suggestions apply to any observational method you select and may also be used in your own classroom with some modifications.

1. Clarify the purpose of your observation. Spend time before the observation to examine its purpose. What is the assignment? Do you understand the method you plan to use? Concentrate on the "big picture" of your observation.

2. Schedule your visit if you are observing in a classroom other than your own. No teacher will appreciate being surprised by your arrival. Phone about a week ahead to obtain permission; arrange the date, time, and length of your observation. Generally explain the purpose of your observation; for example, you might say that you will observe teacher–child interactions. If you describe your observation question in minute detail (e.g., What are the types and frequencies of the questions teachers ask children?), you risk prompting atypical behavior. Leave your phone number in case the teacher needs to contact you before your visit.

3. Come equipped with the necessary materials and a warm smile. For most assignments you will need paper or your observation form, pencils or pens, and something firm to write on. Check in with the school secretary (bring identification). Once inside the classroom, some normal anxiety about being observed can be alleviated by being friendly and greeting each adult individually.

4. Select a position from which to observe. Look around the classroom to note your options. You want to be as inconspicuous as possible; thus you should sit down and keep to the outskirts of activities in progress. You will increase your viewing range if you sit with your back to the wall. You want to find the fine line that will allow you to hear and see what's going on without interfering in or detracting from the activity.

5. Note "the lay of the land." If you are not acquainted with the classroom, spend about 10 minutes becoming familiar with the layout of the classroom, the materials accessible to the children, and what is going on. During this time you want to satisfy your curiosity about general matters so you can then turn your attention to the specifics of your observation. Drawing a rough map of the room is helpful.

6. Check your own biases and emotional responses to the children, teachers, and classroom. Acknowledge them and then try to clear away any judgments that may cloud your focus, such as the labeling of a child (e.g., spoiled, bossy, or stressed).

7. Respond in a natural way to children's inquiries about your presence. If a child asks why you are there or what you are doing, respond with "I'm just visiting to see what preschool (or first grade or whatever) is like." This is usually enough to satisfy and reassure the child as you continue to observe.

8. Fill in the appropriate heading for the observational method you are using.

Observations may be collected inside and outside the classroom or, as this student is doing, through a one-way glass.

Observer Subjectivity

The material that follows discusses the most troublesome skill in sound observation. Consider this scenario. Two observers visit a kindergarten playground to record an individual child's activity for 3 minutes. They watch the same boy, Cyd, who is 5 years and 1 month old (5;1).

Observer A wrote:

The boy I am observing (Cyd, 5;1) is playing all alone with a dinosaur in the sand. He doesn't seem to have any friends. He plays with just one dinosaur all by himself for awhile. Then he gets bored and goes to get some other dinosaurs at the end of the sand area. He demands the teacher's attention, probably the only person who will listen to him. He tells her that the biggest dinosaur is the boss, probably what he wants to be all the time. No wonder he is playing alone.

Observer B wrote:

The boy (Cyd, 5;1) sits in the middle of the sand area, his left foot tucked under his right knee, reaches into the toy bin, and grasps a small plastic dinosaur in his right hand. He stands, leaning on his left hand to push his body upward. Holding the dinosaur, he walks slowly to the edge of the sand area and places the dinosaur to the left of two other plastic dinosaurs lined up on the wood outlining the sand area. In a loud voice he exclaims, "Now you're all here." He spins around to the teacher and announces as he points to them in lined order, "Tyrannosaurus is the boss 'cause he's the biggest. The stegosaurus is the next boss 'cause he's the next biggest. The dimetrodon is the baby. He's not very big."

Both observers watched the same child, at the same time, engaging in the same activity. Yet the accounts are very different. Go back and study the two paragraphs. What are the specific elements that differentiate the two passages?

Observer A tried to explain many of Cyd's actions by drawing on personal impressions or feelings (e.g., "he gets bored," "probably the only person who will listen to him"). Consequently, Observer A has recorded an observation that is influenced by biases, preconceptions, and emotional responses. This observation is filled with obvious examples of *subjectivity*.

In comparison, Observer B recorded more facts and visible behaviors. This observer cautiously avoided evaluations, judgments, impressions, and personal speculations and was as objective as possible by recording accurately what was said and done with nothing added or omitted. This observation is not so much a personal interpretation as Observer A's report. Therefore, Observer B's report is more *objective* than Observer A's report. Review Observer B's exact descriptions (e.g., his left foot tucked under his right knee). Observations like these based on true behaviors are useful in keeping accurate records of the child's developmental growth. The trained teacher would not miss the opportunity to note and record Cyd's display of seriation.

To test whether the observer has been objective to a reasonable degree, ask, "Would another observer concur with the description?" Learning to minimize subjectivity when observing is an ongoing challenge, and Borg and Gall (1989) reminded us that it is impossible to be completely objective all the time.

> Remember that we are all products of an environment that subtly shapes and distorts our perceptions in innumerable ways. As a result, biases can influence the work of even the most competent scientists without their awareness of what is happening. (p. 178)

Continue on the path to sound observation by completing the exercise in Practice Activity 1.3 to sharpen your objective eye.

Practice Activity 1.3
Observation Descriptions

Examine the photo. Then list four statements describing what you see. Give attention to minimizing subjectivity.

Example: The blocks on the left of the middle shelf are not classified or put away in any orderly manner.

1.

2.

3.

4.

Practicing objectivity (to the best of one's ability) is necessary to travel on the road to sound observation. In Action Project 1.1, you have the opportunity to observe on your own. Many people have been surprised to find how obviously subjective their initial observations were. You may find value in saving your initial observation and then comparing it to an observation made at the end of studying this book. This comparison can be valuable feedback and a true measure of the distance you will have traveled.

Action Project 1.1
Practice in Minimizing Observational Subjectivity

Following the general guidelines for observation, visit a school of your choice (preschool or primary) and record six statements (remembering to be aware of subjectivity) that accurately describe what you observe. Be sure to call ahead for permission, go prepared, and stay 15 to 20 minutes.

1.

2.

3.

4.

5.

6.

Take a Moment to Reflect

Most likely you are reading this book because you have a strong affection toward and interest in children. Reflect on the way these feelings and interests came about and how they were nourished over the years.

1. Describe a memorable incident with a child or children that clarified how much you care about children.

2. Recall an incident with a child in which you know your presence was helpful. You may have offered needed security or comfort, supported a complex problem-solving process, explained a troublesome concept, brought fun into learning, or praised significant efforts. The list does not stop here.

CHAPTER 2

Highlights of Development During the Preschool Years

Lupe (2;5) tightly grasps a purple jumbo crayon in her right fist palm down, arm bent parallel to the table about 1 inch above the table. She makes circular strokes of medium intensity. After completing four imperfect circles, she looks up at her teacher with delight and exclaims, "I make doughnuts!"

This carefully worded, detailed vignette records an observation of Lupe's coloring activity made by her teacher. Is the observer's job now complete? No. Once the observational information is collected, it needs to be thoughtfully analyzed and used. The results of this analysis, if applied by the teacher in the classroom, will enrich both the curriculum and the activities planned for the child.

To facilitate Lupe's educational experience, her teacher must understand Lupe's coloring within the context of child development. If the teacher is cognizant of the development displayed by Lupe's coloring and the growth yet to come, then she or he has a developmental framework to guide activity planning. The following questions begin the process. What does Lupe's grasp indicate about her fine motor development? What does her assertion that the purple circles represent doughnuts demonstrate about her cognitive development? What does her ease in sharing her achievements with her teacher suggest about her psychosocial development? Understanding child development goes beyond appreciating children's current interests and skills or rejoicing in their achievements. Teachers need to know enough about child development and appropriate curriculum to make good judgments about what is age-appropriate and individually appropriate for the children in their classrooms (Bredekamp & Rosegrant, 1992).

Chapters 2 and 3 make no attempt to supplant the wealth of information in child-development textbooks. The purpose of these chapters is to highlight selected aspects of early childhood development (ages 2½ through 8) so the observer understands what growth looks like and what to watch for in the classroom. To further serve this purpose, the *growth indicators* for physical, cognitive, psychosocial, and creative development are identified in specified sections, with each section giving examples of individual and cultural diversity. As you read the chapter, keep in mind the ethical responsibility to children noted in the box on page 18.

Selected Highlights of Physical Development

"Oh I wish I had his energy!" remarked Clodine, as she watched her 4-year-old jetting around the play yard late in the day. Preschoolers often appear to be like little firecrackers, sparkling and bursting with fuel. These young children have mastered

Consider Our Ethical Responsibilities to Children

NAEYC Ideal I-1.2

"To base program practices upon current knowledge in the field of child development and related disciplines and upon particular knowledge of each child" (Feeney & Kipnis, 1992, p. 4).

Read on to see how understanding development helps teachers fulfill this ethical responsibility.

walking and have improved their balance and coordination through practice and maturation; now they are engaged in the motor skill adventures of running, jumping, hopping, galloping, skipping, climbing, balancing, kicking, catching, and throwing. Watch young children in your neighborhood, at the park, or in the supermarket. They seem to want and seek out opportunities to exercise a variety of motor skills.

Motor Development

Motor development is defined as "the progressive change in one's movement behavior brought about by interaction of the individual with the environment and the task" (Gallahue, 1993, p. 7). Early childhood educators observe growth in this area by keeping records on children's gross motor development (maturity and capabilities of large muscles, such as those of the arms and legs) and fine motor development (maturity and capabilities of small muscles, such as those of the fingers). Motor development rests on basic developmental principles or axioms (Figure 2.1). Review these axioms, and take time to think about the implication of each axiom for motor development.

Axiom	Motor Development Example
Development occurs at individual maturational rates. Each child possesses his/her own genetic time clock.	In a group of 3-year-olds, some jump by mustering all the energy they can harness for the task; other children jump with quick, easy movements.
Developmental areas (physical cognitive, psychosocial, and creative) and subsets within those areas overlap and are interdependent.	A child who is uncomfortable or shy around others may not participate in gross motor group activities, thus limiting opportunities for physical development.

Figure 2.1.   Developmental axioms.

	"Visual acuity, figure–ground perception, depth perception, and visual-motor coordination are important qualities that are developmentally based and that significantly influence movement performance" (Gallahue, 1993, p. 40).
Motor development is generally predictable.	Children develop jumping abilities before hopping and hopping before skipping.
Physical growth proceeds along a *cephalocaudal* (head-to-tail) pattern.	Babies can lift their heads before sitting. A young preschooler can more easily catch a ball than kick a ball.
Physical development advances in a *proximodistal* (from the center of the body to the outermost part) pattern. Thus, children acquire gross motor control before fine motor control.	Young Morag scurries over to the riding truck on the outside yard, smiling broadly as she plops herself down and powers the truck forward using her strong thighs.
	Four-year-old Tristin spends many happy preschool hours manipulating tiny houses and small wooden people on the "village floor map" made of fabric.
Perfecting motor skills is subject to individual interest, culture, instruction, and practice.	Some children cannot tie shoelaces because no one taught them, they didn't want to learn, or they have always worn velcro-fastened shoes.

Figure 2.1. (*Continued*).

Gross Motor Skills

Identifying basic motor skills and determining needed motor opportunities gear the teacher for active observation. Begin the identification practice by studying the growth indicators in Box 2.1; they describe the key characteristics of gross motor development. "These fundamental movement patterns can be thought of as the building blocks of the more specific skills developed later in childhood" (see Chapter 3) (Payne & Isaacs, 1987, p. 272). Because developmental axioms affect motor skill performance, development is denoted as a continuous process rather than chronological age expectations in Box 2.1.

Another aspect of the identification process is recording how the child performed the motor skill. Adults may easily confirm that a child can run, but the trained observer uses developmental knowledge to ask questions about detail. For example, does the child run with speed, control, smoothness, and endurance? Is the child's hopping balanced and performed with confidence using a spring-like action, or is it stiff and accompanied by large arm movements? When throwing a ball, does the child lead with the same foot or the foot opposite the throwing arm? Observing

Box 2.1
Preschool Growth Indicators of Gross Motor Skills

Skill	*Developing Characteristics*
Increases competency in running	Running begins with a flat-footed forward run and progresses to a forward heel-toe pattern. Child increasingly develops ability to run backward and to run on toes. Child's initial inability to stop, start, and turn progresses to accomplished execution of starts, stops, and turns.
Increases competency in jumping	Jumping down begins with a low jump-down (about 2 feet) from a small crouch position, the child landing with straight legs and arms waving in an uncontrolled manner. It progresses to jumping down from higher elevations in a knee-bent crouch start, with the child moving arms back to front for balance, and landing with knees bent at impact.
	Standing broad jump begins with jump distance of less than 1 foot and continues up to a distance of about 3 feet.
Increases competency in hopping	Hopping begins with only 1 to 3 one-foot hops on one selected foot accompanied by large arm movements. Hop progresses to a stiff-looking 7 to 9 hops, then to 10 or more hops (using either foot) executed with an easy bouncing action using ankles, knees, and hips.
	Hopping forward on two feet begins with feet together, semi-stiff legs and arms waving up and down for 2 or 3 jumps. It progresses to rhythmic jumping with knees and arms bent in pogo-stick fashion.
Increases competency in galloping	Galloping begins with a variation on running. Gallop progresses to a run

Box 2.1 (continued)

Skill	*Developing Characteristics*
	and leap pattern, then to a step-together rhythmic gallop pattern with either foot leading.
Increases competency in skipping	Skipping begins with a hop on one foot and a walk on the other—it appears stiff, usually a flat-footed pattern accompanied by large arm movements. Skip progresses to a smooth rhythmic pattern, using alternate feet with arms bent at the elbow and swinging alternately with foot.
Increases competency in climbing	Climbing stairs begins with a mark-time foot pattern when climbing or descending stairs using hands on the support railing. Climbing progresses to using alternate feet when ascending and descending stairs; hand rails are eventually no longer used for support. As height of climb increases, equipment choice widens (e.g., trees, jungle gyms, ladders, ropes and poles).
Increases competency in balancing	Balancing begins by standing on one foot with help and progresses to standing on one foot for about 10 seconds. In the final stage child can balance on one foot with eyes shut.
	Balancing on a 3 inch wide beam begins with a sideways step-together pattern. Child progresses to taking bigger steps, using an alternating foot pattern with arms extended for balance. In the final stage the child increases speed and uses an alternating foot pattern with arms remaining at the child's side.
Increases competency in catching	Catching begins with straight arms extended in front of body with palms up stopping the ball in arms, head turn-

Box 2.1 (continued)

Skill	*Developing Characteristics*
	ing away. It progresses to elbows bent with lower arm perpendicular to sides of body, palms facing each other with thumbs up, eyes shut at impact—arms used to catch the ball. Child advances to using hands to embrace the ball and adjusting arms to speed and location of ball in a relaxed and appropriately timed manner.
Increases competency in one-hand throwing	Throwing begins with feet stationary, elbow bent, hand with ball about ear height, propelling the ball with the elbow in a forward and downward motion. It progresses to an arm swing over shoulder and behind head; as the body turns to throwing side, ball is propelled with arm over head as the body weight moves forward. Child steps forward using the same-side leg as throwing arm. Child advances to using opposite raised elbow (hand bent downward) for balance as arm with ball is swung backward, elbow is bent, body turns to throwing side, and weight is on rear foot. When ball is propelled, the hips rotate toward target, the weight shifts forward, and child takes a step with opposite foot.
Increases competency in kicking	Kicking begins with using arms for balance and taking a short backward and forward stroke with limited bend in the leg. It progresses to one or more steps forward, with the stroke made by a bent knee on backstroke and follow-through. Child advances to running forward with quick steps, using the hip to propel the leg motion both backward and forward to maximum length

> ## Box 2.1 (continued)
>
> *Skill*   *Developing Characteristics*
>   with a high follow-through. The oppo-
>   site leg bends at impact, and child lifts
>   up on toe.
>
> *Note.* Information in chart compiled from two books by David Gallahue. *Understanding Motor
> Development: Infants, Children, and Adolescents* (2nd ed.) by David Gallahue, 1989, Indianapolis,
> Indiana: Benchmark, and *Developmental Physical Education for Today's Children* (2nd ed.) by David
> Gallahue, 1993, Dubuque, IA: Wm. C. Brown and Benchmark. Adapted and reproduced by
> permission of The McGraw-Hill Companies.

detailed and numerous qualities offers a more complete picture of the child's gross motor abilities. Consider the following classroom anecdote depicting gross motor development. What can be said about how this child exhibits balancing skill?

> 2/6 Amy (4;11). While standing up, Amy brought her left foot up under her left armpit, held it with her left hand, balanced steadily on her right foot as she exclaimed, "Look, I'm hugging my foot."

In programs for preschoolers, children usually have daily outdoor opportunities to exercise their budding motor skills freely. Providing a sufficient number and variety of outdoor motor experiences will support children's development. Teachers can augment the fixed equipment by frequently adding assorted items (e.g., obstacle courses, wooden crawl-through shapes, parachute activities, ring-toss games, jump ropes, or different sized balls). Movement activities assist in motor development and can be carried out even during inclement weather. Children often enjoy moving to recorded music with directions. Planned motor development programs with teacher assistance are necessary for optimum growth (Benelli & Yongue, 1995; Poest, Williams, Witt, & Atwood, 1990).

Fine Motor Skills

Throughout their early childhood years, children display differing skills in fine motor abilities. Some children put puzzles together with the greatest of ease, whereas others appear to be "all thumbs," especially when the pieces are small. In addition, fine motor tasks often require auxiliary capabilities. Picture the young child pouring juice from a small plastic pitcher during snack time. This child must have not only control over her or his fingers but also good concentration, visual acuity, and accurate judgment. The growth indicators listed in Box 2.2 provide the observational focus for these gradual developments.

Well-trained teachers are careful not to base fine motor developmental evaluations on one task; observing the child in a natural setting and identifying the many

---

Box 2.2
Preschool Growth Indicators of Fine Motor Skills

Growth Indicator	*Example*
Increases ability to grasp and control small object	Outside, blowing bubbles, Lorna uses one hand to hold the skinny straw inserted into a hole on the side of the Styrofoam cup. With her other hand she holds the cup, turns it upside down, and dips the rim into a soap mixture. Turning the cup right side up, she blows through the straw; multiple bubbles flow out the top of the cup.
Increases ability to fasten and unfasten	While playing Daddy in the housekeeping area, the child unbuttons and, for the first time, buttons the small fasteners on the coat of the 13-inch doll.
Increases ability to insert and remove small pieces	Prior to December, the puzzles in Maja's classroom contained a maximum of 10 pieces. Today the teacher introduces a 20-piece puzzle entitled "The City." Maja smiles triumphantly as she completes this puzzle on her first attempt.
Increases ability to string or lace	At the art table, several children are creating collages with pieces of beautiful junk. T. J. brings over a long piece of yarn, methodically wraps the ends with tape, and slowly and carefully (sometimes dropping pieces) strings 12 items to make a necklace. He asks the teacher to tie it around his neck.
Increases ability to cut with scissors	Moving from cutting play dough to cutting newspaper strips, the child is reminded by the teacher, "Cut from your belly button forward."

---

fine motor tasks exhibited by the child will provide an accurate picture. To facilitate this expansive approach to assessment, Figure 2.2 identifies many examples of fine motor tools available in different classroom areas. Not all of those tools will be found in every classroom; selections of specific tools are based on the children's developmental abilities, program goals, and teacher supervision.

Opportunities to exercise fine motor skills help build concentration, judgment, and motor coordination.

To check for writing readiness, a frequent observation in the area of fine mo tor development is the child's grasp of tools. The vignette in the beginning of this chapter reported: "Lupe (2;5) tightly grasps a purple jumbo crayon in her right fist palm down, arm bent parallel to the table about 1 inch above the table." To understand Lupe's development consider the following questions for observing advances in techniques using writing instruments (Cratty, 1986).

- Does the child hold the crayon in her fist with only the point touching the paper, controlling the movement from the shoulder and the elbow?

- Or does she use a pincer grip using her hand and wrist as one unit while her lower arm is in the air (not touching the writing surface)? Pincer grip is also called the dynamic tripod, "a finger posture in which the thumb, middle finger, and index finger function as a tripod for the writing implement" (Payne & Isaacs, 1987, p. 255).

- Does her hand rest anchored on the table as her fingers move together using the pincer grip in an adult-like fashion?

Children start to use the last technique between the ages of 5 and 7. Based on Cratty's sequences, the introductory chapter vignette shows that Lupe's "tool-grasping" development is in the beginning stage.

Some teachers of 4-year-olds worry about kindergarten readiness when children in their classrooms cannot competently perform writing and cutting tasks. A

Area	Tools
Art	Paintbrushes, pencils, crayons, markers, scissors, paper punch, staplers, play dough and clay utensils, large needles for stitchery, wire, yarn, pipe cleaners.
Blocks	Small wooden people, small plastic animals, small cars and other small toy vehicles, small signs, small blocks, interlocking train tracks, writing tools/paper for making signs.
Cooking	Can opener, stirring and measuring spoons, forks, paring and spreading knives, spatula, rolling pin, strainer, cheese slicer, vegetable brush and peeler, colander, cookie cutters.
Dramatic Play	Eating utensils, small-handled cups and pouring utensils, dress-up clothes or doll clothes with fasteners (button, zippers, laces), clip earrings, paper play money, writing tools/paper for making grocery lists.
Language Arts	Felt-tip pens; crayons; pencils of various sizes; flannel board pieces; typewriters; computers; hand and stick puppets; plastic magnetic and rubber stamp shapes, letters, and numbers.
Manipulatives and Math Aids	Pegs and pegboards of different sizes, Legos, puzzles, lacing boards, interlocking cubes, Tinkertoys, beads and strings, geoboards, parquetry.
Music and Movement	Hand castanets, xylophone, triangle, handbells, cymbals with small knobs, rainsticks, scarves and streamers.
Science	Magnifying glasses, magnets, toothbrushes for washing rocks, eyedroppers, small items for balancing and classifying, funnels, gardening tools, prisms, timers, tongs.
Woodworking	Nails, hammers, screws with large heads, screwdrivers, vise, saw, small pieces of sanded wood, pencils, markers, rulers or straightedge, glue, Styrofoam squiggles for gluing, pliers, hole punch, string, washers, wire, sandpaper.

Figure 2.2.   Preschool examples of fine motor tools.

specific concern centers around appropriate pencil size in the preschool classroom. Carlson and Cunningham's (1990) research on pencil size concluded "there was some evidence to support the existence of a positive relationship between management and performance. Therefore, the recommendation to early childhood educators is that both large and small diameter pencils be provided for school grapho-motor activities" (p. 279).

In addition to choice in pencil size, the child needs experience with writing tools prior to initial writing attempts that acquaint the child with the tools and aid in developing the needed fine motor control (Kaplan, 1994; Soliv, 1993). The teacher observes and notes whether children have shown an interest, and whether they have had sufficient time and opportunities to practice—beginning with easy tasks, such as using scissors to cut play dough pieces or copying letters in their names using fluid marking pens.

In summary of physical development, understanding the developmental axioms, observing growth indicators, describing performance qualities, and making adjustments for individual needs is the power switch that turns on teacher effectiveness. To more fully assimilate the information on motor development, become an avid informal observer of children. Key into the children's motor skill displays. Discuss your expectations for children's gross and fine motor development with your peers. Check to be sure that your expectations are based on sound developmental information, and use your observations to build an experiential understanding.

The abbreviated treatment of the subject in this chapter does not allow us to discuss all aspects of preschool physical development; our emphasis has been on motor development. You may want to refer to a child-development book to review the areas not examined in this chapter: preschool growth curves for height and weight, bone growth, brain maturation (especially the cerebral cortex), motor perception, and hand preference.

Selected Highlights of Cognitive Development

The boundaries of the concept of cognition are far from clear-cut. Cognition is obviously involved when a child puts a puzzle together for the first time, but the mind is similarly at work when a child watches a friend spin around a playground bar and attempts to do the same. At the very least, both activities involve the coordinated efforts of noticing details, remembering, and making judgments. In this book cognition is viewed as a fertile and complex concept—even though it is not easily defined. It is enough to say, at this point, that cognitive development refers to the changing and expanding intellectual processes of human beings.

The following highlights link children's growth to observable indicators. They offer the following selection of topics rather than an exhaustive accounting: representational abilities, language, reasoning, theory of mind, classification, seriation, number development, and memory. Remember to view each child's development as steps along a continuum rather than as age-segmented skills.

Representational Abilities

Stop and recall your last trip in a car. Who drove, where did you go, and what route did you take? What did you pass along the way? Now analyze your memory of this trip. Did your thoughts contain mental images and/or words? Most readers will answer *yes*. Now let's consider infants. What is their thinking like? We know young infants do not rely on language. Although the study of mental images is complicated, research does indicate that infants do not have the same abilities as young children to think about objects or experiences remote from the present. This is not to say infants do not think; their thinking, though, is somehow different. If a few 8-month-olds are asked to get their teddy bears, they can manage this trip even if it involves crawling through a room, down a hall, and into their bedrooms. These babies have something going on in their minds, but once they reach early childhood, the substance of their thought processes will be altered.

The remarkable advancement in cognition from the infant to the young child hinges on the expanding ability to think representationally, that is, "to make something—a mental symbol, a word, or an object—stand for or represent something else which is not present" (Ginsburg & Opper, 1988, p, 70). Infants demonstrate some symbolic thinking (e.g., they wave bye-bye and know someone will leave), but representational abilities explode during early childhood. Dolls can represent people; toy cars can be models of the vehicles children ride in daily. A scribbled circle can represent a doughnut and an upright block a high-rise apartment building. Words are symbols that stand for people, things, places, actions, and ideas, and numbers designate quantities of objects. Dramatic play often includes complex representations of how children interpret other people's actions (often with a little imagination thrown in).

As preschool children mature, they also learn how to interpret others' representations and are delighted when they recognize pictures of familiar scenes, a city skyline, or a famous landmark. With maturation, experience, interest, and guidance, most preschoolers learn to decode at least some written numbers and letters before they begin kindergarten. Note that numbers and letters are abstract symbols—bearing no physical resemblance to the concepts represented.

Representational thought allows children to solve problems mentally. Rather than trying to bang puzzle pieces into place, preschoolers are able to think of solutions; they may study the shape, color, and details of some pieces before trying to fit them in place. Once children develop representational thought, they are forever changed. Try to fathom thinking without being allowed to use words or mental images. Difficult? Impossible? The ability to think in symbols is, indeed, an integral part of human cognitive processes (see Box 2.3 for growth indicators of representational thought), and one job of early childhood teachers is to provide children with the materials, time, encouragement, and stimulation to represent in depth.

Language

The development of representational thought provides the means for children to understand that words can stand for people, objects, actions, places, feelings, and ideas. Children learn to understand and speak their language remarkably well within their social environments and without formal instruction. This competence is even more impressive when we bear in mind that the bulk of what they hear, comprehend, and speak is newly invented; speakers continually create new sentences. During the preschool years, most children become commendable participants in their native language as they unconsciously learn many rules of their grammar. Furthermore, the number of words in their vocabularies explodes as children add new words to their mental maps of interconnected categories, sometimes after only one exposure (Golinkoff, Hirsh-Pasek, Bailey, & Wenger, 1992). This process is called fast mapping. Although fast mapping quickly builds vocabu-

Box 2.3
Preschool Growth Indicators of Representational Abilities

Growth Indicator	*Example*
Forms mental images	Ayako says, "I want to work with the blue play dough like yesterday."
	Max asks how big the earth is. Parent tries to describe the immensity of our planet but knows the image is inaccurate when Max asks, "Is there a traffic cone at the end?"
Imitates	Josephyne uses fingers to try to represent a spider climbing up a waterspout.
	Two children bark like their dogs and notice the differences.
Uses language	Madeleine asks her caregiver if she can look in the drawer, and the caregiver says, "Sure." Maddy repeats "Sure" to herself, then proudly exclaims to another child, "Tom said yes!"
Pretends	A child pushes a toy car on the floor, saying "Vroom, vroom."
Role-plays	In the house area, Jeffrey takes the role of a dad to three stuffed animals and cooks them breakfast.
Represents in two dimensions	
Represents in three dimensions	Using sand in a large sandbox, Weston constructs the local shopping mall, decorating favorite stores with feathers.
Decodes others' representations	A child carefully studies a pumpkin patch photo to find details observed on a field trip.
	Marissa identifies familiar "EXIT" sign in the adjoining classroom.

lary, children frequently acquire limited or erroneous understandings based on their limited experiences. Think about how the following 4-year-old incorrectly fast mapped a new term in a very concrete manner, and understand his conclusion in the context of his particular store of words and grammar, his previous experiences, and his maturation:

> 6/26 Gregory (4;3) was the prized ring bearer in a relative's wedding, but despite his mother's attempts to quiet him, he persisted in making low growling sounds throughout the ceremony. Afterward, Gregory's mom complimented him on his steady walk up the aisle and careful support of the ring pillow but asked him why he kept making those strange noises. Gregory drew a deep breath that puffed out his chest to proudly explain, "I was the ring bear!"

Achievement in language development goes beyond the obvious communication benefits because language is a vital connector to advancing cognition (Vygotsky, 1987). The growth indicators of language development in Box 2.4 provide a starting point for classroom observations.

Language development during early childhood has practical implications for the early childhood educator. To promote growth, adults talk with children about meaningful topics, take them to interesting places, engage them with other children, read to them, and model a rich and correct use of language—all activities that are part of a productive preschool. These activities guide children from their levels of independent functioning to more advanced levels that children can manage with the help of adults or more competent peers. Vygotsky's *zone of proximal development* describes "the hypothetical, dynamic region in which learning and development take place" (Berk & Winsler, 1995, p. 5):

> The principle of learning is that children can do things first in a supportive context and then later independently and in a variety of contexts. The support of adults and more competent peers provides the necessary assistance or "scaffold" that enables the child to move to the next level of independent functioning. (Bredekamp & Rosegrant, 1992, p. 15)

For example, children learn new words by actively listening to and talking with others; their social environments are keys to vocabulary development. Thus, if *delicious* is in a child's vocabulary, then *scrumptious* is within her or his zone of proximal development (Genishi, McCarrier, & Nussbaum, 1988), and participation in a dynamic interchange with another may serve to add *scrumptious* to this child's vocabulary. This other person (adult or more competent peer) has provided an effective *scaffold*, or support, for the child's language advancement.

Reasoning

Preschool children do not use adult logic to solve problems and usually do not do well on logic or abstract tasks. They manage quite well, however, in their own lives as they encounter objects and events of interest to them. Consider the preschool examples on pages 31 and 32:

With guidance from adults or more advanced peers, children's progress in the zone of proximal development is enhanced.

Box 2.4
Preschool Growth Indicators of Language

Growth Indicator	*Example*
Advances, but does not complete, understanding of grammar	Skyler overgeneralizes some rules and says *foots* to indicate plural and *bited* to form past tense.
	Carlos learns some rule exceptions and uses *feet, sang, bit, taught.*
	A grandmother coaches her young grandchild to record a message for her telephone answering machine.

Box 2.4 (continued)

Growth Indicator	Example
	Ellen: Me and Grandma can't come to the phone right now. . . .
	Grandma: Say, "Grandma and I."
	Ellen: OK. Me and Grandma can't come to the phone right now. . . .
	The grandmother corrects twice more.
	The light seems to go on in the child's head, the grandmother pushes the record button, and the child proudly speaks.
	Ellen: Me and Grandma and I can't come to the phone right now!
Progresses in articulation, but limitations remain	A child explains, "The wight's too bright for the wabbit."
Expands vocabulary	Aaron studies sand stuck at the entrance to a clogged funnel and mutters, "Now this is a perdicament."
Constructs increasingly complex sentences (structure and length)	"This thumb is all right, but this thumb is not," declares Sarah Joy, clutching a sore thumb.
Converses with increasing competence with adults and peers	Steve sits chest-deep in wading pool.
	Steve: I don't need to go under. I'm too little to go under. I'll go under later. I'll go under on Tuesday.
	He cautiously puts face in water and gets out of pool "to think it over."
	Adult: Oh my! How brave you are! Are you going to think about how proud of yourself you are?
	Steve: No, I'm going to think about how it scared me.

- Jose studied a boat being repaired on land and commented, "You need a ladder to get into the boat when the boat is out of the water, and you don't need a ladder to get into the boat when the boat is in the water."
- Rebecca, very familiar with the Berenstain Bears books, listened to a story that took place before Sister was born. "Is Brother really a brother?" she asked.
- "I know two kinds of trip," remarked Frank watching a plane fly by, "one when you go on an airplane and one when you fall down and hurt yourself."

All three examples illustrate thoughtful reasoning about a limited set of factors. Box 2.5 presents growth indicators for the development of reasoning in young children.

Although preschool children have limitations in their abilities to reason, they do not need to be changed. They do, however, need nourishment to develop their reasoning abilities. The nourishment teachers need to provide consists of diverse materials and experiences, time to explore and represent, and an interesting environment in which their support of and participation in children's activities communicate their unwavering commitment. In short, teachers must engage children in their individual zones of proximal development. This nourishment does not spontaneously appear; it is the result of planning based on observation and is part of the early childhood educator's job.

Box 2.5
Preschool Growth Indicators of Reasoning

Growth Indicator	Example
Often reasons and problem solves thoughtfully	A child stands behind a friend at the slide and notices, "I can see your back because I'm not you."
	When Umar's block structure tumbles down on the carpet for the second time, he reaches for a flat board and says, "I'm going to build it again on this."
Often reasons on the basis of perceptions (not logic)	Kelsey compares her broken cracker to her neighbor's whole one at snack time and complains, "Hey, Tillie got more."
Thinks in concrete or tangible terms	When the teacher tells Jackson and Bobby to stick together on the walk around the block, Jackson looks at his hands and asks, "With what?"

Theory of Mind

Theory of mind refers to "an understanding of mental processes, that is, of one's own or another's emotions, perceptions, and thoughts" (Berger & Thompson, 1995, p. 344). Researchers (Wellman & Hickling, 1994; Wellman, Hollander, & Schult, 1996) provide evidence of young preschoolers' awareness that people have mental states different from their own. They therefore realize that a person may be angry even if they, themselves, are not. Furthermore, they understand that thought is not physical, that mental states can determine action (e.g., anger may lead to yelling), and that different people may have different thoughts about the same situation. Moving beyond knowing about the simple existence of mental states, preschoolers later discern that mental states are actively constructed. In a study of how children construe "forget" and "remember," 4-year-olds, but not 3-year-olds, understood that people had to have prior knowledge of something before they could forget or remember it (Lyon & Flavell, 1994). Several more years are required, however, before children view the mind as an independent and active entity constantly at work (Wellman & Hickling, 1994).

> As children become more and more aware of the many different sorts of mental states and activities that the mind can harbor, it may gradually dawn on them that it is a busier, more active place than they had previously imagined. (Flavell, Green, & Flavell, 1995, p. 90)

Appropriate experiences for young children in the process of developing theories of mind are social interactions that stimulate their abilities to consider and respond to others' emotional, social, or cognitive points of view. Indeed, "the number of siblings in a family is related positively to young children's reasoning in theory of mind tasks" (Perner, Ruffman, & Leekam, 1994, pp. 1233–1234). For example, suppose a 4-year-old grabs a younger child's shovel in the sandbox. Should a teacher expect that the 4-year-old can consider the younger child's emotional perspective, at least well enough to imagine the other's hurt, angry, or intimidated feelings? The issue of preschoolers' understanding of others is central to many common interactions in and out of the classroom. The growth indicators in Box 2.6 summarize preschoolers' preliminary theories of mind.

The preschool classroom offers a multitude of opportunities to stimulate and challenge children's evolving understanding of others' points of view. A teacher, Ellie, calls up to Phung at the top of the jungle gym and asks what he sees from way up there.

"I see the pizza place across the street and the big tree and lots of cars driving past," he hollers down.

"What do you think I see from down here?" Ellie asks, interested to discover if the child recognizes that the wooden fence denies her the opportunity to see the pizza store, the cars, and the trunk of the big tree. If Phung's response indicates he understands that her perspective is different from his, she congratulates him for noticing that the fence blocks her view of the street. If, however, he assumes she sees what he sees, Ellie can cherish her next few moments as a teacher.

Box 2.6
Preschool Growth Indicators of Theory of Mind

Growth Indicator	*Example*
Understands that thinking is an internal, mental process	Roland sees a tipped-over trash can and says, "I wonder how it happened."
Understands that others have their own emotional, social, and cognitive points of view	Mayuko builds a block tunnel and calls to a friend to look at her through the opposite end.
	Kurt accidentally spills a glass of juice and quickly looks at the teacher's face to gauge her reaction.
Demonstrates limited interpretations of others' points of view	Using a computer face-making program, Aynsley makes a face and exclaims that her teacher, 15 feet across the room, should see it. Aynsley leans to one side so she no longer blocks the teacher's view but does not understand that her teacher is too far away to discern the details of the face.

"I'll be right up," Ellie calls. "I want to admire your view." The teacher and child stand together on the jungle gym and talk about the tops of children's heads, the entire play yard, and the school roof as well as the pizza store, big tree, and passing cars. Ellie notices Maria jumping next to the fence. "Look where Maria is. I wonder what she can see. Let's go take a look." She promotes Phung's active learning about others' perspectives through this teachable moment.

Let's return to the 4-year-old who grabbed the shovel. Is there reason to believe this child can take the other's feelings into consideration? Most likely, in the heat of the moment (the height of shove desire), the 4-year-old never thought once, much less twice, about how the other child would feel when the shovel was grabbed away. If a teacher talked with the child after the act, however, some perspective taking would probably emerge. Over time, as young children's natural impulsiveness declines with maturation and expanded communication skills and as people help them take notice of others' perspectives (emotional and otherwise), children build their theories of mind and become more aware of and responsive to others' points of view.

Classification

Children and adults rely on classification to deal logically with objects and ideas in their everyday lives. Objects in homes are classified in appropriate rooms; for example, dishes are expected to be found in a kitchen. Classification also serves more detailed purposes. A third-grader might sort a list of spelling words into a group of those mastered and those requiring study. A junior high student may have several alternative ways of sorting baseball cards. For ease of access, a gourmet cook organizes jars of spices, and an expert quilter sorts dozens of fabrics by color. When did this ability blossom? What classification behaviors can we expect to see in the early childhood classroom?

Early childhood classrooms offer abundant opportunities for children to classify objects. Using blocks, children might build enclosures to separate the wild from tame plastic animals, or they might construct a special road just for the trucks hauling supplies. To encourage children to notice similarities and differences and how things go together, the classroom environment may be organized so that children sort toys and supplies into labeled containers or onto labeled shelves and pegboards as they clean up. For example, shaking instruments and percussion instruments might be sorted when stored on the pegboard in the music area. Look for the growth indicators listed in Box 2.7 to evaluate classification skills in the preschool classroom.

Box 2.7
Preschool Growth Indicators of Classification

Growth Indicator	*Example*
Explores diverse attributes of objects	Sophia scrutinizes the parts of a coffee pot while working to reassemble it.
Recognizes similarities and differences	Dorine remarks that the two guinea pigs have the same kinds of wiggly noses and whiskers but different kinds of fur.
Sorts objects with increasing sophistication	An adult gives lettuce, a carrot, parsley, and oatmeal to Hank, who is pretending to be a rabbit. After munching, he exclaims, "I ate all the vegetables and the oatmeal!"
	After a nature walk, Brady groups leaves of similar shape on a collage.

The availability of a variety of materials offer preschool children interesting cognitive experiences.

Seriation

Seriation is arranging things or putting them in order according to one character-istic and is another cognitive ability that progresses as children mature and gain ex-perience in their world. Teachers so often emphasize seriation by size (e.g., blocks or sticks) that they forget about the many other interesting attributes of objects (e.g., grades of sandpaper in the construction area and paint chips of color shades in the art area). Numerous objects available in the preschool classroom enable children to compare along various dimensions:

light to heavy	sweet to sour
short to long	light to dark
narrow to wide	clean to dirty
slow to fast	smooth to rough
high pitch to low pitch	young to old
loud to quiet	

In the preschool classroom, seriation begins with comparisons (Holmann & Weikart, 1995). For example, before children can line up several sticks from short to long, they first need to compare a short and a long stick. Comparisons begin with two objects: for example, wet and dry hands, sweet and sour lemonade, high- and low-pitched singing, fast and slow dancing, light- and dark-green paper, and fine and coarse tree bark. These comparisons support the seriation skills to follow: seriating a few objects through trial and error to seriating many objects systematically. Box 2.8 describes growth indicators of seriation skills.

Number Development

Young children spontaneously and informally learn about numbers before formal schooling (Flavell, Miller, & Miller, 1993). Between the ages of 2 and 8, "children memorize the number words, come to understand that each word represents a different quantity, and develop their counting skills" (Geary, 1994, p. 34). Children seem to understand that *three* is more than *two* at a very early age; however, understanding that all numbers represent specific quantities and learning to count many objects accurately are gradually developing processes. Young children first demonstrate their increasing understanding of numbers with small sets. For example, they can count three objects correctly before they master six objects. Common counting errors include saying more than one number word for an object (e.g., counting five objects as [1, 2]-[3]-[4]-[5, 6]-[7]) and saying a number word without pointing to or counting an object (e.g., counting five objects as [1]-[2]-[3]-[4 in space]-[5]-[6]. The clear awareness that the end number (5, in this example) has to correspond to a specific quantity of objects requires some years of practice and maturation.

The preschool classroom can provide opportunities for children to learn number words, understand that each number represents a specific quantity, and develop counting skills. Over time, such activities will strengthen their understanding of number for use in practical contexts. Box 2.9 explains growth indicators of number development.

Box 2.8
Preschool Growth Indicators of Seriation

Growth Indicator	*Example*
Makes comparisons	At the sand table Teddy says, "Let's make this really soapy water be the ocean and this kinda soapy water be the lake."
Seriates a limited number of objects	Elke arranges three triangles by size and glues them on a flat piece of wood.

Box 2.9
Preschool Growth Indicators of Number Development

Growth Indicator	*Example*
Compares quantities of small sets	"Hey, she's got more!" complains a child with fewer apple slices than a neighbor.
Learns number names	Alvaro counts, "Threeteen, fourteen, fiveteen."
	Children sing a counting song during circle time.
Understands numbers as representations of quantities	Josiah explains to his teacher in the art area, "I need three pieces of paper to make roofs for my office buildings."
Counts limited number of objects with one-to-one correspondence	On a rainy day, Chelsea counts nine umbrellas outside the door.

Memory

In the area of memory, "the basic neurological architecture that supports memory development is established in the first five years" (Schneider & Pressley, 1989, p. 199). Preschoolers and adults thus share the same "basic hardware" because both recognition and recall memory are evident during early childhood. A 4-year-old might hear a song at preschool and instantly recognize it from a visit to his cousin's place 4 months earlier. Recall memory, in contrast, requires mental imagery or language; preschoolers, as we know, are capable of these representational skills. So when a 3-year-old retells her favorite story to a sibling, she demonstrates her recall memory. Although memories certainly advance from early childhood capacities and abilities, the processes of recognition and recall memory are already in place.

"What the head knows has an enormous effect on what the head learns and remembers" (Flavell et al., 1993, p. 255). In other words, what a person knows has a powerful influence on what information that person can store from the environment and remember. For example, chess experts remembered gamelike chess arrangements better than nonexpert players, even when the experts were 10 years old and the nonexperts were adults (Chi, 1978)! The experts' "heads" had more experience and skills with gamelike arrangements and thus were better prepared to remember them.

So it is with young children. Imagine a teacher reading a book about dinosaurs to a small group of children. Manual listens attentively, having been read to at home about dinosaurs, having visited museums of natural history to see dinosaur skeletons, and having played with plastic models of dinosaurs for hours on end.

Tanya plays with dinosaurs at school and is also interested in the book, but Jeremy is content to sit in his teacher's lap as he casually glances from the illustrations to the ongoing classroom activities. After reading about the stegosaurus, the teacher turns the page and asks if anyone knows the name of the next dinosaur.

"Oh, I know, I know," exclaims Manual, struggling to retrieve a name from his memory.

"This is an armored dinosaur," the teacher remarks as they admire the illustration. "Do you remember the name yet, Manual?"

"No, but I know it," he groans.

"Ankylosaurus," says the teacher. "This dinosaur is an ankylosaurus."

"Yes, that's right. I know that. Ankylosaurus," pronounces Manual easily.

The "heads" that Manual, Tanya, and Jeremy brought to the story time were unique. Manual's head already knew a lot about dinosaurs, and he was confidently able to recognize the ankylosaurus's name even though he could not recall it on his own (perhaps next time). Tanya knew less but probably learned something—perhaps that ankylosaurus was an armored dinosaur. Time will tell. Jeremy might not have learned specific dinosaur facts from the conversation, but that's all right; he enjoyed the pleasant company and atmosphere at story time. Thus, even in preschool, children have different heads stemming from their developmental levels and past experiences (see Box 2.10 for growth indicators of memory); teachers cannot expect that everything they say goes into every head in the same way.

Many interesting and important topics were not discussed in this section on cognitive development during the preschool years (e.g., young children's understanding of space and time and their expanding problem-solving abilities); readers may wish to study these topics independently. Also, although this section presented general trends in cognitive development, individual differences between children abound. These differences are normal and reflect human diversity.

Box 2.10
Preschool Growth Indicators of Memory

Growth Indicator	*Example*
Remembers by recognizing	"Oh wook!" exclaims Oleg to Bart while looking at a photo in the block area, "member that 'ky 'craper?"
Remembers by recalling	Jena incorporates a bridge into a block structure, identical to one she observed another child build the day before.
Demonstrates individual knowledge	On a walk to the corner grocery, Hillary asks, "Can I pick these pansies and daffodils?"

Selected Highlights of Psychosocial Development

Human beings are social creatures, and who they become depends in large measure on the impact of their social worlds. Psychosocial development is the third developmental domain to be introduced. Although the domains of child development are categorized for practical study purposes, children are whole beings; their physical, cognitive, psychosocial, and creative developments are interrelated. For example, a preschool child's pumping skills on a swing set depend, in part, on large-muscle strength and coordination (physical development), understanding of when the legs go out and in (cognitive development), and encouragement from others (psychosocial development); once pumping is mastered, the child's creativity might stimulate the invention of new swinging skills. As in the other developmental domains, space and time permit only the consideration of selected topics for the early childhood educator; this section discusses the child's expanding relationships with adults and peers, self-concept, play, fears, aggression, and impulse control.

Expanding Relationships with Adults and Peers

Young children depend on their parent(s), other family members, or guardians for comfort and as communicating liaisons between their personal needs and desires and the larger world. Teachers of young children become sensitive to their own roles as new caregivers when they understand the resources inherent in and intensity behind the family–child bond. For example, perceptive teachers may have a registration form to inquire about each child's routines, needs, interests, and skills so they can make the environment welcoming and somewhat familiar. To reproduce a favorite home activity, dump trucks with pegs for filling and emptying are ready in the block area for one child's first day, and a special blanket is handy for rest time. Furthermore, alert teachers consciously look for opportunities to build up their own relationships and styles of communication with each child. A teacher mixes colors and uses a pump next to a new child at the water table and, with a farewell hug, enthusiastically describes these activities to the parent at the end of the day.

To young children teachers are more than ships passing in the night. They are adults to whom young children reach out for security and companionship. To be effective, teachers establish their own positive relationships with each child in their care. Separation from parents will be less traumatic as children experience the emotional commitment from their teachers and thrive from their new variety of communication partners.

As young children venture away from their homes, they encounter peers in neighborhoods, play groups, preschools, day care, and social gatherings. The success of early friendships hinges "to a great extent on the child's ability to communicate and share a common frame of reference with their partner" (Ladd & Coleman, 1993, p. 72). The quantity and quality of friendships among young children vary considerably as parents control their access to one another. Hints that a friendship is in the making are that the children voluntarily spend time together and share a reciprocal, give-and-take relationship (Hartup, 1992).

Expanding relationships with adults and peers can support young children's prosocial behavior—behavior that reflects concern for others. In general prosocial behavior increases during the preschool years (Zahn-Waxler & Smith, 1992) as children become more aware of others' feelings and ideas. Empathy (the ability to feel *with* other people) generally increases, but not always consistently. For example, if two preschoolers see the same child crying at the bottom of a slide, one may go over to offer heartfelt help and the other may not. Researchers have found that children are more empathic when their parents "call strong attention to the distress their misbehavior caused someone else" (Goleman, 1995, p. 99). Teachers doing the same in their classrooms can encourage children to understand and appreciate others' emotions and to respond with a generous heart and kind actions. Box 2.11 relates growth indicators of expanding relationships with adults and peers.

Self-Concept

Humans are unique as a species in their capacity for self-consciousness. The sense of self is a psychological construct nourished by expanding cognitive and social maturity. During early childhood, children come to understand that they have a physical self that takes up space and has unique physical attributes as well as a psychological self that is not visible from the outside. As discussed earlier in the cognitive section "Theory of Mind," young children understand that they have internal thoughts and emotions as part of this psychological self. Generally, preschoolers are quite pleased with themselves, and their self-evaluations tend to be positive and include overestimations of their abilities (Stipek, Recchia, & McClintic, 1992).

Box 2.11
Growth Indicators of Expanding Relationships with Adults and Peers

Growth Indicator	Example
Demonstrates strong attachment to parents and family	Cecilia asks for the fifth time in one hour, "When's my dad coming?"
Establishes emotional bonds to nonfamilial people	Stuart turns to his teacher to kiss her good-bye at the end of the day.
Forms friendships	Upon arrival at day care, a child asks her teacher, "Is Yvonne here yet? We're painting today."
Exhibits concern and empathy	Eddie looks up from a book in the story area and asks, "Who's crying? I'll go and check."

A critical part of children's conceptions of themselves is their gender identity—that is, knowing whether they are a girl or boy. Most 3-year-olds correctly answer whether they are a boy or girl; if they understand that the genitalia determine one's gender, most also understand that gender is a permanent attribute (Bem, 1989).

In general, conformity to gender stereotyped roles and preferences is already evident in the preschool years. Perhaps because preschool children are only beginning to learn about the complex web of social conventions dealing with gender, they exaggerate their gender roles so as to get them cognitively clear. A 3-year-old girl with short, baby-thin hair publicly reaffirmed her gender every day by adamantly refusing to wear anything except dresses. As levels of moral reasoning advance and children distinguish between moral and social norms, they become less rigid about gender issues (Lobel & Menashri, 1993).

How individual children construe gender roles (see Box 2.12) results from their unique blend of experiences within peer groups, social pressure, imitation and identification, biological influences, and their own self-regulation (Maccoby,

Box 2.12
Growth Indicators of Self-Concept

Growth Indicator	*Example*
Understands that the self has physical and psychological attributes	Colin sits with hands on his knees and declares, "I have hair on my legs like you, Dad."
	After a disagreement with an adult, child exclaims, "I get so mad at you!"
Aware of private, thinking self	"Hi, Sireena. What are you doing?" a teacher says to a child nestled in a beanbag chair. "Just dinkin'," Sireena replies.
Overestimates own abilities	After listening to a story that ends with, "No one's good at everything," a child responds, "I am."
Correctly identifies own gender	Andreas points to self and a playmate and declares, "I'm a boy, and you're a girl."
Often rigidly applies gender roles	Jasmine says she wants to be a nurse when she grows up even though her mother is a doctor.

1980, 1990). Sometimes the strength of social pressure is evident as young children, having noticed the predominant gender of construction workers in their social environment, favor plastic men models to represent these workers in the block area. Personal experiences may, however, help children form some nonstereotypic models. For example, a girl whose mother is a construction worker might well include a woman model in her block play or imitate the role herself.

Play

More than just a diversion to keep children busy, play serves a wide variety of functions during early childhood (Hendrick, 1996) and is "instrumental in children's social and cognitive development" (Pellegrini & Boyd, 1993, p. 118). Although children do not set out to learn about concepts in their physical world when they play, that indeed often happens. In preschool, an observer may be lucky enough to see children playing with materials and, incidentally, learning how to build a sturdy tower or combine effective amounts of sand and water to make a moldable mixture.

Often young children's play facilitates social development (e.g., see Parten's classic 1932 study). Increasing attention is being paid to young children's relationships with peers as they spend more time together in play groups, preschools, and day care than in previous generations. As friendships evolve, children may play independently next to other children, engage in rough-and-tumble play, share common activities, or play cooperatively. Through endless hours of play graced with a multitude of playmates and adult support, young children learn a great deal about how to get along with others.

Through play, children "translate experience into something internally meaningful to them" (Hendrick, 1996, p. 49). A consequence of young children's exposure to people is an interest in trying out various roles; as a result, children further their understanding of themselves, others, and the workings of the mind (Brown, Donelan-McCall, & Dunn, 1996; Flavell et al., 1993; Youngblade & Dunn, 1995). No one will scold children for being bossy if they are only pretending to be the neighborhood grouch. Or in the cloak of pretend roles, shy children can experiment with more assertive behaviors; they might find that the behaviors fit better than expected. Children also learn about their society through play, and they do so without personal risk. They might apply what they have learned about rules and punishments in a game of good guys/bad guys in which no one actually dies or goes to jail.

Play also serves the function of furthering physical development. Strength of large and small muscles, coordination, and flexibility are all advanced as young children play. The gross motor control of a 3-year-old is challenged by maneuvering a tricycle around traffic cones, and the fine motor skills of a 4-year-old are practiced by manipulating water table tools. The next section on creative development discusses the relationship between play and creativity.

Some observers may focus on play with objects versus social play (e.g., Heidemann & Hewitt, 1992), but they always recognize the satisfaction that play gives to children. Although the amount and type of play vary across cultures, keep the growth indicators listed in Box 2.13 in mind for most American children.

Box 2.13
Growth Indicators of Play

Growth Indicator	Example
Explores materials on own	Lesley explores toy trash truck and discovers one lever to raise the truck bed and one lever to open the back hatch.
Expands social interactions	In the sandbox several children industriously dig with scoopers next to one another, speaking occasionally, while others play together to dig a moat around their "castle."
Engages in dramatic play	"Hurry up," one child prods another in the house area. "Hurry up an' get dressed, or we'll be late for work."
Engages in physical play	Monty and Lee race for the adjacent swings.

Fears

"Fears are normal, and they help children solve developmental issues. They also call parents' attention to the child's struggle. They generate support from parents at a time when children need it" (Brazelton, 1992, p. 276). What are young and inexperienced children afraid of? First of all, they might be fearful of real objects, experiences, or people. Fears of this sort might come in the form of bathtub drains that make things disappear, loud noises, high places, people wearing masks, and strangers. Preschool children become increasingly able to think ahead and anticipate potential dangers. Depending on their culture, children might have a healthy fear of fast cars, rushing rivers, hot stoves, or galloping animals.

The origin of some fears might also lie within as preschoolers' representational thought provides entrance to a world of imagination that may feature frightening creatures or experiences. Children may fear what might happen; failure, parents' deaths, war, and abduction may lie in this category for some children.

Adults may help children face their fears by listening to children talk about their fears, reassuring them, helping them find ways to handle fears, maintaining consistent controls on behavior, facilitating learning about the frightening objects, and assisting children in understanding and expressing fears (Brazelton, 1992). Above all, adults working with young children should view most fears (see Box 2.14) as normal and indicative of developmental spurts or adjustments to stress.

Box 2.14
Growth Indicators of Fears

Growth Indicator	*Example*
Fears of real objects, people, and experiences	Margrit backs away from viewing a sea anemone, perceiving it as a sea "enemy."
	Garrett is suddenly fearful of the stenciled designs on his bedroom ceiling that now appear to him as large eyes.
Fears of the unknown or the imagined	After a nightmare Loren sticks close by his teacher for the morning and begins to cry when she goes into a dim closet for supplies.

Aggression

"Aggression clearly has an instinctive component; however, the frequency and intensity of an individual's aggression and the targets selected are influenced by the social environment and the individual's place in the social structure" (Maccoby, 1980, pp. 156–157). Toddlers and young preschoolers usually do not mean to hurt others when they act aggressively; they are simply intent on getting what they want. Their focus may be on a toy, a territory, or a privilege, such as being first to ride a tricycle. This aggression is descriptively called instrumental because the intent is not to hurt. True hostile aggression, however, is not far behind and is evident when children focus their anger on another and the intent *is* to hurt or dominate the other. A general gender difference is noted: "throughout early childhood, most studies find more male than female physical aggression" (Konner, 1991, p. 376). Box 2.15 describes growth indicators of changes in aggression.

Although teachers (and parents) may be assured that aggression declines from early childhood onward, they can foster alternatives to aggressive behavior. Young children are rapidly developing their communicative abilities and can therefore be encouraged to substitute words for blows. The welfare of the victim, not the aggressor, is the focus of the adult's first concern. Adults can also sensitize children to the feelings of others, for example, by involving the aggressor in the care of the victim; this strategy may be related to an earlier discussion of theory of mind in which children are encouraged to understand and take into account others' points of view.

Impulse Control

Parents and teachers often put on narrow blinders and deal with children's misdeeds as isolated events. Instead, they would do well to remind themselves of where young children are in their development of impulse control and what can be done

---

Box 2.15
Growth Indicators of Changing Aggression

Growth Indicator	*Example*
Instrumental aggression	Without making eye contact, Kendra grabs another's play dough.
Hostile aggression	"You big fat baby!" one child yells at another who won't relinquish the lemon-scented play dough.
Increasing reliance on communication to settle disputes	"Can I have the play dough now?" Enrique asks Mary Alice. "No," Mary Alice answers firmly. "Well, gimme *some* then," he counters.

---

to foster it. A brief study of impulse control enables one to see the forest of the development of impulse control rather than the trees of misdeeds.

The fact that young children are naturally impulsive is fundamental to an understanding of the development of impulse control. This fact should carry no harsh judgment. Young children typically act before they think about consequences and respond immediately to interesting or exciting objects, people, and events.

What difference does impulse control make in children's lives? Self-control mechanisms allow children to develop a high quality of solitary play, attend to complex problems, anticipate dangers and guard their own safety, and sustain cooperative play with other children (Maccoby, 1980). Adults who want to foster the development of impulse control in children (see Box 2.16 for growth indicators) can profit from research showing that maternal overcontrol is associated with poor impulse control (Silverman & Ragusa, 1990) and from Maccoby's review of implications for child rearing:

- Provide children with a regular, predictable schedule in which novelty is regulated.
- Minimize the waiting time required of young children.
- Make the environment safe and childproof.
- Make appropriate decisions when children are too young to anticipate the consequences. Provide opportunities for age-appropriate decisions.
- Model self-control.
- Set clear limits and firm controls of children's behavior.
- Engage in joint activities with children.

Box 2.16
Growth Indicators of Impulse Control

Growth Indicator	*Example*
Usually acts before considering consequences	On awaking in the nap room where other children are still sleeping, Nicola calls loudly to teacher.
Has difficulty waiting	Noticing problem behaviors every time preschoolers are lined up and asked to wait, the teacher abandons this procedure in favor of brief, direct transitions.
Makes choices at own developmental level	Kasumi studies two stacks of shirts in a drawer and calls down to parent, "Is it a short-sleeve day or a long-sleeve day?"
Benefits from joint activities with adults	Jessie, who does not often exhibit sustained attention on own, works intently on a sand city when a teacher is involved.

The last strategy deserves a bit more attention, and here again we witness an application of Vygotsky's zone of proximal development. The hours teachers and parents spend working and playing with children will encourage their self-control in the long run. Joint activities allow children to participate in a complex sequence of events they are not yet able to manage on their own and to enjoy the rewards of delayed gratification. Consider a teacher making play dough with a small group of preschoolers. The children gain the experience of following several steps of an activity and produce a lovely product for their efforts. The teacher working alongside the children has the opportunity to model new ideas for children who are easily bored because they tend to work superficially with materials.

Preschool children's progress in learning about themselves and their social worlds is remarkable. "Schools are the first large institution to which children come from their families and home neighborhoods and in which they are expected to participate individually and publicly" (Cazden, 1988, p. 3). At the end of the preschool years, most children are ready to venture further out into the world and meet the expanded social demands of elementary school.

Selected Highlights of Creative Development

Creativity is studied and explored from various perspectives and in many different ways (Edwards, Gandini, & Forman, 1993; Feldman, Csikszentmihalya, & Gardner,1994; Taylor, 1995; Torrance, 1976). Definitions for creativity are also varied.

For this chapter, the definition is linked to the early childhood classroom in which the comparative basis for judging originality is the child herself/himself rather than adult standards mandating that the work be new to everyone (Goetz, 1989). During the preschool years, "creativity is a way of thinking and acting or making something that is original for the individual and valued by that person or others" (Mayesky, 1995, p. 4).

Feldman's work (1980) explored two approaches to creativity taken by psychologists. He labeled one approach the *trait approach* and the other the *process approach*. Feldman explained that the trait approach, fathered by J. P. Guilford, submits that creativity is innate and unfolds naturally; it is motivated from within to express itself and will do so, except under extreme conditions. This approach holds that each person is born with a certain measure of creativity.

In contrast, the process approach "focuses on the interaction between the organism and the environment—the ongoing, ever changing construction of behavior" (Feldman, 1980, p. 90). Creativity is the result of possessing abilities and having conditions that allow for practice and improvement. For example, interested family members and teachers can provide the necessary encouragement and opportunities for children to develop their abilities (Bloom, 1985).

These two approaches, much akin to the nature-verses-nurture controversy, produce implications for the classroom. If we subscribed to the first approach—traits—teachers would need to do little. Today we find in the educational arena, however, the process approach is favored over the trait approach (Cropley, 1992).

Review the growth indicators in Box 2.17 to learn how creativity for young children is identified. Then read on to find out how to facilitate and cultivate creativity through the process approach.

"In preschool children, this putting together of new ideas and products based on past experience is expressed primarily through the use of self-expressive materials, through imaginative pretend play, and through creative thought" (Hendrick, 1994, p. 314). Children of this age are involved with exploration, discovery, and new experiences. If observers slip quietly through the doors of quality preschools, they can see numerous examples of young children engaged in the creative process: constructing block structures and using accessory items; dressing up in high heels, wearing a waltz-length silky nightie, and carrying around precious baby dolls; laboriously struggling to solve puzzle patterns; waving scarves and moving to the music of a favorite record; making mud pies with wet sand; building with nails and wood; drawing with crayons, markers, and chalk; and dictating original stories as an adult's hand races to capture every spoken word. In the famous child care centers in Reggio Emilia, Italy, these abundant forms of creativity are considered languages, specifically referred to as the children's 100 languages (Rody, 1995).

Wise early childhood educators know that simply observing the emerging signs of creative growth listed in Box 2.17 is not enough to support creativity. By using the information obtained from observations of individual children, the teacher makes strategy decisions. The teacher may provide enticing classroom experiences based on a child's interests, offer encouragement related to the child's effort, co-construct a project through the child's lead, ask open-ended questions, arrange the environment to reflect a creative climate, and/or take field trips to appreciate creative expression in the community. Figure 2.3 offers suggestions for the teacher-in-training.

Box 2.17
Preschool Growth Indicators of Creativity

Growth Indicator	*Definition*	*Example*
Expands mental flexibility	Sees alternatives, especially when one idea fails	While playing firefighter, one child uses the only hose. Another child (who usually seeks the teacher's assistance) rummages through the dramatic play materials and uses a vacuum cleaner attachment as a hose.
Expands sensitivity	Tunes into senses and sees details in the surrounding environment	On a walk Effrin carefully observes an ant diligently dragging a bread crumb toward the ant hill and says, "Boy, he's working hard!"
Expands imagination	Composes and utilizes mental images of things not present	Chester, using a block as a microphone and standing on top of an outdoor play structure, sways back and forth as he sings, imitating a popular country western singer.
Expands risk taking	Experiments with possibilities, being open to divergent thinking and acting on it	Olivia adds one more block to a precarious structure.
Expands resourcefulness	Trusts one's own perceptions	A child uses the wheelbarrow to transport selected toys to other side of the play yard.
Expands expressive experiences and skills using creative materials	Develops necessary proficiency through practice and maturation (interrelated with fine	A child's functional explorations and manipulations (stirring and mixing sand) become rep-

<table>
<tr><td>*Growth Indicator*</td><td>*Definition*
motor and cognitive development)</td><td>*Example*
resentational as cakes are created.</td></tr>
</table>

Box 2.17 (continued)

Note. Six growth indicators from *Beginnings and Beyond,* 4th ed. (pp. 472–473) by A. Gordon and K. Williams-Browne, 1995, Albany, NY: Delmar Publishers, Inc. Copyright © 1995 by Delmar Publishers. Reproduced by permission.

Condition	Examples of the Teacher's Role
Psychological safety	Provide "noncritical, nonevaluative and receptive atmosphere where fresh and even wild ideas may be safely proposed" (Davis & Rim, 1989, p. 225). Develop an atmosphere of trust from the first day forth.
Real experiences	Provide experiences that develop the senses. Provide experiences with creative materials Plan abundant field trips. Tune into children's questions and interests on walks and field trips. Point out changes in nature.
Uninterrupted time blocks	Plan large time blocks for children to use materials of choice in ways that are congruent with their development. Permit important projects (e.g., block structures) to be left as is and worked on later.
Sufficient space	Provide space appropriate to selected activity (e.g., easel painting protected on the side, central space for overflow block structures, specified space for group activities, such as mural painting and dramatic play).
Open-ended materials	Use a help-yourself shelf in the child directed art area Provide a choice of tools to create with; items to draw, paint, paste on, or fold and tear; alternatives for fastening things together; and an assortment of everchanging materials. Provide multiuse materials and equipment for all areas.

Figure 2.3. Preschool classroom conditions affecting creative climate.

Condition	Examples of the Teacher's Role
Accessible and organized materials	Minimize the child's need to hunt for materials and tendency to become distracted from selected activity by labeling and classifying materials within the areas.
	Define distinct areas of the room using low moveable shelves or large area rugs of various colors.
Varied and abundant materials	Change the dramatic play area from time to time: include props for role-playing varied life experiences (e.g., store, hair salon).
	Survey the avenues for creative expression in the classroom. Observe and determine why some areas are more popular than others. Consider the materials and the activity choices. Are baskets of small wooden people or plastic animals offered with the unit blocks? Are easel painting and another set-up activity (e.g., collages) offered as well as a help-yourself shelf in the art area?
	Count the children. Are there enough items, or will children need to wait a long time to have a turn to express themselves?
Teacher's supportive attitude	Respect each child as unique and important; accept the child's level of expression, and use comments that enhance rather than stifle the creative process. Address the child's effort or the process rather than approve of the result. "Children's motivation and creativity can be destroyed if evaluation, reward, and competition are misused" (Amabile, 1989, p. 69).
Teacher modeling	Exhibit curiosity, recognize curiosity in children, and encourage curiosity in daily experiences. Use your senses to explore with the children.
	Promote flexibility and sensitivity by asking open-ended questions rather than giving answers.
Aesthetic appreciation	Display art prints with themes that correspond to various centers (e.g., science, books, blocks). Play a variety of musical selections during free-choice time or nap time.
	Include children's books about artists, musicians, and writers in the book corner.
	Invite local artists, musicians, or writers to visit the class.

Figure 2.3.   (*Continued*).

Let's take a closer look at two specific components of creativity: art and block play. When you are observing children engaged in these two activities, knowledge of typical growth is advantageous.

As children grow and develop at their own pace, so does their representational drawing. The individual growth rate is influenced by the child's cognitive development (e.g., representational thought), physical development (e.g., motor control), perceptual development (e.g., sensory awareness and space perception), and art experiences (e.g., opportunities to explore). Therefore, if the teacher understands and can identify the characteristics represented by a child's art work, an observational window opens.

While studying the growth indicators of children's drawing presented in the Box 2.18, be aware of the development sequence from scribbling to the advancement of picture forms. The classroom teacher can collect a few samples of each child's drawings over time, dating each sample. Box 2.18 is a handy reference for interpreting children's developmental growth in drawing.

Teachers can also observe and keep notes of the sequential development of three-dimensional art materials. When the children are working with clay, the teacher can expect to see the following (Wolfgang & Wolfgang, 1992):

1. Random pounding
2. Controlled pounding
3. Rolling clay into snake-like rolls and later into circles
4. Adding pieces to the rolls and circles (facial features and body parts)
5. Combining products, such as people in cars or a boy on a horse (p. 31)

When evaluating art experiences (two- or three-dimensional), consider the following warning: fostering creativity mandates art activities that are process oriented (exploratory) rather than product oriented (crafts). In November many classroom walls are filled with paper-plate turkeys that have strips of colored paper glued on to represent feathers. The head and feet are cut by the teacher and glued on by the children. All the turkeys look alike. Did the children express themselves creatively? No, they simply followed the teacher's directions. "If art products look as though they were done by one person, there was not enough room for creative self-expression. If they all contain the same symbols in a similar way, the experience was overdirected" (Hoffman, Kanter, Colbert, & Sims, 1991, p. 23). Art activities that duplicate a model or dictate a specific product stifle creative growth. Schirrmacher (1993) advised as follows:

There are too many activities that masquerade as creative art. Some of these include

- photocopied, or mimeographed sheets
- cut-and-paste activities
- tracing patterns
- coloring-book pages
- dot-to-dot pages
- crafts
- holiday gifts
- seatwork (p. 9)

Box 2.18
Preschool Growth Indicators of Drawing

Preschool (ages 2½–5)

- Scribbles, loops, zigzags, waves lines, makes jabs and arcs—often partially off the paper at first
- Produces chance forms or shapes
- Tries out different effects
- Finds meaning in the act itself, not in results or product
- Experiments with leaving a mark, using colors and motions to leave a sign or have an effect
- Makes separate lines, circlelike shapes; combines straight and curved lines
- Makes other basic forms and controlled marks; formulates first schema (personalized representational symbols), mandalalike shapes

Early primary (ages 4–6)

- Combines shapes into schemas; makes intentional image repetition of schemas; develops preferred schemas
- Begins drawing representations, often of people, animals in profile, letterlike forms, and basic forms represented consistently—houses, flowers, boats, people
- Portrays meaning (subject matter) in an increasingly readable manner
- Repeats repertory or symbolic forms (schemas) practices, and adds new elements
- Shows beginnings of individual style (e.g., typical way of drawing a house)
- Isolates figures, each discrete (no overlapping of whole or of parts); shows no context or baseline and draws size and details according to perceived importance or interest (e.g., long arms)
- Presents several figures on the page; begins representing events or narratives; places schematic figures in a larger concept, for example, knowing an elephant is a four-legged animal with a trunk, the child uses a well-established routine, or schema, for drawing animals—cats, dogs, and so forth—and adds a trunk to the elephant.

Note. Adapted and reprinted with the permission of the National Association for the Education of Young Children. From *Considering Children's Art: Why and How to Value Their Works* by B. S. Engel. Copyright © 1995 by National Association for the Education of Young Children.

Children's three-dimensional
art develops in predictable
sequences.

Practitioners must be diligent not to cheat children from the most obvious and basic creative experience by substituting product art for process art.

Another important pathway to creative expression that deserves extra attention is blocks. They are one of the most universal toys at home and school, and block play has been a part of early childhood education for more than 75 years. The developmental values of block building are numerous. Blocks help children develop imagination; awareness of balance, form, and spatial relations; representation and classification abilities; patterning skills; size, shape, area, volume, and equivalency understandings; eye–hand coordination; and fine motor skills. Eventually blocks are used by children to set the scene for dramatic play, a rich source of language and cooperative play.

When first exposed to unit blocks, children need plenty of time to explore with them. Progressing at their own pace through sequential stages (see Box 2.19), children make new discoveries, including how to structure bridges, enclosures, or patterns; repetitions of these creations are commonly observed from day to day. Children who enter block play at older ages (4 through 6) pass quickly through all beginning stages, but they skip the first, elementary one (Hirsch, 1996). Making sketches or taking photos of children's expanding block development is an excellent observational aid.

Blocks seem to hold a magnetic attraction for young children. There can be times, however, when children ignore the block area. To rejuvenate enthusiasm, the teacher may add accessories reflecting the children's current interests (e.g., small plastic sea creatures), actively participate in block building, or change the location of the block area. Strategies for teacher observation and interventions in block play are addressed in Chapter 11.

Chapter Conclusion

This chapter gives a brief overview of the preschool child's multifaceted growth and development. Certainly no two children develop along the exact same course; individual children show different progression rates of physical, cognitive, psy-

---

Box 2.19
Preschool Growth Indicators of Block Play

Stage 1   Child carries block around not used for construction.

Stage 2   Child makes mostly rows, either horizontal (on the floor) or vertical (stacked). There is much repetition in this early building pattern.

Stage 3   Child makes bridges.

Stage 4   Child makes enclosures.

Stage 5   Child makes elaborate designs using pattern and balance.

Stage 6   Child names structures related to their functions (houses, boats, stairs).

Stage 7   Child reproduces or symbolizes familiar structures with buildings.

Note. From *The Block Book* (pp. 142–148) edited by Elisabeth S. Hirsch, 1996. Washington D.C.: National Association for the Education of Young Children. Copyright © 1984 by the National Association for the Education of Young Children. Adapted and reprinted with permission from the National Association for the Education of Young Children.

chosocial, and creative development. Yet development generally follows a predictable path. Understanding development and growth indicators along that path allows the teacher to identify each child's advances, missing neither the baby steps nor the giant leaps. This process enables the teacher to fulfill one of our ethical responsibilities to children (NAEYC Ideal I-1.2) highlighted at the beginning of this chapter: "To base program practices upon current knowledge in the field of child development and related disciplines and upon particular knowledge of each child" (Feeney & Kipnis, 1992, p. 4).

Take a Moment to Reflect

One of the developmental axioms (see Figure 2.1) holds that each child develops at an individual maturational rate, that each child possesses his/her own genetic time clock. Using information from your own or your child's preschool development, reflect on and answer the following questions (you may have to consult one of your parents):

1. What were the unique qualities of you or your child?
2. Choose one of the four developmental domains and describe the significant strides you or your child made during the preschool years.
3. Discuss one example of how an adult (teacher, parent, or significant other) enhanced or hindered the developmental process.

CHAPTER 3

Highlights of Development During the Primary Grade Years

From *Life* magazine comes an article (Follmi, 1989) about a child from Tibet making a perilous journey from her remote and isolated village in the Himalayas to a school 100 miles away. In a small entourage, Diskit and her brother traveled single file on a frozen river following the leader who, with a long stick, tapped the ice to test for strength. Stop and think for a moment how Diskit's secluded mountain life and unusual travel protocol might have shaped her perceptions of the physical world. Then read on.

> On the twelfth and final day, the landscape changes. The white of eternal ice gives way to the brown hills surrounding the valley of Ladakh. The exhausted travelers trade the frozen skin of the mighty river for a dirt road, and Lobsang and his children hitch a ride on a transport truck. Diskit cowers: The driver is a Sikh with a turban and a long moustache. She has never before seen an Indian who was not a Tibetan Buddhist. The vehicle overtakes a man on horseback. She tugs on her father's coat. "Abale," she asks, using the native word for father, "have you seen? Here the donkeys walk backward."
>
> "No," her father replies. "It's just that we're moving faster than it is." (p. 116)

Extraordinary, isn't it, from our Western, industrialized perspective that a primary grade child could perceive an object being overtaken as traveling backward? How can this be explained?

Diskit was a child with all her mental faculties intact. Her perceptual error of thinking that a man on a donkey was traveling backward as she overtook him on a truck was understandable in the context of her cultural experiences. Growing up in a small mountain village dedicated to growing barley in the summer and surviving frigid winters had not yet taught her about the traffic patterns she first observed, without understanding, in town. As she learned from new experiences, Diskit would doubtlessly become incredulous that she was ever capable of such a misinterpretation.

As you reflect on the development of preschool children as described in Chapter 2 and read about the development of primary grade children (K–3) in this chapter, think about how the various cultures familiar to you influence and moderate development. While reading, look for examples that illustrate this chapter's featured ethical responsibility to children (NAEYC Ideal I-1.2) and answer the following question: In what ways can teachers be responsive to developmental needs that reflect cultural diversity? Selected highlights of physical, cognitive, psychosocial, and creative development are presented to document general growth trends. As in Chapter 2, however, remember that individual and cultural diversity is always evident.

Consider our Ethical Responsibilities to Children

NAEYC Ideal I-1.2

"To base program practices upon current knowledge in the field of child development and related disciplines and upon particular knowledge of each child" (Feeney & Kipnis, 1992, p. 4).

Read on to see how understanding development helps teachers fulfill this ethical responsibility.

Selected Highlights of Physical Development

Body Growth

As the active primary grade child's internal developmental timetable continues, the child proceeds to grow in a general stepwise pattern increasing in height and weight. During these years the child's first permanent teeth appear, and the need for regular naps ceases.

Early childhood teachers respect that "the range of normal development is quite broad" (Berger & Thompson, 1995, p. 296). This range in physical development is illustrated in the photograph on the next page. Each child possesses an individual genetic rate of maturation. Therefore, differences in children's stature (even within homogeneous age groups) are noticeable. Attention to this factor is necessary when observing and assessing a child.

In a room full of first or second graders, a general trend in physical growth development is evident, but individual differences in this area can be easily spotted. Think back for a moment to your primary years. Were you an "average" child? If not, did you get dubbed with a nickname reflecting your physical development—half pint, peanut, lefty, freckle-face, four-eyes, or boney maroney? Maybe you knew someone who did. Do you think these individual growth deviations from the norm affect the primary age child? Consider how physical development may influence a child's self-esteem as you read the psychosocial development section in this chapter.

Motor Development

Motor development encompasses the changes in movement ability and body control. In this section, both gross motor development (the growth toward movement competence of arms, legs, and torso—large muscles of the body) and fine motor

And they are all the same age!

development (the growth toward efficient control of fingers, hands, feet—small muscles of the body) are explored in an abbreviated form.

Gross Motor Skills

During the primary grade years, two stages of gross motor development are apparent. Some children still engage in perfecting the fundamental motor skills listed as growth indicators of gross motor development (Chapter 2, Box 2.1)—running, jumping, hopping, galloping, skipping, climbing, balancing, catching, throwing, and kicking, whereas other children move forward to a more complex stage of coordinating two or more skills to create a new skill, such as playing basketball, which combines running and dribbling. Accomplishments in the latter stage allow the child to use these more specialized skills in a number of activities, such as dance, sports, and other recreational games (Gallahue, 1993).

Given abundant practice opportunities, the primary grade child shows continuous advancement of muscle strength, balance, reaction time, and eye–hand coordination. This growth facilitates gradual improved performance of motor skills with age (Clark & Phillips, 1985; DuRandt, 1985; Kerr, 1985). Compare the physical activities on the K–3 playground to those on a preschool yard. Notice the individual differences in the children who play jacks, climb the bars, jump rope, or cross a balance beam. As motor-skill performance becomes more complex and specified, increased strength and judgment are required to carry out the task. When were you able to engage in combining motor skills in sports, such as baseball, basketball, tether ball, soccer or volleyball? What about your sister or brother? Skillful participation in these second-stage activities are more likely in the primary grade years than the preschool years.

The primary grade growth indicators of gross motor development listed in Box 3.1 help guide ongoing observations and record keeping. Be sure to assess each child as an individual. "Do not compare children's movement skills based on chronological age, as is usually done, but remember that many performer factors (e.g., heredity, culture, and environment) contribute to the development of each child's skills" (Burton, 1992, p. 4).

The complex process of motor development is enhanced by appropriate experiences.

Box 3.1
Primary Grade Growth Indicators of Gross Motor Skills

Growth Indicator	*Example*
Increases strength of legs and arms	Mandy's knuckles whiten as she gives an extra kick with her legs while reaching for the last rung on the overhead parallel bars. Today she finally makes it all the way across!
Increases speed	In the fourth game of neighborhood "hide and seek," whining complaints of the preschoolers echo in the streets, "Why do we always have to be *it?*" "Because you never catch us," laugh the older brothers and sisters, scampering off.
Increases coordination	Sheyenne dribbles the ball four times as she runs toward the basket, aims, and makes a successful jump shot.
Increases agility	The boy begins to feel confident as he successfully dodges the ball again and again and again in the second-grade game.
Increases endurance	Having just run eight laps around the track, Patrick smiles and heads for the water fountain, remembering that last year he could only run six laps.
Increases specialized skills in sports	The child dribbles the soccer ball for 7 yards before passing it to a teammate.

Fine Motor Skills

Most children approach the primary grade years having had a variety of experiences using small muscle tools (e.g., puzzles, crayons, magnifying glasses, and clothing fasteners). As with gross motor skills, genetic makeup and maturation play key roles in the development of fine motor skills along with suitable experiences. As K–3 children gain increased small muscle control and eye–hand coordination, they can, with appropriate opportunities and practice, successfully engage in such activities as coloring within chosen lines, cutting out intricate pictures, and using writing, drawing, and building tools.

During the primary grade years, observations of fine motor skills are often focused on the complex and advanced ability of handwriting. Teachers keep in mind that proficiency in this process involves not only coordinated arm, wrist, hand, and finger movements but also honed perceptual skills, proper posture, appropriate instruction, and practice time (Kalverboer, Hopkins, & Geuze, 1993; Soliv, 1993). In kindergarten, handwriting begins with printing of unevenly formed letters and numbers from ½ inch to 2 inches high and advances to printing horizontally aligned letters and numbers about ¼ inch high (Payne & Issacs, 1987). Remember that when a child reverses letters (e.g., prints the letter *b* instead of the letter *d*), the child's perceptual skills are still developing; reversals are not uncommon in children up to the age of 8 (Corbin, 1980). With this in mind, it is understandable that children are not introduced to cursive writing until the second or third grade.

Optimal observations and recordings in the early childhood classroom (see Box 3.2 for fine motor growth indicators) are accomplished by viewing children as individuals developing at their own rate. These wise words exemplify that idea:

> One of the most well-established premises of human development is that there is a wide range of individual variation that is well within the range of "normal" and, of course, the inclusion of children with disabilities and special abilities further expands the range of individual differences in any one classroom. (Bredekamp, 1992, p. 31)

Elements Affecting Motor Development

Throughout this section of physical development, two major factors that influence the development of motor skills have been identified—maturation and environment. Figure 3.1 on page 66 summarizes the main components of these factors. While reading them, think about the implications of these factors for observation and planning.

Developmentally appropriate curriculum planning based on observation keeps in mind the primary grade child's need for ample school opportunities to practice, exercise, and engage in physical play. In addition, special attention is paid to the following:

- Children who have poor diets and are overweight.
- Children who have long bus rides and then go directly into the classroom.
- Children who have not developed social skills and appear to withdraw or attach themselves to the teacher on the playground, seldom entering into physical activities.
- Children who continually use the outdoor play equipment for dramatic play rather than motor development.
- Children who spend most of their out-of-school hours watching television or playing computer games.

Box 3.2
Primary Grade Growth Indicators of Fine Motor Skills

Growth Indicator	*Example*
Increases ability to skillfully use writing tool, scissors, and small objects	The boy cuts an intricate snowflake out of folded paper, while his younger sister struggles to cut out a heart shape.
Increases ability to arrange numbers and letters uniformly	Kindergartner Kristen wrote:

1 2 3 4

Second grader Blake wrote:

1 2 3 4 5

| Increases eye–hand coordination | While playing Stak Attack, 8-year-old Sally carefully and slowly removes the bottom block from the stack, adding it to the top without toppling the 15-inch stack. |

- Children in city schools when Stage 3 smog alerts prohibit them from playing outdoors.
- Classroom schedules that do not allow for ample movement and rigorous activity during the day. Is one recess at 11:00 A.M. the best way to aid attention span?

Overall K–3 children are moving into a social environment in which motor skill performance is necessary for success in sports participation and other recreational activities. Fine motor skills are necessary for classroom success in writing, computer operation, and manipulation of art tools for creative expression. The knowledgeable teacher observes and understands maturational and cultural differences, provides practice opportunities, gives instruction and encouragement based on observations of individual interests, and maintains realistic expectations.

Factors	Examples
Rate of body growth, increased strength, and maturity of the nervous system have an impact on physical development, delaying or advancing the process.	A tall kindergarten child has difficulty synchronizing the timing of the hop and step movements to be an effective skipper. A child, frustrated because he cannot coordinate his eye–hand movements while playing jacks, never gets beyond the "threezes."
Ease in social participation and physical activities are mutually linked	In a study on children's feelings of loneliness and their relationship to physical fitness, it was reported that "lonely children were less physically fit and physically active than were those who were not lonely" (Page, Frey, Talbert, & Falk, 1992, p. 211).
Encouragement, instruction, and opportunities to practice influence the development of motor skills.	When learning to print letters, the child is taught to form the circles in letters *o, g, d,* and *q* by starting at the top and circling to the left, so the transition to writing those letters in cursive will be quicker and easier than trying to form new habits if the printed letters are learned with a motion of circling to the right.
Practice is often linked to interests, motivation, cultural expectations, and geographic location.	Children living in southern California may easily combine the fundamental motor skills into more complex skills through regularly riding a skateboard, playing baseball, or perhaps swimming in the ocean. Children living in Vermont may perfect their skills through regularly skiing, ice skating, or playing basketball.

Figure 3.1. Elements affecting motor development.

This chapter section on physical development is far from a comprehensive discussion of physical growth. To review the areas not covered (e.g., fundamental skill progressions, brain maturation, motor perception, and hand dominance), consult a child-development book.

elected Highlights of Cognitive Development

Representational Abilities

As children move from the preschool through the primary grade years, the complexity of their representational activities expands. (Recall from Chapter 2 that a representation is something that stands for—or represents—something else.) For example, children's role play, drawings, and models exhibit more details, concepts, and sophisticated designs than those produced a few years earlier. Further, primary grade children are prepared to construct and decode abstract symbols. Older children can listen to a book with few picture aids and rely on their own mental imagery to augment the text. Their understanding of the meaning behind letters and numbers becomes more secure and skilled. Consider this example of growing familiarity with the representational meaning of numbers. A prekindergartner (4;9) arranged magnets on the refrigerator in spite of a missing 3 and 0.

1   2   ΨΨΨ   4   5   6   7   8   9   1●

The child explained that she used three sucker magnets because she didn't have a 3 and that a small round magnet was "almost like" a zero; clearly she understood the representations involved.

Because nothing about the symbol 3 suggests what it stands for, understanding numbers (and letters) as abstract representations is a critical cognitive step for primary grade children. This step results from maturing perceptual skills and from instruction. On the one hand, maturing perceptual skills allow children to make increasingly fine distinctions between symbols (e.g., between b and d). On the other hand, no amount of contemplation of an "M" or "Σ" will result in children's correct deciphering of the letter unless they have been taught its meaning. Elementary schools are responsible for teaching children the abstract representational systems of letters and numbers. Box 3.3 summarizes the growth indicators of young children's representational abilities to observe and support in primary grade classrooms.

Language

The most far-reaching change in language during the primary grade years stems from children's growing understanding of language as a means of communication. Primary grade children become able to think about how they and others use language. Most children enjoy conversing with others and become aware of themselves and others as givers and receivers of messages. Hopefully, teachers and parents of primary grade children provide encouragement as language skills (see the growth indicators in Box 3.4) develop in speaking and writing.

Box 3.3
Primary Grade Growth Indicators of Representational Abilities

Growth Indicator	*Example*
Expands complexity of preschool growth indicators	Shonnie, Buddy, and Abdul engage in "school" dramatic play and sound remarkably like the people they represent!
• Forms mental images	
• Imitates	
• Uses language	A third grader draws a person in profile.
• Pretends	
• Role-plays	
• Represents in two dimensions	Detlof constructs a personally designed car out of Legos.
• Represents in three dimensions	
• Decodes others' representations	
Decodes and uses abstract symbols (letters and numbers)	A second grader competently reads *The Cat in the Hat* to a kindergartner during after-school care.

Children need encouragement and a trusting environment in which to talk, write, and try out new words. Although more attention is paid to primary grade children's technical use of language (e.g., spelling and grammar) than to that of younger children, continued emphasis on content before form reduces risks of failure. Teachers want to encourage children to speak and write fluently, and that requires lots of practice, experience, and confidence. If children are continually under the critical eye of adults waiting to pounce on a misspoken or miswritten word, they are apt to pull back from language. On the other hand, engagement in their zones of proximal development (see Chapter 2) appropriately challenges children in a supportive environment.

A first-grade teacher delighted in the content of a child's story and ignored the many errors and lack of a title. Try to figure out the words, and enjoy a chuckle.

> The day the teacher vanisted we panted the room fluorescent. Spied on the other classis. We acted up for 2 hoers and theen went home, for louch. Back at school we rearranged the classroom. We never saw or teacher agin. Intell we fowd out she had moived to massachousits.

Primary grade children can construct complex representational models.

At the beginning of third grade, this child was a prolific and able writer. Consider this short piece about a grandparent.

Gaga and the Raccoons

My grandma's name is Gaga. She died when she was 70 that was 3 years ago. Gaga's real name is Marge Gaede. She taught first, second, and third grade before she retired. After she retired gaga worked at the hands on museum in ann arbor. Gaga loved raccoons very much and to her great joy discovered that many raccoons lived in the forest behind her house. Every night Gaga would make peanut butter samwitchs and then she would throw them all over her yard. My family, Gaga and her husband Gampa and I all sit on the porch and wait and watch. Soon the raccoons began to come they ate and ate and ate. When the raccoons were full they slowly began to leave and I went to bed. When Gaga was still teaching her stutents gave her a shirt that said Fuzzies and Raccoons go togather. Fuzzies are little balls of thered with eyes that Gaga loved to make. When I was at Gaga's feunroll all I could think was Raccoons and Gagas go togather.

This child's language development flourished in an environment that encouraged talking about a wide range of interesting topics, reading books regularly, seeing adults read, and writing as a method of communication about personally meaningful subjects.

Box 3.4
Primary Grade Growth Indicators of Language

Growth Indicator	*Example*
Expands vocabulary	Vinnie describes a new friend as "very considerate."
Understands there can be literal and figurative meanings of words	To describe her grandparents, Hannah sums up, "They're very old, and they can't talk very good; their voices *ruffle.*"
	During a first-grade story time, children laugh heartily as Amelia Bedelia literally follows directions to dust furniture, draw drapes, and dress chickens.
Discerns subtle differences among words	Tuong-Anh says, "Today the rain sounds sharp, not plunking like usual."
Uses and understands many grammatical rules and exceptions	A second grader is not confused by the passive sentence construction, "Trent was teased by Riley."
Becomes a proficient communicator with adults and peers	Nicholas contributes his viewpoint to the class discussion: "The color of the wind is whatever's behind it."
	To emphasize her anxiety before her first class play, a 6-year-old declares she has "monarchs" in her tummy.
Constructs increasingly complex sentences (structure and length)	Carmela informs a friend, "My favorite dinner is barbecued ribs with extra sauce on the side, cole slaw, and creamy potatoes, and for dessert I like baked apples with cinnamon."

Note. (See Figure 6.1 in Chapter 6 for information on writing development.)

Logical Thought

A major cognitive advancement during the primary grades is children's increasing ability to reason logically about problems with real objects (Piaget & Inhelder, 1969). Primary grade children's experiences and expanded mental flexibility allow them to understand logical operations, such as addition and subtraction. First graders who are beginning to learn math facts often treat $3 + 4 = 7$ and $7 - 3 = 4$ as two independent problems. Before the year is out, most will understand the logical connection between the two.

Primary grade children's logical thought may be demonstrated by asking them questions about conservation (the concept that something remains the same if nothing is added or taken away). In a conservation-of-length problem, two rulers are aligned and then one is simply moved over in full view of the child. If a young primary grade child asserts that the two rulers remain the same after the re-arrangement and is asked why, the child is likely to justify this conclusion with a statement that focuses on the maintained identity of the objects: "It's the same stick" or "You just moved it over."

Given a variety of conservation problems, a primary grade child (particularly a 5- or 6-year-old) typically answers some correctly and some incorrectly. For example, the child who was right about the preceding conservation-of-length question might answer incorrectly on questions about conservation of matter and liquid 2 minutes later. This inconsistency is a bit perplexing. One would think that once a child understands that something remains the same if nothing is added or taken away, this reasoning could be applied across the board on a variety of tasks. If the child said that two rulers are the same if one is moved over, why wouldn't the child also say that two equal globs of play dough remain equal if one is reshaped and two amounts of juice are the same if one is poured into a differently shaped container? Although the basic concept of conservation is the same across tasks, children do not become logical thinkers all at once. Some tasks are more difficult than others, even when they theoretically draw on the same cognitive concept. In addition, children have had varying experiences and have varying cognitive strengths. Adults should expect to see primary grade children draw on logical thought sometimes (but not always) and to observe individual differences among children. Box 3.5 describes growth indicators of logical thought.

The thinking of primary grade children remains concrete, based in the tangible world, so they reason best about the here and now. For example, an 8-year-old listened to an older child tell a joke about two friends, Joe and Casey, who loved baseball. The friends agreed that whoever died first would try to return to earth and let the other know if baseball is played in heaven. Joe died first, and one day Casey returned home to find him sitting in his living room. The 10-year-old delivered the punch line:

10-YEAR-OLD: So Joe said, "I've got some good news and some bad news. The good news is there is baseball in heaven. The bad news is you're scheduled to pitch tomorrow."

8-YEAR-OLD: I don't get it.

Box 3.5
Primary Grade Growth Indicators of Logical Thought

Growth Indicator	*Example*
Often reasons flexibly and logically about tangible problems	A child studies the groups of math manipulatives and exclaims, "Oh, I get it! A remainder is like leftover stuff. There's not enough to make another whole group."
Continues to demonstrate concrete thinking	Cassie looks at a photo book of Amish families with a parent who describes their religion and simple life. To exemplify the connection between beliefs and daily life, the parent explains the Amish reliance on hooks and eyes rather than modern zippers to fasten clothing. After attentive listening, Cassie asks thoughtfully, "Do they believe in elastic?"

10-YEAR-OLD: Well, see, for Casey to pitch in heaven, he's gotta die first.
8-YEAR-OLD: [No laughter but a moment of thought] So what did Casey die of?

The joke bombed! Concrete thought simply did not allow the 8-year-old to discern the hidden agenda.

Metacognition

Building on preschool children's theories of mind, primary grade children gain specific knowledge about thinking. Metacognition is knowledge about cognition, and "metacognitive knowledge can be roughly subdivided into knowledge about *persons, tasks,* and *strategies* (Flavell, et al., 1993, p. 150). Metacognition is at work when you monitor your understanding of information, take a list of growth indicators on an index card with you during an observational session, and adjust your study procedures for an essay versus a multiple-choice exam. Similarly, children increasingly understand and make judgments about what thinking is like and how people are similar and different as thinkers. They learn about the varying requirements of cognitive tasks and how they and others can best approach them. The growth indicators in Box 3.6 introduce metacognitive knowledge of primary grade children.

Box 3.6
Primary Grade Growth Indicators of Metacognitive Knowledge

Growth Indicator	*Example*
Demonstrates increasing knowledge about people as cognitive processors	"I only need to work on these four spelling words 'cause I already know the others," the third grader explains.
	"Ask Rob Allen; he knows where everything is," suggests his brother.
Demonstrates increasing knowledge about cognitive requirements of tasks	A first grader glances at the instructions booklet of a new game and says, "You read it, Dad, and tell me how to play. I can't read all that, you know."
Demonstrates increasing knowledge about cognitive strategies	Annika rehearses spelling words by writing them down whereas Dekker does so orally.

Classification

Classification skills undergo substantial development during the primary grade years. Although preschool children are generally content to sort a limited number of objects once, primary grade children can be challenged to sort and re-sort a larger number of objects. Thus, their greater mental flexibility enables them to select classifying attributes that guide their sorting and then abandon these attributes and begin again. Re-sorting is a notable achievement and one that they enjoy immensely; appreciate the collections and hobbies of school-age children that involve sorting and re-sorting.

A first grader sorts and re-sorts a collection of leaves into the following piles and then says no more groupings are possible.

1. Big leaves
   Little leaves
2. Green leaves
   Brown leaves
   Yellow leaves
3. Pointy leaves
   Roundish leaves

This child sorted real leaves on the basis of some concrete similarities and differences. First, size differences guided the child's groupings, then color, and then shape. This was a fine demonstration of sorting and re-sorting for a first-grader.

As children's thinking becomes increasingly flexible (see Box 3.7 for growth indicators of classification abilities), they can sort and re-sort objects according to various concrete attributes. Young primary grade children, like the first grader who sorted the leaves, tend to select attributes of the objects themselves as the basis of classification and produce a limited number of groupings. As they mature and gain knowledge about the objects being sorted, children produce more abundant groupings but remain predominantly concrete in their approach to classification tasks. By the end of elementary school, however, children might draw on their per-

---

Box 3.7
Primary Grade Growth Indicators of Classification

Growth Indicator
Sorts and re-sorts objects flexibly and usually by concrete attributes

Example
Amanda sorts model horses:

1. Bays   Grays
   Chestnuts   Blacks
   Paints   Whites

2. Black mane
   Brown mane
   Gray or white mane

3. Albino hooves
   Brown hooves
   Black hooves
   Gray hooves

4. Face markings
   No face markings

5. Famous or related to famous horses
   Unknown horses

Note: Grouping 5 stems from Amanda's own knowledge about horses rather than concrete features of the models.

Growth Indicator
Compares whole class with its parts with increasing accuracy

Example
"Here's my stack of left-handed pitchers and here's the right handers, but look at how many pitchers I have all together!" exclaims Donnie while sorting his baseball cards.

sonal stores of knowledge and, for example, sort leaves into an evergreen pile and a deciduous pile; thus they are no longer tied to the objects' concrete attributes.

Number Development

Children entering elementary school build on their number knowledge and counting skills as they begin to deal successfully with increasingly large sets of objects and numbers (Geary, 1994). By the end of third grade, they understand that the last number counted in a set represents its total number of objects (the cardinal principle). Given a "tricky" conservation-of-number task with 12 marbles heaped in a pile compared to 12 arranged in a line, 8-year-olds are not tempted by their perceptual information to erroneously conclude that the sets are not equal; their correct judgments are based on numerical reasoning, not perceptual cues.

Primary grade children also understand that numbers are serially ordered and, further, that any given number is made up of a group of smaller numbers (Geary, 1994). This concept enables them to understand that 10 is composed of 1 and 9, or 2 and 8, or 3 and 7, and is vital to their grasp of addition and subtraction. Skill comparing relative quantities and employing measurement strategies to assess length, volume, weight, and the like also improves. Children's early success in arithmetic is based on the number concepts and fundamental skills outlined in Box 3.8.

Memory

Although preschool and primary grade children share the same basic memory processes (recognition and recall), memory skills become honed during the elementary years. Processing speed increases, and "a number of memory strategies emerge and develop" (Schneider & Pressley, 1989, p. 199). Most notable during the primary grades are the strategies of rehearsal (repeating items to be remembered either mentally or aloud) and organization (clustering similar items to facilitate remembering).

During the primary grade years, children begin to use rehearsal and organization spontaneously. First graders faced with the task of learning their very first set of spelling words simply do not realize that rehearsal would be an appropriate study strategy. By the third grade, however, most children can use rehearsal on their own and, if encouraged, can use this strategy effectively. The same is true of organization.

What makes the deliberate selection of memory strategies possible is the development of metamemory—knowledge about memory—and a component of metacognition discussed earlier. Even during the primary grade years, children know something about memory. In an early metamemory study, for example, when kindergarten and first-, third-, and fifth-grade children were asked if it would be easier to learn the names of birds in town for the first or second time, many of the children (even the kindergartners) knew intuitively that the relearner would have the advantage (Kreutzer, Leonard, & Flavell, 1975). Ideas about memory (and the mind) gain clarity as 8- and 9-year-olds begin to distinguish between what they understand and what they have merely memorized (Lovett & Flavell, 1990). Further, not only do primary grade children have some knowledge about memory as a cognitive process, but they also become more aware of when they must put out some

Box 3.8
Primary Growth Indicators of Number Development

Growth Indicator	Example
Counts increasingly large sets of objects	Before boarding a bus for a field trip, Lydia counts her 19 classmates, herself, and her teacher.
Understands cardinality	A kindergartner counts the lunch boxes and mentions to his friend that there are 13.
Develops measurement strategies	A second grader uses a ruler to measure the perimeter of the art table.
	Given responsibility for distributing the after-school snack, a third grader equally divides 4 packages containing 3 peanut butter crackers among his 2 siblings and himself.
Adds and subtracts objects and numbers	Yohana studies 6 cup hooks, 4 of which are empty, and says, "I know what 6 take away 4 is."
	Rowley practices his addition flash cards with a parent.

effort to store or retrieve information; think about the growth indicators of memory presented in Box 3.9 in this light.

The cognitive development highlights presented in this section are not comprehensive. You may be interested in reading about problem solving, reading comprehension, spatial relations, additional math concepts, and so forth. Although this section describes general trends in cognitive development, individual differences are always apparent. These differences are normal and reflect the beauty and complexity of human diversity.

Selected Highlights of Psychosocial Development

Self-Concept and Self-Esteem

In Chapter 2, we left the preschool child with a beginning understanding of the self as both a physical object and a psychological being. Children's ideas about the self grow more complex during the primary grade years. They realize their minds and

---

Box 3.9
Primary Growth Indicators of Memory

Growth Indicator	*Example*
Increasingly uses memory strategies spontaneously and deliberately	"I'm going to write that word five more times without peeking; it's still kinda blurry," reports Paula, preparing for a spelling test.
Exhibits early development of metamemory, including knowledge about people as rememberers, varying task difficulty, and appropriate memory strategies	Samyr writes homework assignments in his notebook to avoid trying to remember them.
	Children discuss pros and cons of stage plays versus radio plays and remark that the latter require less memorization.
	A third grader practices flash cards to study for a math test and review chapter self-quiz to prepare for a social studies test.

---

the minds of others are constantly active (Wellman & Hickling, 1994), regardless if one's thinking is obvious to an observer. Gradually, through the primary grade years and beyond, children's self-concepts include more psychological assessments (e.g., "animal lover"), characteristics uncommon to others (e.g., "the shortest kid in the class"), and descriptions of active abilities (e.g., "a really good gymnast") as well as many of the concrete characteristics cited by younger children (e.g., "curly hair"). Elementary school children also understand their own specific strengths and weaknesses, but their self-evaluations, in contrast to preschoolers' sunny reports, grow more critical. They can judge their often varying competencies in multiple areas (e.g., math, reading, sports, music), and their judgments are differential, not global (Eccles, Wigfield, Harold, & Blumenfeld, 1993).

Although primary grade children feel more like unique individuals, they also feel more closely bound to a social network (Maccoby, 1980). As a result, primary grade children are likely to include membership in a group (e.g., an ethnic group, a sports team, or a scouting troop) when asked to describe themselves. Sustained experience in groups offers tremendous growth opportunities. Ethic groups may guide children's development in many ways (e.g., expectations of how children treat their elders) and help them forge their identities. Within groups, children also are stimulated to acknowledge how their behavior appears to others (e.g., bossiness is not valued), to monitor their behavior, and gradually to make appropriate adjustments.

Children gain "extensive knowledge of gender stereotypes" and gradually become aware that "both males and females *can* have the same traits or engage in the same activities and occupations" (Serbin, Powlishta, & Gulko, 1993, p. 64). Young children (and adolescents) regarded "the crossing of stereotyped gender boundaries as more wrong and expressed a greater personal commitment to sex-role regularity, than [did] children in middle childhood" (Stoddart & Turiel, 1985, p. 1241). Primary grade children's increased freedom from rigid adherence to gender stereotypes stems partly from their secure understanding that their gender is constant and that gender roles are societal conventions rather than absolute requirements. As Western society formally and informally continues to reduce its gender-stereotyped expectations and restrictions, children may recognize and embrace their life options wholeheartedly.

Self-esteem is the evaluative component of the sense of self, and positive self-esteem is possible when children's physiological needs and needs for safety, belonging, and love have been met (Maslow, 1970). Two essential ingredients that contribute to self-esteem are the warmth, acceptance, and respectful treatment given a child as well as the child's success as "measured against personal goals and standards" (Coopersmith, 1967, p. 242). Thus the origins of self-esteem lie not only with how children are treated by the important people in their lives but also with how well they do in the world. Children need not excel in everything they do in order to feel good about themselves, but reasonable competence in selected arenas is important to self-esteem. Children's beliefs in their own motivation and learning abilities fuel their performance accomplishments (Bandura, Barbaranelli, Caprara, & Pastorelli, 1996).

A person's self-esteem is linked to his or her aspirations in specific fields of interest. If you try an unfamiliar activity and do not do well, you might be mildly embarrassed but your self-esteem should not suffer. After all, you are a fish out of water. However, you care very much about your performance in areas in which you have chosen to compete—perhaps becoming a competent observer of children. This is your pond, and your performance is connected to how you feel about yourself.

The same process is true of children. Children, however, are just beginning to find their ponds, and adults need to assist them in their searches by exposing them to a wide range of experiences. Trying out new activities includes the possibility of failure, so adults working with primary grade children can encourage this risk taking by being low-key and minimizing pressure. Adrienne, age 6, made a list of all the things she wanted to try; included were soccer, softball, ballet, violin, Brownies, jazz dancing, horseback riding, and gymnastics. Her parents supported her interests with the stipulation that she had to commit herself for a season or school year. At the end of first grade, she crossed off three of the four activities she had tried that year: soccer (too hot and too much running), softball (too boring), and ballet (too embarrassing), and anticipated sticking with Brownies and trying out jazz in the second grade. Through this process Adrienne learned more about the kinds of activities she enjoys and can do well. Her self-esteem will be enhanced as she discovers the ponds in which she wants to swim, develops competence, and is encouraged by those who love and teach her. Box 3.10 lists indicators of the growth of self-concept and self-esteem in primary grade children.

> ## Box 3.10
> ## Growth Indicators of Self-Concept and Self-Esteem
>
> | *Growth Indicator* | *Example* |
> |---|---|
> | Includes psychological assessments, uncommon characteristics, active abilities as well as concrete characteristics in descriptions of self and others | Heidi reports to parent after school, "I really like the new kid in my class; he's kinda shy like me, and I think he likes the monkey bars too!" |
> | Considers group ties as part of self-definition | Stavros proudly wears a scouting uniform to school. |
> | | Child shares photos of the Aroma Pueblo and says, "I'm this kind of Native American, just like my mom, who lived here when she was 10." |
> | Does not rigidly adhere to all stereotyped gender roles | "I'm really good in math," Nellie proudly tells her mother after school. |
> | Becomes aware that gender roles are societal customs | Spencer reads *Little House in the Big Woods* and compares the diversity of his sister's activities to those of Laura Ingalls. |
> | Searches out areas of interest that contribute to self-esteem | Much to the children's delight, a second-grade class plans a hobby/collection/interest day so that each child may share her or his personal "passion." |
> | Gains more accurate understanding of strengths and weaknesses | "I bet Mr. Yonce will say something really good about me in reading on my report card," anticipates Stacey. |

Advances in Play

During the elementary school years, children increasingly participate in cooperative play with other children and enjoy games with rules (Schickedanz, Schickedanz, Hansen, & Forsyth, 1993). Cooperative play is sustained as maturation and experiences stimulate children to give and take actively in their encounters. Board games are popular as primary grade children readily learn rules and understand that these should apply equally to all players. Even in children's unstructured play (e.g., school, spies, house), rules command an increasingly prominent role (see Box 3.11 for growth indicators of play).

Box 3.11
Growth Indicators of Play

Growth Indicator	*Example*
Participates in cooperative play	"Ya wanna play fort?" Meleah calls to two friends. "I'll build the walls, and you can build the roof, and we can all decorate it. OK?"
Participates in and makes up games with rules	"You're out!" several children call to a child hit by the ball in dodgeball.
	"Let's say you don't really have to go to jail when you land here," says George to Duncan while playing Monopoly.

Cooperative play and games with rules characterize play during the primary grade years.

Relationships with Peers

Children's relationships serve as important models of future relationships (Hartup, 1992). Primary grade children increasingly choose friends who come to their aid and stick up for them, share their secrets, and engage in leisure-time experiences with them. Generally, "children find same-sex play partners more compatible, and they segregate themselves into same-sex groups, in which distinctive interaction styles emerge" (Maccoby, 1990, p. 513). Children learn the useful skill of how to disengage from conflict to "increase the likelihood that [their] relationships will continue once the disagreement ends" (Hartup, Laursen, Stewart, & Eastenson, 1988, p. 1600).

Peer relationships provide unique benefits for children. Children with friends are better able to consider others' points of view and are more altruistic than those without them (Dunn, Brown, & Maguire, 1995). "Children who see their friendships as a source of validation or aid tend to feel happier in school, see their classmates as supportive, and develop positive school attitudes" (Ladd, Kochenderfer, & Coleman, 1996). In addition, children's expanding psychological understanding of themselves goes hand in hand with their increasing appreciation of their friends (Hartup, 1992).

Increasingly throughout the school-age years, peer groups offer the individual security and a sense of belonging, but they also exert pressure to conform. Much of this conformity centers around participation in activities (e.g., playing four-square at recess), clothing (e.g., wearing the "right" brand of T-shirts), and allegiance to peer-group members. Some peer groups expect conformity in antisocial activities. In general, children are inclined to go along with their peer groups until they reach midadolescence (Shaffer, 1993); therefore the types of peer groups primary children are involved in warrant scrutiny. Box 3.12 lists growth indicators of primary grade children's relationships with their peers.

Box 3.12
Growth Indicators of Relationships with Peers

Growth Indicator	*Example*
Increasingly focuses friendships on loyalty and intimacy as well as on mutual interests	"I like Melody more now 'cause she really stuck up for me at recess," Jocelyn reports.
Usually prefers same-gender playmates	Shirley invited only girls to her birthday party, and her brother asked to invite a friend of his own.
Is aware of and sometimes vulnerable to peer-group influences	"I can't wear this shirt to school, Mom," Mikio whines. "All the kids will laugh."

Prosocial Moral Development

Preschool children tend to base moral judgments on the material outcome of an action rather than the intent of the person involved. In contrast, primary grade children begin to understand that many moral questions pivot around a person's intent. Their earlier preoccupation with surface details (e.g., how much paint was spilled) is gradually abandoned for a deeper evaluation of the situation's complexities and relevant issues (e.g., Was the spill accidental? Was the person being careless? Were any rules broken? Was anyone hurt?). Developmental changes in moral reasoning generally parallel cognitive development, but children's levels of sympathy and the social context are also factors (Carlo, Koller, Eisenberg, DaSilva, & Frolich, 1996). In addition, their maturing theories of mind help them become adept at understanding the perspectives of others. See Box 3.13 for growth indicators of prosocial moral development.

Although children gain increasing maturity in judging what is the right thing to do in a hypothetical situation, whether they choose the right thing in a real-life situation is another matter. There are, however, strategies to promote children's prosocial moral behavior.

Box 3.13
Growth Indicators of Prosocial Moral Development

Growth Indicator	*Example*
Increasingly evaluates the intent of the actor	"We know you told us to stand still," a brave child tells the substitute teacher, "but Robby would have gotten hit by the ball if Shuichi hadn't knocked it away. He really wasn't being bad."
Increasingly takes into account the relevant issues of a moral situation	"No way!" Caleb vehemently argues. "Marcin shouldn't get any 'cause he didn't help."
Demonstrates perspective-taking skills in many, but not all, situations	Aware that a friend dislikes scary stories, Brock advises against reading a particular book.
	"Come on, just jump," Jillian impatiently urges Bonnie on the swings. "There's nothing to be scared of."
Expands prosocial behavior	"Would you like to sit with me at lunch?" Renata asks Carol on her first day at a new school.

First, the relevance of the zone of proximal development to children's growth of social competence should be explored (Maccoby, 1992). Seizing opportunities to help children think about others builds and challenges their perspective-taking skills. For example, parents may talk about others' experiences or discuss inferences from stories or television programs; such early experiences at age 3 contribute to children's understanding of emotions at age 6 (Brown & Dunn, 1996). Furthermore, adults may "promote each child's comfortable, empathic interactions with people from diverse backgrounds" (Derman-Sparks, 1994, p. 69).

Second, a reasonable amount of control over their own lives provides children with experience in responsibility. Third, power-assertive discipline that undermines children's sense of control and responsibility is rejected because conscience development is enhanced by encouraging "internalized regulation, growing empathy, and awareness of wrongdoing" (Kochanska, Padavich, & Koenig, 1996, p 1433). Clear connections between a child's actions and their consequences will help the child consider consequences when faced with moral choices. What is our long-term goal for children? Consider the model posed in the classic novel from South Africa, *Cry the Beloved Country*:

> I shall no longer ask myself if this or that is expedient, but only if it is right. I shall do this, not because I am noble or unselfish, but because life slips away, and because I need for the rest of my journey a star that will not play false to me, a compass that will not lie. (Paton, 1995, p. 208)

Managing Stress

Everyone has stress in daily life, and children are no exception. How children cope depends on two factors: their competence (social, academic, and creative) and their social support (Werner & Smith, 1982). Critical problems arise when these factors are in short supply and/or when the stresses multiply (e.g., divorce plus a move plus the mother returning to work plus lower family income).

The modern tendency to pressure children to hurry through their childhoods has resulted in unnecessary stress (Elkind, 1988). Parents hold high expectations for their children's successes, but their demands may be inappropriate to the children's developmental levels. Typically, children are enrolled in an abundance (often an overabundance) of extracurricular activities and allowed access to information formerly reserved for the more mature (e.g., adult problems, violence, and sex in the media). What can adults do? Here are some of Elkind's (1994, 1988) suggestions:

1. Reinvent our adulthood. Children are not born with an internal set of rules and controls; they rely on adults to set standards. "When we try to be pals with our children . . . , we deprive them of their most important source of internal rules, limits, standards, and controls" (Elkind, 1994, p. 227).

2. Cut back on the demands placed on children and increase adult supports. Look for a reasonable balance of developmentally appropriate responsibilities and adult support and commitment. For example, a teacher encourages the parents of a 7-year-old who goes home each day to an empty house for 3 hours to enroll

their child in an after-school program. After the child becomes noticeably happier, the parents decide to devote half of a weekend day to a leisure-time activity with their child.

3. Provide opportunities for unstructured play, such as opportunities for creative expression—a natural antidote for hurrying. Competitive and instructional activities, although they may be an important part of children's lives, do not reduce stress. Be sure children have physical space to call their own for their projects and relaxation.

4. Identify, appreciate, and acknowledge each child's uniqueness.

5. Model living in the present and smelling the roses in your own life. Remember that children carefully observe and imitate the important adults in their lives; through example, you can model ways to enjoy life and moderate stress.

These suggestions are further supported by research on the relationship between stress and school activities. Children in developmentally inappropriate classrooms exhibited more stress than did children in appropriate classrooms; particularly stressful times were transitions, waiting, and workbook/worksheet activities (Burts et al., 1992). Moreover, "compared to children in didactic programs, children [ages 4–6] in child-centered programs rated their abilities higher, had higher expectations for success on school-like tasks, selected a more challenging math problem to do, showed less dependency on adults for permission and approval, evidenced more pride in their accomplishments, and claimed to worry less about school" (Stipek, Feiler, Daniels, & Milburn, 1995, p. 220).

Psychosocial development is affected by children's individual natures, developmental strengths and limitations, unique social surroundings (their family, friends, school, and extended social networks), and cultures. Against the backdrop of the developmental trends discussed above, cherish the inevitable differences among children.

Selected Highlights of Creative Development

Imagination, innovation, problem solving, rearrangement, originality, risking, inventions—these are the elements of creativity ("a complex mental process used to solve problems through novel solutions" [Kapel, Gifford, & Kapel, 1991, p. 145]). Feldman (1980) suggested that there are two approaches to the study of creativity—the *trait approach* and the *process approach*. As recalled from Chapter 2, the trait approach proposes that people are born with various amounts of creativity; it unfolds on its own. The process approach, favored by educators (Cropley 1992), explains creativity as an interaction between the person's abilities and the opportunities to explore, practice, and perfect. This chapter section focuses on identifying the growth indicators of creativity and learning how the primary grade teacher facilitates interactions with children and their environments.

Advancing from preschool to the primary grades, children's expressions of creativity become increasingly clarified and intricate. Two examples follow. A 4-year-old may draw a person, a house, or an animal disproportionately in space, whereas a 6-year-old may recall and illustrate a favorite scene from a field trip using detailed figures in an organized drawing that includes a baseline and a skyline with air in between (Lowenfeld & Brittain, 1987). Preschoolers may shake musical instruments to the rhythm of a favorite song; K–3 children may construct their own music-making devices. During the early elementary years, nonverbal, verbal, and written expressions become representational and more elaborate than they were during the preceding years.

Another difference between preschool and primary grade children's creative development is more pronounced individuality in the primary grade years. Children's creative interests and strengths begin to bud during the preschool years, but they bloom during the primary years. Comparing the dictated stories of two preschoolers, Ona and Whitney, would probably reveal some observable differences. If, however, Ona continues to nurture her interest and ability in writing and Whitney finds writing less appealing than science experiments, the differences in these two girls' third-grade stories will become increasingly pronounced. Ona and Whitney, along with other primary grade children, begin to recognize and develop their individual creative talents through abundant and varied opportunities.

In the primary grade classroom, common forms of creative expression are writing, thinking, creating, making music, acting, dancing, building with blocks, and storytelling (Engle, 1995; Gardner, 1980). Many children this age delight in organizing and participating in plays and backyard circuses, building tree houses, and inventing new games or revising old ones. In the classroom, evidence of creativity is proudly displayed at open house: artwork, science and social studies projects, and original stories.

During these important years, maturing individual strengths can be appreciated and supported when creative interests and abilities are identified. The growth indicators of creativity listed in Box 3.14 provide the basis for teacher observation that leads to recognition of development and curriculum planning based on individual needs.

One specific pathway, creative art, has been singled out and spotlighted over the years. Art growth has been studied and defined through adolescence (Herberholz & Hanson, 1995; Kellogg, 1970; Linderman, 1990; Lowenfeld & Brittain, 1987). Development of representational drawing follows a predictable pattern as children are given bountiful opportunities for unrestricted practice and experimentation. A word of caution—art activities duplicating a model are not creative; they stifle growth (see Chapter 2).

The growth indicators in Box 3.15 are the target for observing the characteristics of representational drawing occurring in the primary grade years. The characteristics for early primary grade drawing (found in Chapter 2) are repeated, together with the characteristics of drawings by middle primary grade children. Remember that growth is continuous and ages are only general guidelines.

"Is creative expression really important?" ask educators who are pressured to demonstrate classroom proficiency in academic areas. Absolutely! Creativity assists independent thinking, fosters self-esteem, relieves emotional tension, and helps children discover that their own uniqueness is special, valued, and important in the world (Cherry, 1990; Dixon & Chalmer, 1990; Wright & Fesler, 1987).

Box 3.14
Primary Growth Indicators of Creativity

Growth Indicator	Example
Expands representations, moving from a single idea to interrelated ideas	Chase's preschool drawing of his family displays each member as distinct and separate, without background. Chase's second-grade drawing of his family shows each member involved in roles: Mom is at the computer, Dad is cooking dinner, and his two brothers are working on homework—all in one room!
Expresses individual strengths	The child enthusiastically volunteers for the lead in the first grade play. *Are You My Mother?* The boy shares a poem he wrote after his kitten was run over.
Expands flexibility	"Two 5-year-olds, Missy and Eric, want to build a school, but they have no blocks or pieces of wood. They consider using shoe boxes, which are fairly durable and stackable, for a base" (Schirrmacher, 1993, p. 53).
Expands sensitivity	The child leafs through the *Great Book of French Impressionism*, looks up and says, "Why do they paint pictures of people without their clothes on?"
Expands imagination	Tori is whirling around and clapping her hands in patty-cake fashion. She tries frantically to keep the beat of the rock music that's playing. She flaps and flops her hands over her head. Then she opens and closes her hands quickly like little signal lights. She calls out, "I'm dancing like a peacock."
Expands risk taking	Having had a lot of practice riding her two-wheeler with training wheels, Najeeba seeks out her big brother. She says, "I want you to take off these training wheels. I'm going to teach myself how to ride without them."

Box 3.14 (continued)

Growth Indicator	Example
Expands resourcefulness	While four children are playing an electronic memory game, the pattern with four different colored buttons becomes too difficult to duplicate. One child suggests that each child concentrate on only one color. Therefore, as a team, the group could successfully reproduce long patterns.
Expands expressive experiences and skills in using creative materials	"This is the best story I've ever written about dinosaurs," the child says. "I think I'll illustrate it. Let's see, should I use watercolors, tempera paints, clay, markers, or block prints?"

Note. Flexibility, sensitivity, imagination, risk-taking, resourcefulness, and creative-skills indicators adapted from *Beginnings and Beyond*, 4th edition (pp. 472–473) by A. Gordon and K. Williams-Browne, 1995, Albany, NY: Delmar Publishers, Inc. Copyright © 1995 by Delmar Publishers. Reproduced by permission.

How can creativity be promoted in the classroom? If "a primary goal of education is to enable children to develop their minds and intellectual capabilities, using all forms of creative intelligence as means for achieving this goal" (Getty Center for Education in the Arts, 1985, p. 11), then employing a curriculum design that embodies creative development becomes a critical choice for the teacher. The integrated curriculum approach, based on thematic units (Schwartz & Pollishuke, 1991), is an excellent example of such a design. Children's language arts experiences are related to a theme (sometimes originating from the children's interests, sometimes offered by the reading program). All other curriculum areas are woven around the language arts experience but taught "full strength" (Gunderson, 1989). This approach promotes creativity by providing an atmosphere of directed exploration, accepting individual ideas, and linking disciplines together. In Figure 3.2, Crosswhite (1995) illustrated how the integrated curriculum approach centered in literature facilitates development of creativity in the primary grades.

In summary, promoting creativity is one of the teacher's main challenges. The primary grade child's maturing creative expression and emerging strengths develop best when

- Creativity is incorporated into the curriculum.
- Indicators of creative growth are fostered.

One avenue of self-expression is drawing.

Box 3.15
Primary Grade Growth Indicators of Drawing

Early primary (ages 4–6)

- Combines shapes that become schemas (personalized representational symbols); makes intentional image repetition of schemas; develops preferred schemas
- Begins drawing representations, often of people, animals in profile, letterlike forms, basic forms represented consistently—houses, flowers, boats, people
- Portrays meaning (subject matter) in an increasingly readable manner
- Repeats repertory or symbolic forms, practices, and adds new elements
- Shows beginnings of individual style (e.g., typical way of drawing a house)
- Isolates figures, each discrete (no overlapping of whole or of parts); shows no context or baseline, and draws size and details according to perceived importance or interest (e.g., long arms)

- Presents several figures on the page; begins representing events or narratives; places schematic figures in a larger concept, for example, knowing an elephant is a four-legged animal with a trunk, the child uses a well-established routine, or schema, for drawing animals—cats, dogs, and so forth—and adds a trunk to the elephant.

Middle primary (ages 5–8)

- Draws elaborations and variations of schematic figures and experiments; shows repetition of imagery by practicing "set pictures" (always drawn the same way), such as racing cars
- Produces details traditionally or formulaic, such as windows with tie-back curtains, chimneys with smoke coming out at an angle, girls with skirts and long hair
- Draws narratively, illustratively, and inventively; often shows baselines as multiples; draws "see-through" houses and most figures are in their own space, without overlapping

Note. Adapted and reprinted with the permission of the National Association for the Education of Young Children. From *Considering Children's Art: Why and How to Value Their Works* by B. S. Engel. Copyright © 1995 by National Association for the Education of Young Children.

The teacher's guide contains information for reading, vocabulary, structural analysis, and guided and independent reading. Beyond reading, the following activities are some samples of using the story across the curriculum.

Themes: Nap time, bedtime, families
Story: *The Napping House* by Audrey Wood

Sample Activities.

- Have the students select rhythm instruments to represent each of the action words in the book, such as sandpaper blocks for snoring, triangle for dreaming, drums for bumps. Read the story a second time adding the sound effects.

- Play "Charades" by having individual children act out bedtime/morning activities as the other students determine the activity.

- Discuss bedtime/nap time experiences. Encourage the children to share a time when a nap was disturbed or something funny happened. Then invite the children to write a story and illustrate the event.

- Assist the children in creating their own family mobiles (including pets). Discuss several ways to make a mobile including the use of straws, string, and construction paper.

Figure 3.2. Integrated curriculum example.

Source: From *A Guide to a Shared Reading Experience* by L. Crosswhite, 1995, Jacksonville, IL: Perma-Bound. Copyright © 1995 by Perma-Bound. Adapted by permission.

- Children's creative interests are encouraged.
- Ample opportunities for children to grow at their own rate are provided.

To avoid redundancy the expanded explanation of the approaches to creativity (trait versus process), conditions of creativity, and the teacher's role are excluded from this chapter. Review the creativity section in Chapter 2 if you wish this information.

Chapter Conclusion

The primary grade child is developmentally different from yet similar in many ways to the preschool child. Children within both age groups show individual maturational rates, follow general predictable patterns, and draw on their own experiences and genetic makeup. In this chapter, however, development is highlighted as an ongoing process with each child making advances physically, cognitively, psychosocially, and creatively. Identified growth indicators help the teacher zero in on developmental strides through continued observation and fulfill the ethical responsibility (NAEYC Ideal I-1.2) exemplified in this chapter: "To base program practices upon current knowledge in the field of child development and related disciplines and upon particular knowledge of each child" (Feeney & Kipnis, 1992, p. 4).

Take a Moment to Reflect _____

In an interview with David Elkind (Scherer, 1996), he purported that the general trend of the family today shows a change from a cohesive unit to autonomous individuals. "Today soccer practice or a business meeting takes precedence over dinner because personal needs are more important than the family" (p. 7). Reflect on the implications of that idea and answer the questions below.

1. What examples have you seen in which families have replaced togetherness with autonomy? Think about your own, relatives', and television families.

2. How might the individual focus of some families today strengthen or limit the developmental process of their primary grade children?

Observing Individual Children

The adventure of *Through The Looking Glass* continues in Part II. Before we proceed, however, check to see that you possess the keys from Part I. Do you understand *why* and *what* to observe? Do you have a grasp of the basic developmental growth indicators? If the answers to those two questions are yes, you are ready to reach for the next set of keys—the *how* keys of observation in the methodology chapters.

Part II begins with an investigation of five methods for observing individual children: running records in Chapter 4, anecdotes in Chapter 5, checklists in Chapter 6, rating scales in Chapter 7, and ABC narrative event sampling in Chapter 8. Each chapter gives ample opportunities for practicing and mastering the various methods. In addition to explaining how to use each method, each chapter offers two detailed examples, one from preschool and one from the primary grades, to show how educators effectively use the observational method, interpret the data, and initiate follow-through plans. The chapters are arranged to build on the reader's expanding understanding of observation.

Chapter 9, the last chapter in Part II, explores yet another key—the *communication* key of observation. This chapter shows how to systematically organize observations in portfolios and effectively communicate the results through dynamic parent conferences. This key widens the door to include family–school partnerships.

You will complete Part II knowing the methodology for observing individual children. In Part III, the looking glass expands further as the observational subjects broaden to include groups and environments.

CHAPTER 4

Observing Development of Individual Children Using Running Records

When Fiona thinks of one of her students, Warren, her ponderings often begin with "if only." If only Warren would wander less. If only Warren would pay more attention in class. If only Warren would complete his assignments. If only Warren found school interesting. If only. If only.

Warren does, however, wander in class, and he does not pay attention or complete assignments or find school interesting. How can Fiona begin to understand this child who frustrates her best intentions as a second-grade teacher?

Given the daily demands of teaching a child who is challenging, Fiona worries she is overlooking clues that help to explain Warren's behavior. Perhaps there are consistencies or patterns where she sees none. Fiona plans time to observe Warren as he goes about his usual school activities. The aim of this chapter is to describe how to write running records that portray an array of children's developmental characteristics within their natural contexts; a running record is Fiona's observational method of choice.

Overview of Observing Using Running Records

Description

The *running record* is a "narrative or continuous recording of everything a child says and does within a unit of time" (Veale & Piseitella, 1988, p. 8). Researchers in child development depend on running records (at times called specimen records or descriptive narratives) to gain insights into development. Piaget, for example, relied on his detailed observations of children to help him conceptualize and describe cognitive growth. In many of Piaget's books, portions of running records are reproduced to demonstrate his theoretical points; these original accounts are thus available for you to study.

In a running record the observer writes down in the present tense what the child says and does during a specified length of time or designated activity. Detailed, factual recordings are made in sequential form while the event is happening. "The observer in making a narrative record records a wide slice of life. No attempt is made to filter what occurred in any systematic way" (Evertson & Green, 1986, p. 177). The observer does not look for or interpret any specific behavior; the goal is simply to gather as much raw data as possible. Because of the high yield of information, the running record is a valuable observational method for teachers of young children.

Perhaps an imaginative analogy is in order. Compare writing running records to observing as a human video camera. The observer's eyes are focused on the subject, and the observer records what is seen and heard. The qualification of *human* is essential; although the observer would like to be able to capture absolutely everything, keeping up with an active child and being as objective as possible makes recording a challenging task. Practice allows the observer to become increasingly proficient at collecting a large quantity of facts.

Acknowledging that recording *everything* a child says and does is impossible, the observer makes reasonable judgments about the amount of detail to record. The best guideline to follow is to keep the purpose and setting of the observation in mind. This focus will help determine which facts are essential to record and which may be safely omitted. In a running record in Chapter 1, for example, Cyd's language in the sand area was recorded as clear evidence of his ability to seriate three objects by size; noting his clothing, however, would not have added useful infor-

Teachers learn about the development of individual children through careful observation.

mation. In contrast, if a child being observed interacts with several unfamiliar children, recording what each child is wearing could be vital in distinguishing one child from another. The observer, always improving with experience and practice, makes on-the-spot decisions regarding the appropriate amount of detail to record.

A well-written running record is a rich account of naturally occurring behavior. The observer can return again and again to its deep well of details to study a child with a new purpose or perspective. To heighten the future value of a running record, a brief conclusion is added to its end. Imagine teachers preparing for parent conferences and sifting through the contents of a few running records on each child to refresh their memories, and then consider the time involved in this task. If, however, the teachers had written a conclusion at the end of each running record, the contents would be quickly and effectively accessible. A conclusion, written in the past tense, briefly summarizes the development demonstrated by the behavior or events observed and recorded in a running record. Pay attention to this valuable service provided by the conclusions in the running records in Figures 4.1 through 4.4.

On a general note, observational studies may be quantitative or qualitative. "Quantitative studies are dependent on numerical or statistical treatments of data; qualitative studies are not" (Genishi, 1982, p. 567). Clearly, the narrative data collected in running records are qualitative; observers scrutinizing the data focus on "holistic chunks of information" (Brause & Mayher, 1991, p. 137) rather than numbers.

Purpose

The intent of the running record is to learn more about the many aspects of a child's total development from the precise recording of this child's actions and language. Running records can be particularly helpful to teachers getting to know a new child in the classroom or trying to understand individual children's problems. Reading a running record at the end of the observation day or a week later or 2 months later provides a replay option that allows the observer to note each child's developmental strengths or limitations and draw conclusions.

In addition to helping teachers learn more about individual children, running records support classroom planning. Teachers may use their observations and conclusions to plan supportive and stimulating daily activities. More specifically, as we begin the observational method chapters, remember as Bredekamp and Copple (1997) declared:

> Teachers use observational assessment of children's progress, examination of children's work samples, and documentation of their development and learning to plan and adapt curriculum to meet individual children's developmental or learning needs, identify children who may have a learning or developmental problem, communicate with parents, and evaluate the program's effectiveness. (p. 133)

The brief running record reproduced in Figure 4.1 provides diagnostic information about a child's incorrect (but consistent) mathematical procedures. This information may guide the teacher's planning of follow-up math activities for this child.

Running Record of Felipe During Math

School/Grade: Delta Elementary/Third Grade

Date: 3/6   Time: 9:07–9:09 A.M.

Observer: Seth   Child/Age: Felipe/8;11

	Comments

Given the problem $\begin{array}{r} 56 \\ \times 32 \\ \hline \end{array}$, Felipe hunches over his desk with his eyes about 10 inches from the paper, taps his right foot rhythmically, and whispers, "2 times 6 is 12; put down the 2 and carry the 1." He methodically writes "2" in the ones' column and a "1" above the 5. In a louder voice he says, "3 times 5 is 15 plus 1 is 16." He unhesitatingly writes "16" in the hundreds' and tens' columns. His answer is 162.

9:07

Seems confident but works slowly

Conclusion: Felipe displayed an incorrect understanding of two-digit multiplication problems. He vertically multiplied the ones' digits and the tens' digits, skipping the intermediate steps.

Figure 4.1.   Brief example of a running record.

Teachers may also use running records to augment information contained in other observational formats. For example, in the next chapter a running record provides the data for an anecdotal record. When completing a checklist or rating scale to assess a child's growth (topics of Chapters 6 and 7), a teacher may draw on running records for supportive accounts. The information gathered in running records also serves to enrich parent conferences as teachers share specific, wide-ranging accounts of children's behavior, language, interests, and interactions in the classroom.

Guidelines for Writing Running Records

Typically, running record observation times are 10 minutes or less, and observers first practicing their skills might begin with short spans of 3 to 5 minutes. The raw data of a language specialist's 6-minute running record in Figure 4.2 provide information about a child's difficulties keeping up with the pace of an activity and suggest teaching adjustments.

What guidelines smooth the transition from reading about running records to actually writing them? The following suggestions have been helpful to many observers viewing children's development through the observational lens of running records.

- Employ the running record observational method when the details of a child's naturally occurring behavior are desired. Because this method is time-consuming

---

Running Record of Taki During Listening Lotto

Center/Age level:	Center for Speech and Language/3- to 6-Year-Olds
Date:	7/17
Observer:	Naoki

Time: 10:20–10:26 A.M.

Child/Age: Taki/4;11

Comments

10:20

Taki is seated on the floor with Kyle (4;8), and Camille, teacher, is in a corner of the classroom; both children have their backs to the center of the room. Taki sits with her right leg tucked under her bottom and her left leg bent with her foot flat on the floor. The Listening Lotto card is in front of her on the floor, and she holds a bunch of red, plastic markers in her right hand. Camille begins the tape.

No intro of game

The first sound is of a baby crying. Taki looks up at Camille, who says, "What's that?" Taki looks at Kyle, who has already placed his marker on the crying baby. Camille says, "That's a baby crying," and points to the picture on Taki's card. Taki places the marker with her left hand as the next sound, beating drums, begins.

Hearing aide working

Taki looks at Kyle as the drumming continues. Camille points to the picture of the drums on Taki's card, and Taki places her marker.

Understands process

The next sound is of a toilet flushing. Taki looks at Kyle and points to the drums. Kyle says, "Good, Taki. We heard drums banging." Taki smiles. Camille says, "Do you hear the toilet flushing?" as she points to the correct picture. Taki places her marker and repositions herself to sit cross-legged. She continues to hold the markers in her right hand and place them with her left.

10:22
Kyle supportive of Taki

When the tape plays the sound of glass breaking, Taki looks at Kyle, Camille points to the correct picture, and Taki places the marker.

Taki behind stop tape?

The sound is of a bouncing ball. Same process. Taki looks at Kyle, Camille points to the picture of the ball, and Taki places the marker.

A lion roars on the tape. Taki looks at the markers in her right hand (3 left) and scoops up more from the floor. Camille says, "Do you hear the lion?" She points to the picture, and Taki places the marker with her left hand.

The sound is of sizzling bacon in a frying pan. "What's that, Taki?" asks Camille. Taki looks at Kyle, Camille points to the picture, and Taki places the marker.

Camille looks up at another group finishing an art activity, checks the clock, and says, "One more." The sound is of a radio and the jarring changing of stations. "Where's the radio?" She points to the radio, and Taki places a marker.

10:24

Figure 4.2. Language specialist's running record example.

"Time to clean up," announces Camille. Taki opens the
3″ × 6″ plastic bag with her left hand and slides her remaining
markers in from her right hand without spilling one. She picks
up the remaining markers on the floor with her right hand and,
making a trough-like shape with her right hand, slides the
markers into the bag. She zips the bag closed (holding it with   *Knows exactly*
her right and zipping with her left), puts the bag and her game   *what to do*
card in the box, stands, and walks to her snack table.

Conclusion: Taki followed the teacher's directions in Listening
Lotto but did not demonstrate success on her own. Her fine
motor control was in evidence as she handled small markers.
She observed Kyle and smiled at his praise.

Figure 4.2. (*Continued*).

and requires the observer's complete attention, it is used selectively; anecdotal
records, introduced in the next chapter, are recorded most frequently.

- Begin by reviewing the general guidelines for observation in Chapter 1.
- Prepare a heading to include the setting (center or school/age level or grade, date, and time) and people present (observer, child). This format will also be the standard used for checklists, rating scales, ABC narrative event sampling, tally event sampling, and time sampling.
- Record only the facts. Try to minimize subjectivity, and do not add any inferences. (In the example in Figure 4.2, the observer crossed out "jarring," realizing she had assumed Taki shared her own reaction to the radio sound.)
- Record events in sequence, as they are occurring.
- Write exactly what is happening in the present tense.
- Stay focused on the child being observed. Conversations, noise, or activities going on simultaneously in the classroom may be distracting; resist!
- Provide space in the right margin for comments. Use this space to jot down notes that are not a part of your running record (e.g., additional information about an activity or impressions you may want to think more about later). Also periodically note the time, and note when the activity changes. Knowing how long a child was engaged in an activity can provide information about the child's interests and attention span.
- Use abbreviations or short phrases if helpful. The flow of activities can be so rapid that even an experienced observer can have trouble keeping pace with the action; you should, however, write complete quotes of a child's language ability. The exact words a child said will be difficult to remember and fill in later.

- When you have completed the observation, go back and fill in the needed details as soon as possible while they are fresh in your mind. Running records are rich with description.

- At the end of the running record, write a brief conclusion using the past tense to summarize the development (cognitive, psychosocial, physical, or creative) demonstrated by the child.

- Keep the records confidential; do not leave them lying around the classroom.

- Organize each child's running records in his or her portfolio. (More on this in Chapter 9.)

A major hazard of running records is writing general and vague descriptions. Capturing children's developmental moments in detail is a valuable observational skill to cultivate; using explicit words is the key. After writing a running record, the observer checks to see if some words are general or vague and need to be replaced with specific words to thoroughly describe an observance. For example, a general statement might be, "The girl plays with the blocks in the carpeted area." What specific words would explain how she might have played with blocks? Did the observer consider stacks, forms enclosures, or balances? Descriptive words can precisely characterize the child's behavior and provide the teacher with accurate developmental information. Practice Activity 4.1 presents an opportunity for you to apply your practical understanding of word choice.

Practice Activity 4.1
Descriptive Word Practice

Write some descriptive verbs to further specify the following activities of children. You may use a thesaurus if you wish.

Example: Looks—squints, peeks, stares, scans

1. Builds

2. Colors

3. Tells

4. Runs

5. Writes

Detailed running records will provide developmental information about these children.

Descriptive modifiers (e.g., adjectives, adverbs, and prepositional phrases) increase the clarity of each observation. Study the following examples, and find the modifiers. How are they helpful to the reader of the observations?

Example A

Delia rolls balls down
   different-sized ramps
   made of blocks.

Example B

Delia (4;2) stacks three blocks and places a long, flat board from the top of the blocks to the ground. Then she rolls a ball down the incline, watching where it stops. Next, she adds two more blocks vertically so that the incline is even steeper and rolls another ball down the higher ramp. As the second ball races down the incline and speeds past the first ball, an ear-to-ear smile fills her face. Quickly, she constructs a ramp seven blocks high and again rolls a ball down the ramp.

Descriptive words can provide information about the child's facial expressions, movements, appearances, tones of voice, gestures, and problem-solving methods. Accurate conclusions cannot be drawn without these details.

Striving to record an accurate picture is the job of the trained observer. Avoid the pitfall of vague descriptions, and remember that details, details, details pave the way to useful observations in running records.

Integration of Developmental Theory and Observation

Preschool Example

A teacher committed to studying the development of her day care students observed a 3½-year old boy in the dramatic play area. Jeffrey, as usual, was the first child to arrive at the day care center, and his teacher, Gita, thought she would have 10 to 15 minutes to observe him working alone before the next child needed to be welcomed. After Gita hugged Jeffrey good morning and he put his jacket in his cubby, he headed straight for the dramatic play area. This area seemed to be his favorite spot in the early morning, but Gita knew she was unaware of the fine points of his play. A running record was made to order because she was interested in observing his natural play rather than assessing a predetermined skill or behavior. Gita sat on a small chair next to a low shelf with her notepad and filled in her heading; she was about 12 feet away from Jeffrey where she could maintain full view of the dramatic play area and the entrance door. Read Gita's running record in Figure 4.3.

Interpreting the Data   Later in the day, when Gita reads over her running record (Figure 4.3), she is able to draw detailed conclusions about specific areas of Jeffrey's

---

Running Record of Jeffrey in the Dramatic Play Area

Center/Age level: Peaceable Kingdom Day Care/3-Year-Olds

Date: 2/8   Time: 6:40–6:55 A.M.

Observer: Gita   Child/Age: Jeffrey/3;6

	Comments
Jeffrey stands at the entrance to the dramatic play area, yawns, and rubs his hair with both hands. Then with his hands on his hips, he slowly turns his head from one end of the area to the other, looking at the materials. He stands, without moving, looking back and forth at the area for 50 seconds. He slowly walks heel-to-toe to the far corner and looks down at the heap of dolls and stuffed animals. He bends over, picks up the brown bear with his right hand, and holds it under his left arm while he pulls out the rabbit and pink bear. He takes this load and dumps the three animals on the round table and goes back to the pile. This time he goes down on his knees and rummages through the heap of mostly dolls. He extracts a dog with a torn ear and missing eye and nose; after turning it all around, he discards it to the side. He pulls out a dirty, limp lamb and without hesitation puts it with the dog. He rummages again. Lifting his head, he calls to me, "Hey teacher, we got any more animals?"	*6:40*
"No," I reply, "I think you found them all."	*6:45*
Standing up, Jeffrey returns to the round table. He puts the animals in three of the four chairs around the table and scoots each one in. He picks up the pile of full-sized plates from the stove with both hands and goes to the brown bear. Holding the plates in his left hand, he pats the brown bear on the head with his right hand and announces, "Gregory." He puts a plate in front of Gregory. Moving clockwise around the table, he reaches the pink bear. "Mimi," he says and gives it a plate. He pauses with his hand on the rabbit's head for 15 seconds. "Casey," he says tentatively; then, "No—Wally." He gives Wally a plate.	
Jeffrey walks to the cupboard and gets the plastic fruit and a large, long-handled spoon from the bottom shelf. Using his left hand, he puts the plastic tomato on the spoon held in his right hand and, balancing it carefully, walks over to Wally.	
"Here you go, Wally," Jeffrey says with a smile and a slightly raised voice. "Your favorite, bacon an' eggs." He tips the tomato onto the plate.	
"Now for you, my little chickadee," Jeffrey sing-songs on his way back to the fruit. "What my little darlin' want to eat?" He pauses, looking through the fruit. "Oh? We got some that too." He puts the plastic apple on the spoon, carries it over to Mimi's	*6:50*

Figure 4.3. Preschool running record example.

plate, and tips it on. He briefly glances at two children who are being greeted by Dolores (the aide).

After studying the animals at the table, Jeffrey rummages through the stove, sink, and cupboard without removing anything. Opening the refrigerator, he smiles and uses both hands to collect an oversize handful of real flatware from the top shelf. Walking slowly toward Gregory, he transfers the flatware to his left hand; as he tries to pull out a fork with his right hand, several pieces drop to the floor. He picks them up and tries again. Again, he loses several pieces, but this time he gives Gregory a fork before collecting the pieces. The fork he tries to pull out for Mimi gets tangled, and the whole handful tumbles to the floor. Frowning, Jeffrey scoops the flatware up and dumps the pieces in the sink.

Yipes! Clean up.

6:55

Noah and Lene arrive at the entrance to the dramatic play area and are greeted by Jeffrey. "Hi, wanna play with me? I'm feeding my babies. He got bacon an' eggs, and she got pancakes with 'nanas. I'm the dad, OK?"

Conclusion: Jeffrey's dramatic play with stuffed animals, dishes, and plastic fruit demonstrated his focused representational ability, and he maintained one-to-one correspondence with three animals and three plates. He used a long-handled spoon with his right hand to balance and dump plastic fruit. His initiation and independence allowed him to play on his own, although he also welcomed other children.

Figure 4.3.   (*Continued*).

development. First, there is wonderful evidence that Jeffrey enjoys using his cognitive ability to represent.

- Jeffrey allows one thing to stand for another. The animals were given names and referred to as *babies.* He pretended that the tomato was bacon and eggs and the apple was pancakes with bananas.

- Jeffrey is able to take on a role. He pretended that he was the dad and talked to the animals with raised intonation. He gave each animal a plate and started to pass out forks.

- Perhaps he is imitating action and language he has observed. Perhaps he has heard someone use the phrase "my little chickadee" and watched the table-setting process.

Gita also finds information about Jeffrey's developing number skills.

- Jeffrey is able to maintain one-to-one correspondence with small numbers. He successfully passed out plates to the three animals, although he took the whole

Children's interests and abilities are continually on display in the classroom.

stack with him to the table rather than counting out three at the stove. It appeared that he planned to give each animal a fork but abandoned the idea when the handful of flatware proved to be unwieldy.

This running record also provides information about Jeffrey's development in other areas that will not be pursued at this time. In the psychosocial realm, for example, Gita observed a child who worked beautifully by himself and yet was cordial to arriving children. Running records often provide a wealth of information in various developmental areas.

Follow-Through Plans While learning to be a successful observer, you will practice the observational methods presented in this book as part of your study. As a result, you will learn about the potentials of the various methods and how to utilize them competently. As a teacher (future or present), however, you want to conduct observations in order to enrich the lives of the children in your classroom. You will want to press your running records and interpretations into service. Remember, "teaching is not one activity and inquiring into it another. The ultimate aim of inquiry is understanding; and understanding is the basis of action for improvement" (McKernan, 1991, p. 3).

Therefore, in anticipation of teaching responsibilities, let's examine how Gita puts her running record to practical use. She notices how long it took (nearly 15 minutes) for Jeffrey to set up his role play. The dolls and stuffed animals were all jumbled together. The plates, flatware, and plastic fruit seemed to be located in random places; the flatware was in the refrigerator and the plastic fruit in the cupboard. Gita wonders how much more Jeffrey's role-play might have developed if he could easily have located his props in predictable places. Consequently, Gita decides to do a general housecleaning and organization of the dramatic play area.

Gita continues to study the materials-and-equipment issue. She concludes that plastic fruit is a poor substitute for bacon and eggs or pancakes and bananas because it does not allow the child to mix things together or practice fine motor skills by ladling food onto dishes. Further, because plastic fruit clearly represents real fruit, some children might feel constrained to use it only as fruit. She plans to fill one canister with open-ended materials, such as various wooden shapes, which will add to the ease and enjoyment of the children's pretending.

Gita ponders what else might be changed in the dramatic play area to support children's representational thought. What else can Jeffrey do as a make-believe grownup? Are there materials to support pretending to write checks, make a shopping list, read a cookbook, take care of a baby, and chat on the telephone? If Jeffrey wants to pretend to be someone other than a family member, could the dramatic play area provide the foundation? Are props and space available to be a shopkeeper, bank teller, doctor, office worker, chef, fire fighter, and the like. Gita's running record stimulates an evaluation of the materials available and the use of space throughout the classroom.

Noticing that Jeffrey exhibits one-to-one correspondence with three animals and three plates, Gita wants to find out if this skill extends to larger numbers. She decides to ask Jeffrey to pass out napkins to the eight children at the snack table tomorrow. She plans to provide Jeffrey with opportunities to count objects so as to evaluate his number development further.

Gita's running record also gives her pause to appreciate Jeffrey's thoughtfulness; he did not act impulsively in the dramatic play area. He studiously surveyed the area before commencing play. He was not distracted during his cumbersome search for the stuffed animals. Jeffrey appeared to plan his role-play mentally and carry it out with great deliberation. Gita recognizes the importance of being responsive to this individual characteristic. If she rushes him, she will not bring out the best in Jeffrey.

Primary Grade Example

Consider Our Ethical Responsibilities to Community and Society

NAEYC Ideal I-4.2

"To promote cooperation among agencies and professions concerned with the welfare of young children, their families, and their teachers" (Feeney & Kipnis, 1992, p. 10).

Read on to see how Pablo fulfills this ethical responsibility.

Going one step further than being a "human video camera," a primary grade teacher arranged (with parental permission) for a student teacher to videotape Thienkim, a child in his kindergarten class. To minimize classroom disruption, the camera was set up near a wall and the zoom feature used to follow the child. Pablo, the teacher, was concerned about Thienkim's behavior in the classroom and scheduled a preliminary child-study team meeting of the principal, resource specialist, and himself to explore the necessity of special help for Thienkim. Pablo promised to supply a videotape so the team could share a common frame of reference, and he transcribed a portion of the tape in the form of a running record (Figure 4.4) for Thienkim's file.

Interpreting the Data   After the child-study team views the videotape, Pablo presents Thienkim's problems as he sees them. Pablo describes an insecure, timid child whose behaviors limit her potential enjoyment of friends, school, and learning. Pablo is bewildered by some of Thienkim's behaviors: Thienkim said she did want to work with Luciano and then chose not to; further, she held up her index finger while recognizing two ducks on a Lotto card. Pablo admits feeling unsuccessful with Thienkim and begins to wonder if she should be placed in a special class with more individualized attention.

Fortunately for Thienkim, the resource specialist is of Vietnamese ancestry and is able to explain some of Thienkim's behaviors to Pablo and the principal. In Thienkim's culture, shaking hands and hugging are not acceptable methods of greeting between teachers and children; a slight bow is appropriate. As an indication of courtesy and comprehension, Vietnamese often answer a question with "yes" and then go on to reply to the message. Regarding Thienkim's ability to count, the resource specialist notes that Vietnamese begin counting with their thumbs—so the index finger is the usual sign for two (Buell, 1984).

A running record is often the key to an expanded understanding of a child.

Running Record of Thienkim During Greeting Time

School/Grade: Glade Elementary/Kindergarten

Date: 9/17   Time: 8:00–8:20 A.M.

Observer: Pablo   Child/Age: Thienkim/5;4

	Comments
Thienkim arrives at school, barely visible behind the coat of her mother. With a gentle nudge, the mother guides Thienkim through the doorway into the classroom and departs quietly. Thienkim stands motionless with her eyes cast downward.	*8:00*
"Good morning, Thienkim," Pablo says cheerily and reaches out to grasp Thienkim's hands, pull her close, and hug her. Thienkim's body stiffens, and she recoils from Pablo's embrace as soon as she is released.	
Thienkim goes to the cubbies via the outskirts of the classroom, keeping her eyes focused on the floor. She puts her lunch away, sits on the rug circle, and studies her hands until the class is gathered to begin the day.	*8:03*
During Pablo's calendar and counting activities, Thienkim remains motionless and silent. Pablo begins free-choice time and asks, "Who wants to work with blocks?" Thienkim does not volunteer nor does she express interest in any other available activity. All children leave to start on self-selected activities. Only Thienkim remains on the circle.	*8:10*
"Would you like to work with Luciano and the puzzles?" Pablo asks.	
"Yes, I don't want to," replies Thienkim in a barely audible voice. She gets up, walks swiftly to the small-toys area, chooses a Lotto game, and spreads the cards out on an empty table with her back to the center of the classroom. She studies each picture card for a second or two before putting it in place. She completes 12 matches on 2 cardboard sheets.	*works 10 minutes on this*
"How many ducks are there?" asks Pablo later, pointing to a card.	*8:20*
"Two," answers Thienkim without hesitation, holding up her hand with her middle, ring, and pinky fingers bent down.	*Holds up one finger—why?*
Conclusion: Thienkim withdrew from friendly interactions with the teacher and class participation. She chose to work alone with a structured game and orally enumerated two objects.	

Figure 4.4. Primary grade running record example.

Follow-Through Plans   Grateful for the resource specialist's gentle and gracious cultural education, Pablo resolves to make his classroom more hospitable to Thienkim. Review Pablo's running record in Figure 4.4, and write down your suggestions in the exercise below.

Practice Activity 4.2
Practical Applications of Pablo's Running Record

List ways Pablo can make use of the information from his running record of Thienkim.

Example: Greet Thienkim with verbal warmth but physical restraint.

1.

2.

3.

Applications

Strengths and Limitations

The fundamental benefit of using the running record method is the collection of detailed, narrative data, usually on one child. The data are usually gathered in short periods (5–10 minutes) because of the method's stringent attention demands, although an experienced observer may effectively manage a longer session. This observational method records a child's behavior and language and allows developmental conclusions to be drawn. Running records may be saved and used throughout the year (or longer) for discovering, assessing, and marking the changes in children over time. They may also serve to stimulate plans for developmentally appropriate activities and the evaluation of the classroom.

Both the experienced and the inexperienced observer can easily recognize the major difficulty with the running record. The setting alone, an active early childhood environment, can be problematic. A young child may change activities frequently as the observer frantically writes or may move to a place where sight and hearing are hindered. Perhaps classroom noises or interferences distract the observer. Myriad factors might cause the observer to neglect to record some behaviors or verbalizations. Being a "human video camera" requires the constant use of imaginary blinders, a well-tuned ear, and a fast hand.

Another problem is scheduling. Even though the running record method requires only a paper and pencil, the busy classroom teacher encounters many obstacles to finding time to observe a child. Given the day-to-day demands on an early childhood teacher, running records are best spaced out and employed judiciously. It takes a diligent teacher who is willing to plan for (and an administration that is willing to support) the practical implementation of observational time.

A running record for Warren, the child discussed in the chapter's opening vignette, might have yielded a wealth of understanding; for example, it might have revealed his interests, his active concern with practically oriented problems, how long and under what conditions he worked on task, and how he responded to peers. Warren's busy teacher, however, probably would have required help from the principal, a specialist, or a parent to accomplish this running record. Fiona could have asked this person to free up her time so she could give Warren her full attention for a short period, or if the person were trained in observation, Fiona would have had the option of asking him or her to use the running record method to observe Warren.

As you gain expertise in the observational methods presented throughout this book, you will become able to put the running record in perspective: one plate in a smorgasbord of observational options. You will use the running record selectively when you need raw, factual data to learn more about a child or profit from an overall picture. Then, the time investment required by the running record will pay off; review the educational follow-through plans for Jeffrey and Thienkim if you have any doubts.

Action Project 4.1
Running Record Activity

Observe a child working alone for 3 to 5 minutes, and record her or his actions and language in a running record. Consider using a tape recorder that you can start and stop at your convenience as you write your final copy. As you select your observational subject, remember that you will want to draw some conclusions about the child's development in all pertinent areas. Also remember to include the following information on your recording form.

Running Record Title

Center or School/Age level or Grade:

Date: Time:

Observer: Child/Age:

Comments

Running record:

Conclusion:

Points to Remember

Running records offer observers the means to explore the development of individual children, especially those who are most puzzling. Teachers who make the time to use the running record are well rewarded for their efforts. They have a descriptive narrative, unhampered by premature interpretations, that reports the actions and verbalizations of a child in detail. The running record stands alone as raw, qualitative data and is available for later study—stimulating evaluation and profitable follow-through plans. To maximize the usefulness of each running record, check that it

- Includes the informative heading used throughout this chapter
- Is written sequentially in the present tense
- Is as objective as possible
- Uses explicit words, modifiers, and details to describe behaviors
- Summarizes the subject's exhibited development in a conclusion written in the past tense

Take a Moment to Reflect

Frequently we have suspicions about how the data of our observational study will turn out, particularly if we know the children involved. Pablo in the primary grade example is no exception. Before he collected his running record data, he scheduled a child-study team meeting to explore the necessity of special help for Thienkim. He anticipated documenting her problems with the running record so that the other professionals in the meeting would agree with his assessment. What happened? When the resource specialist inter–

preted some of Thienkim's behavior within her cultural context, Pablo viewed this child in a new light. He immediately began to make plans to support Thienkim's development in his classroom and abandoned his proposal for a special placement for Thienkim.

Fortunately Pablo had an open mind and did not stubbornly stick to his preconceptions. He was open to the information presented by his data. Think about the openness of your own mind in a similar situation, and reflect on strategies to cultivate it.

1. Recall an incident in your own work life in which you were either open or closed to surprising, unanticipated information. What happened? With hindsight, what would you do differently?

2. If you publicly voice a strong opinion before you have the supportive information, you risk digging yourself an embarrassing hole. What helpful questions could you ask yourself to avoid forming premature conclusions?

3. List some practical values of maintaining an open mind in the workplace and in observational settings.

CHAPTER 5

Observing Development of Individual Children Using Anecdotal Records

Gita, the teacher in the preschool example in Chapter 4, is sitting on her chair with notepad in hand when Noah and Lene arrive at the entrance to the dramatic play area. Jeffrey cordially invites them to play. Gita's running record of Jeffrey's role-play has progressed smoothly, and she has the time and the desire to continue. She anticipates that Jeffrey's interactions with the other children will be interesting to observe. What problems do you foresee if Gita chooses to use the running record method in this situation?

While a running record is an excellent method to use when the observer wants to gather wide-ranging data on one child, can you imagine Gita's frantic attempt to write down every action, reaction, interaction, and verbalization of all three children if she chooses a running record?

Gita certainly collected an impressive display of developmental information about Jeffrey in a running record, and now she wants to extend her understanding of Jeffrey's social skills by recording the behaviors of the trio. There is, however, another observational method for efficiently summarizing incidents that is especially useful when detailed accounts are not feasible. It is the anecdotal record.

This chapter investigates the use of the anecdotal method as a powerful teacher's tool for building an understanding of the whole child; it is an easy way to collect and analyze significant happenings. Although this chapter features the observation of individual children, anecdotal records can also be helpful for teachers observing small groups of children, students observing master teachers, supervising teachers observing student teachers, or principals observing teachers. What then are anecdotes? Read on, and learn about one of the most popular observational methods in the early childhood classroom.

Overview of Observing Using Anecdotal Records

After returning from a vacation or, as in this instance, a family celebration, I frequently delight in sharing brief accounts or memorable moments with friends. Often, the happenings are humorous or heartwarming; often, they are unusual or unfortunate; always, they are anecdotal. One such recent anecdote is as follows:

> Having been to preschool and learned the song *Jesus Loves Me, This I Know*, my niece's son (3;0) looked up at her while they snuggled on the couch and said, "Momma, I love you. This I know."

Have you had similar experiences of recounting personal happenings? Most likely we all have. An anecdote, then, is not a new idea to any of us. We all seem to have a sense of what it is all about.

Description

In the early childhood classroom an *anecdote* is more than something interesting, emotive, or amusing to share. It is a short, concise, nonjudgmental narrative summarizing one directly observed incident. The focus of a classroom anecdote is a specific incident or event that the teacher identifies as notable (Diffily & Fleege, 1992). The difference, then, between a classroom anecdote and a personal anecdote is purpose; the classroom anecdote is chosen for its developmental significance whereas the latter is usually chosen for its emotional appeal.

The three steps to take when keeping classroom records using anecdotes are as follows. The teacher first observes the incident, then identifies the incident as valuable (developmentally significant), and completes the process by writing it down after it has occurred. This transcribed memory account of a important classroom happening traps golden developmental moments and provides a permanent record of individual children's growth trends. Figure 5.1 displays three examples of classroom anecdotes for one child. Read through them and appreciate the developmental significance that each represents. Notice that the data available for study are qualitative.

Anecdotal records are most reliable if jotted down as soon as possible after the event, thus capitalizing on a clear memory (Sax, 1989). In bustling classrooms writing a detailed anecdotal entry immediately after the observed incident is not always possible. Reread the first anecdote of Kristi and the firefighter in Figure 5.1. The teacher, in this example, having acquired the competence to spot significant behaviors, observed a noteworthy incident and had time to make only a quick memorandum using key words on a nearby scratch pad.

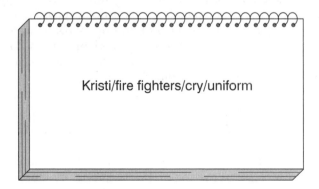

Kristi/fire fighters/cry/uniform

As time permitted later in the day, the teacher transcribed the key words into a few meaningful sentences (Figure 5.1) and placed the anecdote in the child's portfolio. This same technique, using key words, was practiced by the teacher in each of the anecdotes in Figure 5.1. What key words do you think the teacher wrote for the

10/5 Kristi (3;3). During the fire fighters' classroom visit, Kristi cried and crawled into the teacher's lap when Ryan's mom (one of the fire fighters) put on her uniform. (Psychosocial—Fear)

10/12 Kristi (3;3). At the art table, when given a choice of assorted sizes of brushes, Kristi picked up four various-sized brushes in each hand, dipped them into two different colors, and with long strokes painted the entire paper. (Creative—Expanding risk taking).

10/15 Kristi (3;3). Choosing the outside obstacle course, Kristi steadily walked with even paces, one foot in front of the other, on a four-foot balance beam. (Physical—Gross motor)

Figure 5.1. Examples of preschool anecdotes.

other anecdotes about Kristi? Many teachers find that using key words relieves the pressure of recording their anecdotal observations while they are teaching.

When based on key words or short phrases, anecdotal records take little time and are easy to record on a daily basis (Tull, 1994). Anecdotes require no particular setting, no forms, and no time structures. The observer needs only to capture the essence of what occurred—the child's actions, reactions, and responses during the incident (Veale & Piscitelli, 1988). The observer may draw on the *journalistic approach* and record the factual accounts of the *who, what, where, when,* and *how* of a single incident. Reporting the specifics of *when* and/or *where* may not always be necessary; it is up to the observer's judgment. For example, if a child chooses the

The journalistic approach assists the observer in remembering the essential components of anecdotes.

planned art activity for the very first time when it is set up outside, then stating where the event transpired may be an important factor and should be included.

An important component in learning to write anecdotes is the content. A well-written anecdote gives brief information to build a visual image of the setting, summarizes how the incident happened, and uses descriptive words to tell what was said and done. "The use of direct quotes and descriptions of the child's expressions and gestures are important to include because they provide valuable information for review" (Smith, Kuhs, & Ryan, 1993, p. 11). As additional examples, consider the language anecdotes shown in Figure 5.2 that were extracted from individual portfolios. Analyze their content. Did the observer satisfy the requirements of the journalistic approach?

Language development is one of the major growth areas in the early childhood classroom. The teacher recording the language anecdotes in Figure 5.2 considered them developmentally meaningful; in so doing, the teacher appraised the child's age, the vocabulary choice and usage, the expression of relationships, and the concise communication of a complex idea. Language anecdotes may also be collected to evaluate sentence length, articulation/clarity, word order, and conversation skills. In addition, K–3 teachers may observe and record children's use of expanded sentences, pronouns, and accurate grammar, just to mention a few examples.

Purpose

The fundamental aim of the anecdotal record is to note significant and ongoing evidence of children's development or growth through selected observations. Teachers observe and record behavioral patterns, changes, progress, milestones, or un-

---

Example 1
10/5 Tatiana (2;0). While sitting on the floor in the art area peeling the wrappers off crayons, she looked up as the caregiver drew near and said, "I making the crayons all naked." (Cognitive—Language)

Example 2
5/19 Maggie (4;8). I listened as Maggie chattered on and on while the two of us cleaned up the block area. Finally I winked and said, "It all sounds like baloney to me." Maggie quickly asked, "What's baloney?" I replied, "It's a word that means you made all that up." She thought for a few seconds and said, "No, it's salami!" (Cognitive—Language)

Example 3
2/24 Matthew (7;4). While discussing *In A Dark, Dark Room and Other Scary Stories* by Alvin Schwartz, Matthew thoughtfully shared, "Do you know what kind of scary things I like best? Things that are halfway between real and imaginary." The teacher started to ask, "I wonder what . . . ? Matthew quickly replied, "Examples would be aliens, shadows, and dreams coming true." (Cognitive—Language)

Figure 5.2.   Examples of language anecdotes.

common happenings (Kapel, Gifford, & Kapel, 1991) based on the growth indicators explained in Chapters 2 and 3. Typical topics for early childhood anecdotes are language and literacy development, social interaction patterns, problem-solving skills, aggressions, and achievements. The recordings may involve only a single child or child–child interactions or adult–child interactions.

Anecdotes chronicling a child's development can provide the basis for the teacher's planning of appropriate environmental support, activities, responses, and experiences. Posting one or two anecdotes a week for each child gives the teacher a collection of valuable information to offer a learning program that germinates from emerging individual needs.

"Taken regularly, anecdotal notes become not only a vehicle for planning instruction and documenting progress, but also a story about an individual" (Rhodes & Nathenson-Mejia, 1992, p. 503). Recordings gathered over a period of time and representing all requisite domains of development (physical, cognitive, psychosocial, and creative) supply enough information to create a story and, thus, a holistic understanding of the child. In addition, parents can fully appreciate this story when well-selected anecdotes are shared at conference time.

Educators with teaching experience may believe they know the strengths and weaknesses of the children in their classrooms and conclude they do not need to

Teachers observe and record anecdotes to note developmentally significant incidents.

write down individual observations. It is, however, impossible to remember the wonderful growth, in detail, of 8 to 15 (let alone 20 or 30) children over the course of the year. "Memory leaves just the impression. The written word is an opportunity to check impressions and opinions against the facts" (Gordon & Williams-Browne, 1995, p. 169). Regular and systematic recording documents up-to-date information needed for individual planning and productive parent conferences.

Guidelines for Writing Anecdotes

Over the years, researchers, teachers, and observers have developed helpful hints to ensure success using each of the various observational methods. The following are suggestions to assist in writing useful anecdotal records:

- Employ the anecdotal record method when you want to document significant developmental incidents. Use the information from anecdotes to help chart developmental growth, plan curriculum (based on children's needs and interests), design environments, and write summary forms for parent conferences. Anecdotes are recorded frequently in the early childhood classroom; they are the backbone of portfolios.

- Begin with a clear understanding of the developmental characteristics of the age group being observed. (Review Chapters 2 and 3 or reread the growth indicators in Appendix B.) Be able to identify growth indicators for physical, cognitive, psychosocial, and creative development.

- Be aware of significant happenings in each child's daily activities.

- Jot down brief notes using key words on paper or adhesive note paper or dictate into a small tape recorder as soon as possible after a directly observed incident. Record important language passages verbatim. Tuck them away in a folder or in a pocket designated for anecdotal records. (Remember that all records must be kept confidential.)

- As soon as possible, transcribe those key words or cursory notes into readable sentences.

- At the beginning of each anecdote, enter the date of the observation and the child's age (year; month).

- Use the journalistic approach, and write in the past tense.

- Be factual, objective as possible, and concise; summarize.

- State the developmental significance (e.g., physical, cognitive, psychosocial, or creative) in the anecdote itself or in parentheses at the end. In the primary grades, cognitive development may be categorized into the relevant subject areas (e.g., language arts, math, social studies, and science).

- Guard against haphazardly tossing individual anecdotal records into a catchall file. Enter the finished anecdote in the child's portfolio of observational records.

- Check portfolios periodically to verify the recording of a variety of developmental incidents for each child.

To practice using the guidelines, slowly read the anecdotal record examples listed in the next activity and determine if each is an acceptable or unacceptable anecdote. For each incorrect anecdotal example, decide what changes should be made.

Practice Activity 5.1
Anecdotal Examples for Analysis

If the anecdote meets the guidelines, place an *X* in the box marked correct. If, on the other hand, the anecdote does not meet the guidelines, place an *X* in the box marked incorrect. In each case, describe your reasoning in the space marked *analysis*. While working through the following examples, ask yourself the following questions:

Does this example
- use the correct form (stating the date of the observation and the child's age)?
- concisely describe only one incident?
- use a journalistic summary rather than an overall appraisal?
- give too much or not enough information?
- use descriptive words to recount what occurred?
- provide quotations of the child's language when appropriate?
- state the developmental significance?

Example:
5/8 Willie (4;5). Willie is cognizant and watchful while playing with others. He can communicate well. Does like to create own play with other objects but keeps his playmates in mind. (Psychosocial   Play)

☐ Correct

☒ Incorrect

Analysis:
The observer has written an overall evaluation using inferences rather than a journalistic summary of one specific incident. Recording quotes would indicate Willie's communication skills. The last sentence is subjective.

Example:
11/24 Meghan (3;9) with Ernestina (3;3) When Meghan saw Ernestina in the doorway crying and clinging to her mother's leg, she walked over and gently placed her cheek touching Ernestina's cheek. The girls stood quietly cheek to cheek for a few moments, and Ernestina's mom departed. (Psychosocial—Empathy)

☒ Correct

☐ Incorrect

Analysis:

The observer has identified a significant incident in the psychosocial development of Meghan and Ernestina. The narrative summary is written concisely yet contains information on the *who, what, where,* and *how* of a single incident. This anecdote could be filed in each girl's portfolio. What would the developmental significance be for Ernestina's anecdotal record?

2/15 Jeffrey (3;6) with Noah (3;8) and Lene (3;3). At Jeffrey's invitation Noah and Lene joined in dramatic play. Jeffrey directed and Lene cooperated in the feeding and napping of Jeffrey's "babies." Noah dressed up in men's clothes and pretended to wash the dishes. (Psychosocial—Play)

☐ Correct

☐ Incorrect

Analysis:

12/7 Hien (4;2). Hien picks one marker out of the container with his left hand, smelling it (scrunching up his nose). "Um pink," he says. He draws carefully constructed horizontal parallel lines with it and puts it back. He sorts through the container and picks up a thinner marker, smells it, and looks it over. Hien asks if all the markers smell as he drops the thin one back into the container. He takes out a green marker, smells it, and draws on the paper using a circular motion. He uses his right hand to steady the paper. "I'm gonna make a target for us," he says. Putting back the green marker, he takes out the red marker and bangs it on the table and then lays it down. Next, he takes out the blue marker and uses a circular motion to draw inside the green circle.

The teacher asks, "So that's a target?"

"Not yet," Hien says. He returns the blue to the container and takes out a purple marker. Quickly, he draws with purple in a circular motion inside the blue circle and says, "Now, that's a target." (Creative—Representations)

☐ Correct

☐ Incorrect

Analysis:

4/11 Thelma Lou (6;4). I am quite worried about Thelma Lou's fine motor development. While working with small puzzles, she seems to have a plan to begin with but asks for help over and over.

☐ Correct

☐ Incorrect

Analysis:

6/23 Cassandra (7;11). In a small, cooperative math learning group assigned to create a new pattern using plastic links, Cassandra stood up and gathered the links that had been placed in the center of the table. After unlinking each one, she announced, "We all have to have the same amount; I'm going to pass them out!" (Psychosocial—Relationship with peers)

☐ Correct

☐ Incorrect

Analysis:

Integration of Developmental Theory and Observation

Knowledgeable teachers jot down anecdotal records that reflect all areas of development. Periodically they check each child's portfolio to see if they are collecting a variety of anecdotes in different settings. Individually or as a team, teachers read the newly added anecdotes and a sample of the old ones to broaden their understanding of each child. They look for developmental growth patterns as they study individual recordings and plan activities based on assessed needs.

Two classroom anecdotes are reproduced in Figure 5.3 to represent preschool and primary grade topics. As you read through them, see if you can determine why

---

1/13 Song (3;3). While watching a puppet show in another classroom, Song responded with tear-filled eyes when he was mocked by the two 4-year-old boys sitting next to him. One boy poked the other and said, "Look at him; he's Chinese. He looks like this." With his hands he pulled down the corners of his eyes until they were partially closed.

9/18 Lissy (7;5). In the computer lab Lissy asked how to spell *through*. I responded, "Let's sound it out together." Lissy said, "I know how to write it that way, but I want to know the correct way to spell it."

Figure 5.3.   Examining anecdotal records.

the teacher chose to write each one down (the developmental significance has been omitted for your practice), and begin to think of some plans the teacher could make to further each child's growth.

Although not all anecdotes necessitate follow-through plans, the examples in Figure 5.3 beg for teacher interpretation. "Interpretations are constructed through our active mental work; they are not part of the immediately given environment. They grow out of our theories, our past experiences and our present observations" (McCutcheon, 1981, p. 5). Listed are possible teacher plans based on the anecdotes in Figure 5.3. These plans model the process that teachers follow when interpreting anecdotal information to further individual growth.

Preschool Example

Consider Our Ethical Responsibilities to Families

NAEYC Ideal I-2.3

"To respect the dignity of each family and its culture, customs, and beliefs" (Feeney & Kipnis, 1992, p. 6).

Read on to see how Song's teacher fulfills this ethical responsibility.

Preschool Anecdotal Example—Song

1/3 Song (3;3). While watching a puppet show in another classroom, Song responded with tear-filled eyes when he was mocked by the two 4-year-old boys sitting next to him. One boy poked the other and said, "Look at him; he's Chinese. He looks like this." With his hands he pulled down the corners of his eyes until they were partially closed. (Psychosocial—Self-concept)

Interpreting the Data   At the moment this incident happened, the teacher looked firmly at the two boys and had time only to say, "Song is not Chinese; he is Korean. You hurt his feelings when you make fun of his eyes. Eyes can be all different shapes." And then the teacher looked at Song and said, "It's OK to tell them that you don't like that."

After the children have gone home, the team teachers in Song's class evaluate the day. They begin by looking at the anecdotes they have written. Song's is first. The teacher who interacted with Song and the two boys shares her feelings related to this incident. She says she is a little surprised but very pleased with her response. In the past she had not responded this assertively to delicate situations. The other teacher readily responds that he personally has been afraid to step in when sensitive matters occurred. Both teachers spend time talking about their own discomfort. Realizing that their biggest fear is uncertainty regarding the right words to say, they review other responses teachers might make in similar situations.

"That's very hurtful when you say _____. I can't allow you to hurt someone's feelings."

"I'm sorry Logan and Ricardo hurt your feelings."

"I think you're wonderful just the way you are."

The teachers agree that knowing the kind of words to say is important, but they must steer away from pat answers that become litany. Each situation will be different; their responses must come from an active involvement.

The teachers then shift their attention to Song's discomfort and inability to stand up for himself with 4-year-olds. They discuss how they could affirm Song. In their 3-year-old classroom they continuously represent several cultures, including Korean, with dolls, pretend food, cooking tools, books, snacks, and pictures on the classroom walls. As the teachers read back through other anecdotes they have collected about Song, they see a clear picture that Song shows confidence in dealing with and communicating his feelings to children his same age in his classroom; however, he is the first child of young parents and could benefit from more exchanges with older preschoolers in their school.

Follow Through Plans   After much discussion about Song's reticence and the other boys' insensitivity, the teachers decide to invite the same class of 4-year-olds back to share a diversity awareness party with the help of parent volunteers. Their party will have several different activities set up throughout the room; the children will freely choose one activity to participate in.

Song's teachers confer with the teachers of the 4-year-old class and choose the theme, "I'm Me and I'm Special" (York, 1991, p. 73). The teachers referred to the books *Anti-Bias Curriculum* (Derman-Sparks & A.B.C. Task Force, 1989) and *Roots and Wings* (York, 1991) for some of the following ideas.

At the first table the teachers decide to have hand mirrors, skin-toned construction paper, and several boxes of crayons, including assorted skin-tone crayons. The children who choose this activity will be invited to look into the mirrors and draw what they see. The teacher at this table will talk with the children about differences and similarities as they come up, affirming that it's wonderful and important to be who we are—"you and me."

At the second table there will be long pieces of butcher paper, many shades of skin-tone tempera paint, primary-color tempera paints, various sizes of paint brushes, craft sticks for mixing paints, paint cups, crayons, pencils, scissors, and a full-length mirror. The children will be offered the big paper to trace around each others' bodies on the floor. Then, with the aid of an adult, they will mix the skin-tone paints to reflect the color of their own skin and help each other paint their portraits on the butcher paper, adding hair, facial features, and clothes. The adults at this table will talk about our skins' many beautiful shades of color and how no two seem to be exactly alike.

At the third table will be magazine pictures of eyes of various shapes and colors along with scissors and glue for making collages. Again, mirrors will be handy to help the children identify their own eye shape and color.

At the fourth table, close to the sink, will be long strips of butcher paper, skin-tone tempera paints to be mixed to individual shades, buckets of soapy water, paper towels, and paintbrushes. Here, the children can take their shoes off, mix paint the color of their feet, paint the bottoms of their feet, and make footprints on the paper. Perhaps they will also want to make handprints. The teacher at this table can talk about the marvelous variety of sizes, colors, and shapes.

In addition, two other large tables will be available on the periphery of the room. One of these tables will be left empty for children who want to work independently. The other table will be designated the resource table with an array of other materials that children from any table may need: yarn, crayons, marking pens, glue and tape, various colors of construction paper, large and small pieces of fabric, and wallpaper sample books.

After all the projects are completed, the adults plan to assist the children in displaying their creations in the classroom for everyone to admire. The teachers from both classrooms will help the children to talk about and celebrate their differences and similarities.

The diversity awareness party takes place 2 days later and is a success for all. The teachers of the two different age groups plan more times when the two ages can be mixed: a trip to the park, a snack time, and a musicfest. Subsequent anecdotal records note that Song slowly and steadily gains confidence with older children. The two 4-year-old boys become more accepting of diversity, and the use of the anti-bias curriculum begins to gain momentum in the school. Daily the teachers are more aware of their own reactions as well as those of the children to cultural diversity. They are watchful not to ignore subtle comments. They use opportune moments to point out differences, likenesses, options; they model acceptance of and joy in who each person is. They agree that working toward a bias-free environment is a perpetual process necessary to help children develop a positive sense of self and others.

> Never has our nation been as diverse in its population as it is today. Nor has any previous generation of children been confronted so urgently with the task of learning to respect and empathize with one another and to recognize a common humanity. (Clinton, 1995, p. 193)

Primary Grade Example

Anecdotes are also useful in the primary grade classroom. Consider the example of Lissy in the computer center.

Primary Grade Anecdotal Example—Lissy

9/18 Lissy (7:5). In the computer lab Lissy asked how to spell *through*. I responded, "Let's sound it out together." Lissy said, "I know how to write it that way, but I want to know the correct way to spell it." (Cognitive—Language)

Interpreting the Data   Lissy, an enthusiastic second grader, has been going to the computer laboratory since kindergarten. In this laboratory, the children are encouraged to write words phonetically, using invented spelling, so as to avoid being bogged down by spelling refinements. She writes terrific stories, many about the exciting adventures of a female, underwater photographer. One of her stories was recently chosen for the school newspaper.

As the teacher enters this anecdote and checks previously logged anecdotes, she notes Lissy's continuous literacy development. Lissy enjoys writing and reading her stories and readily shares them with other class members. Her stories already have well-developed plots, thus showing her ability to comprehend sequence. The incident recounted in the anecdote was, however, the first evidence that Lissy is aware that printed materials need to be consistent for readers. Documenting Lissy's emerging personal interest in spelling illustrates the natural step children can make when they are ready and able to use correct spelling without it limiting their creative writing. Lissy's teacher is pleased to see that Lissy has made this connection on her own.

Follow-Through Plans   As often happens, the teacher notes other children who seem to have the same need: in this case, an interest in correctly spelling words of their choice. The teacher plans a small-group time to demonstrate ways to spell words using different sources. Lissy's teacher shows the children how to use their well-known reading stories to locate the spelling of a word that they know, and she introduces the use of the picture dictionary. The teacher also helps the children create their own personal dictionaries—blank papers stapled together with one letter of the alphabet on each page. When the children need to look up a word in the picture dictionary or if they need teacher assistance for spelling, they can record the word in their personal dictionaries, thus having it for future reference.

A child's enthusiasm for writing soars with the opportunity to use a computer to compose stories.

Enthusiastic about the small group information, Lissy shows avid interest in using the picture dictionary. She is also delighted to have her own personal dictionary. She immediately inscribes words on several pages. Her teacher later observes that Lissy sometimes illustrates the new word she adds to her dictionary. (What a resourceful idea!) To capitalize on the children's spelling interest, the teacher gradually puts up charts on the walls with lists of commonly used descriptive words, action words, and prepositions. Lissy's enthusiasm for writing continues to increase because her developmental need is met at the right time.

If teachers view each child as an important and unique person, they will observe and record carefully, then consciously select curriculum activities and experiences based on identified individual needs. Analyzing anecdotal records unlocks the doors to the appropriate curriculum cupboards.

Anecdotes and Other Forms of Recording

A cohesive portrait of each child's development is drawn through the use of many forms of classroom observation. The use of various methods allows the teacher to see through the looking glass with clarity and confidence. Some teachers find it difficult to work with the large amount of raw data collected through running records. Although many running records document abundant and varied happenings, their conclusions cannot stand alone without the running record. Running record conclusions are seeds for several anecdotes (for clarification review the running record and conclusion in Figure 4.2). For this reason teachers pick out individual incidents in each of their running records, rewrite them as anecdotes, and file them in the child's portfolio. These shortened, one-incident recordings usually prove to be much more useful than the long descriptive passages of running records when the teacher is analyzing, planning, and conferencing.

Likewise, anecdotes are a possible source for some of the information requested by checklist or rating scale assessments discussed in the next two chapters. For example, a child's gross motor abilities recorded in several anecdotes could be transferred to a motor development checklist or rating scale. Language anecdotes are also a likely topic. Think about other potential topics as you are introduced to checklists and rating scales in Chapters 6 and 7.

Applications

Strengths and Limitations

In the early childhood classroom, anecdotes are among the most widely used observational methods; their strengths are numerous. To begin with, "teachers report that they see and hear with more clarity when using anecdotal records, by focusing more intensively on how children say things and how they interact with each other" (Rhodes & Nathenson-Mejia, 1992, p. 508). Many times the teacher's attention is on whether the child is able to complete the task instead of on the process the child is using while engaged in the task. When the teacher is cognizant of growth indicators and on the look-out for significant developmental incidents, the teacher's focus is on the child's process. In those focused moments, the teacher will be able to respond appropriately to each child and can effortlessly move the child ahead in his or her zone of proximal development (see Chapter 2). This can happen when anecdotal recordings are one of the primary classroom observational methods.

Developmentally appropriate programming requires that the curriculum be age and individually appropriate. Anecdotal records are one of the vehicles teachers use to meet this criteria. Weekly anecdotal recordings supply the teacher with specific examples of each child's growth patterns and developmental characteristics; the focus is the individual rather than the group. These valuable records are then analyzed and, when suitable, used in planning to facilitate individual learning and provide a program that serves the individual needs of each member.

Many teachers maintain that an important advantage of anecdotal records is their ease in use. Writing anecdotes takes no more than paper and a pencil (or a pocket-size tape recorder). Anecdotes are written at the teacher's convenience after the event has occurred. Because an anecdote is a concise statement, little time is needed to record the major elements. Using the key word method to jot down significant words at the time of the observation helps teachers' memories remain accurate, especially at the end of a long day! Time can also be saved when using a computer. "This year I discovered how much easier it is to make quick notes during the day and write up the incidents later on the computer. Word processing allows anecdotal records to be created in one-quarter the time, sometimes less" (Diffily & Fleege, 1992, p. 13). Many experienced teachers also enlist the help of assistants who can be trained effectively in anecdotal record collecting; some schools provide excellent in-service training for assistants.

Anecdotal records are a treasure chest of documented incidents that can be compared and contrasted with other recorded observations. These gems, used in conjunction with other kinds of observational records, can help the teacher form a precise understanding of each child's unique growth patterns, changes,

Teamwork enhances the observational process.

interests, abilities, and needs. These records, when read weekly, provide the teacher with an ongoing portrait of the individual developmental composition of the class. This wealth of information is the foundation for teacher planning and conferences. Teachers report that conference preparation and participation are smooth and efficient when based on anecdotal records; parents have high regard for the teacher who offers true-to-life illustrations of their child's development.

Many would argue that teachers' biases may influence what they choose to record (Borg & Gall, 1989; Sax, 1989). Teachers may fail to see an important developmental step if they have formed preconceived ideas (either positive or negative) about a particular child or children in general. For example, a primary grade teacher may think boys are better than girls in math. Or a preschool teacher may judge a child's behavior on the basis of a sibling's competence displayed in a previous year. Practicing anecdotal writing and receiving feedback from others is an excellent way to uncover hidden biases and avoid this potential limitation.

On the other hand, the teacher may unknowingly miss an important milestone for one or more children because of the many demands for a teacher's attention. Teachers avoid this pitfall by using aides or enlisting parent volunteers as classroom helpers, relying on well-organized systems of record keeping (more on this in Chapter 9), and offering a program that has a variety of child-directed activities. "Sand and water play, blocks, and dramatic play, for example, tend to anchor children and free teacher time for observation" (Benjamin, 1994, p. 17). In addition, devising effective classroom management techniques allows for needed "release time" to stand back, observe, and listen to individual children as they play and work.

Action Project 5.1
Anecdote Exercise

You are now ready to practice writing some anecdotes of your own. One of the best ways is to turn on a videotape of prerecorded incidents. (Beginning writers of anecdotes think that the replay button is mighty helpful!) Because we cannot play a videotape in this book, we will move to the next best option. This exercise gives you the opportunity to practice writing anecdotal records by extracting them from a running record.

Study the running record for Evan at the workbench, and then write one anecdote embedded in the scenario. Remember, an anecdote is a summary of one incident.

Write your chosen anecdotal record for Evan (5;2) or Shaina (5;4). Use the correct form, concisely summarize the incident, use the journalistic approach along with descriptive words, write in the past tense, and state the developmental significance. Think through any needed follow-through plans.

Running Record of Evan at the Workbench

School/Grade: Cornerstone School/Kindergarten

Date: 9/25   Time: 10:15-10:23 A.M.

Observer: Mariah   Child/age: Evan/5;2

Comments

As the door swings open to the outside yard, Evan makes a beeline to the workbench. He leans over and roots around in the large scrap-wood box, finally selecting two long (about 15-inch) rectangular pieces. As he places the wood pieces on top of the bench, he arranges one piece of wood perpendicular and on top of the other, forming a T shape, both lying flat. As he holds the top rectangle in place with his right hand, his left hand retracts the hammer from its hanging position on the pegboard attached to the back of the workbench. He lays the hammer down on the workbench and lets go of the wood with his right hand. The two wood pieces stay in the T position without support. Evan opens the drawer under the workbench top with both hands and picks out three nails with his left hand and places each one on the workbench. He grasps the hammer in his left hand and a nail in his right hand. Holding the nail at the intersection of the two wood pieces, he raises his left arm almost shoulder height and whacks the nail; he misses and instantly pulls his right hand away. The top wooden rectangle falls off the bottom one, and Evan lets go of the nail. Still holding the hammer in his left hand, he once again repositions the wood into a T shape. He picks up another nail with his right hand and holds it in the same place. Again, he raises the hammer shoulder height and brings it down toward the nail with great speed. Again, he misses! With the hammer in his left hand and the nail in his right, he puts both hands on his hips and sighs deeply.

Shaina (5;4) approaches the workbench and says, "Wanna play chase?" "No," responds Evan, "I'm making 'un airplane, but this nail's falling." Shaina walks around the workbench, looking at Evan's structure as Evan re-joins the two pieces he has been working with. "Wait, wait!" hollers Shaina as she raises her hands into the air. "You gotta use the vise." "The what?" asks Evan. "This thing," Shaina replies as she reaches up and takes the vise from its position on the pegboard. "My daddy showed me how to use this; it works!"   *10:18*

Evan steps back one step with eyes glued on Shaina's actions   *Very skilled* as she clamps the two pieces of wood together and securely fastens them on the edge of the workbench with the vise. "Now it won't move. Try it and don't pound so hard," she says as a broad smile fills her face.

With his right hand he chooses another nail and moves it into   *10:21* position. This time, he holds the nail with his whole hand. Evan bends slightly at the knees, raises the hammer about 1 foot above the nail and, with a slower speed, taps the nail. This time he makes contact. With tongue now gripping the right side of his mouth, he lifts the hammer and strikes the nail again. He repeats his successful motion six times, each time making contact. When the nail is securely driven in, he looks up at Shaina, eyes wide, lips together, and gives one nod of his head. Before Evan has time to utter one word, Shaina exclaims, "I'll bet that's a DC-10!"

Conclusion: (The conclusion has been omitted so that your selected anecdote will not be influenced.)

Points to Remember

One definition of a classroom anecdote is "a written log containing specific accounts of a student's behavior" (Kapel et al., 1991, p. 32). Observing and recording a child's developmental progress through anecdotal records requires little time. Anecdotes can easily be used to collect qualitative data in all areas of growth. Contents state the *who, what,* and *how,* and sometimes the *where* and *when* of an observed behavior. Using an in-the-nutshell recording format, anecdotes are written after the incident occurs. They are placed in each child's portfolio and used in planning. As preserved treasures, anecdotes enrich parent conferences.

Anecdotal record keeping necessitates the use of objectivity to the best of one's ability, a thorough understanding of child development, the ability to proficiently capture an incident in a concisely written form, and the commitment to regular recording for each child. Anecdotes are often considered the backbone of portfolios.

Take a Moment to Reflect

In the classroom authentic (naturally occurring) observations take place as the child experiences the daily program; anecdotal records are authentic observations. If the teacher collects weekly anecdotes for each child in all areas of development, a comprehensive and true-to-life picture of each child's current and evolving strengths becomes apparent and is readily available. Two scenarios follow. Read both, then reflect on one.

1. Suppose you were the only teacher at your school collecting anecdotes—doing authentic observations. The other teachers seem to scurry around

the last week before conferences trying to get some idea where the children are developmentally. You see your colleagues pull children aside and "test" them. You feel compelled to share your knowledge about authentic assessment at the next staff meeting. You worry, however, about how to do that without offending other teachers. You are aware that not all of the teachers have had an observation class. What approach would you take? How would you proceed to be a child advocate in this situation?

2. Search your own memories. Have you had experiences that prompted you to think that everyone was out of step except yourself? What feelings surface as you think about a particular example or situation? If you courageously came forward and shared your thoughts or took action, what was the outcome? Explore how your past experiences may influence how you handle current and future child advocacy concerns.

CHAPTER 6

Observing the Development of Individual Children by Using Checklists

Nicole is the teacher of an early childhood group. Today she has set up an obstacle course outside. She has carefully designed the course to challenge and assess the children in several areas of gross motor development, such as climbing, hopping, jumping, and balancing. The play yard is a busy place, with two classes of children outside at the same time; these children may also choose to use the obstacle course. Nicole plans to target her observational attention on the developmental skills of the children in her group. How might she best accomplish her goal?

When Nicole observes the children in her class going through the obstacle course, she wants to document their abilities. She rejects the running record method because her hand could never keep pace with quickly moving children. Anecdotal records would also be cumbersome. Imagine writing something like this for each child: "In my prepared obstacle course, Linnea (5;7) ran with a steady, moderate pace around the tree, hopped in two Hula-hoops on her right foot, jumped over the 12-inch foam cube from a standing position, and balanced halfway down the balance beam." Nicole wants to assess each child's gross motor abilities efficiently; this chapter introduces an observational method for her to consider.

Recall how you brush your teeth at night, and check off which of the following descriptions apply to you.

- Uses fluoridated toothpaste
- Brushes for at least 1½ minutes
- Uses dental floss
- Uses gum massager of some kind

You have just completed a short checklist that requires no special skills other than knowledge about your toothbrushing practices. You have used a checklist—the topic of this chapter.

Overview of Observing Using Checklists

Description

A *checklist* is a register of items that the observer marks off if they are present; behaviors or details not on the checklist are ignored. Good checklists have clear items that leave little room for observers' subjective interpretations, and checklists usually investigate skills or easily observed behaviors within their natural contexts. For example, children's prosocial or motor skills or teachers' story-reading skills might be studied on one or more occasions. In the introductory example, Nicole wants to assess the presence of specific abilities—that is, whether each child can run in a coordinated fashion, hop on one foot, jump over a low obstacle, and walk on a balance beam; a checklist is the appropriate observational method.

Checklists may be filled out during or after an authentic observation as children engage in their normal classroom activities. In either case, the observer brings the checklist and paper for note taking to the observational session. The quality of data recorded on checklists depends on the clarity of the items and the observer's ability to assess each item accurately. Therefore, the observer must be familiar with the content of each item and know what constitutes an earned check; instructions on checklists may serve to clarify potential ambiguities.

Information to complete a checklist may be gathered from a single or several observations, or the observer may want to include data from other observational records (e.g., anecdotes) on the subject. The choice depends on the purpose and type of checklist used. A one-time observation may be sufficient to assess an environment, whereas a teacher completing a multiple-subjects checklist for a primary grade child would want to draw on the widest possible information base.

This chapter examines checklist items that focus on children's development, the environment, and explicit teaching skills. First, let's look at portions of a checklist (Figure 6.1) assessing children's progress in emergent writing (Houghton Mifflin, 1989). Appreciate how the ordering of items illustrates developmental growth and how the heading introduced in the chapter about running records efficiently organizes introductory information at the top of the sheet.

High/Scope Educational Research Foundation developed checklists to evaluate the implementation of its curriculum (Hohmann & Weikart, 1995). The checklist that evaluates how spaces for children are arranged and equipped includes the following item. (Note that High/Scope chose to use lines instead of check boxes.)

_____ Labels make sense to children. They are made from

    _____ The materials themselves

    _____ Photographs, photocopies

    _____ Pictures

    _____ Line drawings, tracings

    _____ Written words in addition to any of the above (p. 147)

These clear and straightforward choices are responsive to the curricular goals of accessible and well-organized materials to support children's interests, autonomy, and intentions; the observer records their presence or notes their absence.

Other portions of the High/Scope checklist assess the skills of teachers in supporting the program's goals. Building on the preschool growth indicators of seriation summarized in Chapter 2 (Box 2.8), consider these relevant items on p. 138.

Writing Developmental Checklist

School/Grade:

Date:

Observer: Child/Age:

Date	Skill
[ ]	Mimics writing; scribbles
[ ]	Draws recognizable pictures of people, animals, and objects
[ ]	Dictates words and short phrases
[ ]	Dictates complete sentences
[ ]	Dictates stories
[ ]	Traces upper- and lowercase letters
[ ]	Traces words and sentences
[ ]	Identifies and forms uppercase letters
[ ]	Identifies and forms lowercase letters
[ ]	Uses letters and numerals to mimic writing; no sound–symbol association
[ ]	Is aware of left-to-right sequence of letters and words
[ ]	Is aware of spaces between letters in words
[ ]	Is aware of spaces between words in sentences
[ ]	Copies words and short phrases
[ ]	Copies sentences
[ ]	Writes words and short phrases using invented spellings; demonstrates awareness of sound–symbol associations
[ ]	Writes complete sentences using invented spellings; demonstrates awareness of sound–symbol associations
[ ]	Writes stories using invented spellings; demonstrates awareness of sound–symbol associations
[ ]	Writes stories that include some words with standard spellings
[ ]	Writes stories with a distinct beginning, middle, and end
[ ]	Writes detailed, imaginative stories that reflect an awareness of standard spelling, capitalizations, punctuation, grammar, and usage

Figure 6.1. Checklist example.

Source: From *Houghton Mifflin Literary Readers. Selection Plans and Instructional Support, Book 1.* Teacher's Guide in *Houghton Mifflin Reading/Language Arts Program* by William K. Durr et al. Copyright © 1989 by Houghton Mifflin Company. Adapted by permission of Houghton Mifflin Company.

Comparing attributes (longer, shorter, bigger/smaller)

_____ Provide materials whose attributes children can easily compare

    _____ Sets of materials in two sizes

    _____ Materials children can shape and change

    _____ Materials with other contrasting attributes

_____ Store and label materials in a way that encourages children to compare attributes

_____ Listen for and support the comparisons children make as they play and solve problems (Ibid, p. 472)

The High/Scope checklists focus on precise teaching skills that serve to keep teachers on track in meeting program goals.

Purpose

Checklists are used primarily to assess the current characteristics of an observational subject (child, teacher, curriculum, or environment), to track changes in these characteristics over time, and to provide information for program planning. First, consider the examination of current characteristics. A teacher might be interested in verifying which of the children in a preschool classroom heap blocks or build rows, bridges, and enclosures and which are beginning to name, add details to, and pretend with block structures. Having observed children's developing building skills over the first few months of school using anecdotal records, this teacher now wants to condense these observations onto an accessible and easy-to-read form. A checklist is an appropriate observational method to meet this teacher's needs.

The following example shows the use of checklists to examine current characteristics of teachers-in-training. A college professor of children's literature devises a checklist to observe students reading stories to children in the laboratory school. The first few items on this checklist are the following.

During story time, the practicing student

❑ provides a brief introduction connecting the story to the children's experiences.

❑ maintains eye contact with the children.

❑ asks the children open-ended questions throughout the story.

❑ provides opportunities for the children to comment about the story.

After pilot testing the entire checklist (trying it out and making appropriate revisions), the professor adds space for comments at the bottom of the form. Here, particular strengths, words of encouragement, areas of concern, examples, or suggestions may be jotted down.

The second purpose of checklists is to track changes in characteristics over time. Nicole, from the opening vignette, may reuse her checklist to monitor children's advances in gross motor skills. The teacher mentioned earlier observing block-building skills can use the same checklist periodically over the course of the year to chart children's developmental growth. Over the semester, the college pro-

Checklists are used for assessment. In this photo a college professor consults with a student about her story-reading techniques.

fessor can document the students' progress by using the story-time checklist as a pre- and post-test.

The third purpose of checklist assessments is program planning. Checklists not only provide teachers with information about the skills and development of the children in their classrooms, but they also provide a foundation for teachers' daily plans. For example, after studying the checklist results, the block-building observer concludes that he needs to plan exploratory experiences for the novice builders and add more diverse building materials for the experienced builders. Checklists (and observations in general) are not completed just to be entered in children's portfolios or cumulative records. Rather, the information they provide about individual children is for teachers to use in planning supportive activities, in evaluating program effectiveness, and in planning appropriate curricular adjustments.

Guidelines for Constructing a Checklist

Many useful checklists are available to the early childhood educator, and portions of two of these have served as examples (a writing checklist and a curriculum checklist). As a beginning observer, however, you should gain the ability to construct your own checklist to explore early childhood issues that are of specific interest and concern to you. Box 6.1 provides guidelines for designing a checklist.

Box 6.1
Designing a Checklist

1. Select an appropriate topic.
2. Research the topic in libraries and classrooms.
3. Identify clear, distinct items.
4. Design a recording form with the traditional heading and check boxes. Decide if instructions are necessary.
5. Consider adding space for comments at the bottom of the form.
6. Pilot test the instrument.

Checklists are constructed to assess children's or teachers' skills or behaviors or the specific characteristics of programs and environments. The topic under examination is thoroughly researched, and the checklist items are carefully worded. The checklist, now a form on a piece of paper, is called an instrument—"a device used to collect data, information, and evidence" (Wheeler & Haertel, 1993, p. 72). Pilot testing (trying out the observational instrument) is essential because new items may not be added after data collection has begun (Evertson & Green, 1986). Chapter 12 addresses pilot testing in greater detail, but for now, participate in the following activity by selecting some appropriate subjects for checklists.

Practice Activity 6.1
Checklist Topics

List five topics that may be appropriately assessed by checklists. You may include topics concerning children, teachers, curricula, and/or environments.

Examples:

- Children's understanding of numbers
- Presence of culturally diverse materials

1.

2.

3.

4.

5.

Return to the introductory toothbrushing checklist, which I made up at my desk after reviewing what I know about toothbrushing. You and I have no confidence that my checklist identifies the essential components of good toothbrushing. I failed to research my topic in the library and in the field; consequently, the checklist suffers. If I want to design a checklist that accurately assesses a person's oral hygiene, I must do some research. I might visit a school of dentistry, interview professors about proper oral hygiene, and ask them to critique my checklist. I could also talk to my own dentist, observe people brushing, and then move to a literature search.

What are the possible flaws in my checklist? Perhaps to do a thorough cleaning job, the brusher needs to brush for 3 minutes rather than 1½ minutes. I simply don't know how long an effective toothbrusher brushes, but the experts may. If not, this item should be omitted. Furthermore, I worry that my last two items overlap and, therefore, are not mutually exclusive—that is, one item might be included in another. Does flossing serve to massage the gums in addition to cleaning between the teeth? Or should a gum-massaging agent be used in addition to floss for optimal results? Additionally, I do not know if the advice my dentist has given me about my own teeth is universally applicable or if mouths, like children, vary considerably.

On the surface the topic of toothbrushing appears simple and straightforward, yet we quickly learned that the construction of a checklist, regardless of the topic, requires research and care. I hope you conclude that I had no business constructing a checklist without researching the topic, despite my years of brushing. Apply this lesson to early childhood education, and understand that even knowledgeable researchers review the relevant literature to ensure an accurate and current list of items.

Integration of Developmental Theory and Observation

Preschool Example

To experience the process of constructing a checklist, we join Cecily and Dave, inexperienced preschool teachers of 4-year-olds, who want to know what gross and fine motor abilities the children in their classroom possess. Because these teachers do not yet have a clear understanding of the range of normal physical development, they read and take notes on several chapters about the physical abilities of preschoolers in reputable child-development texts. They are drawn to the convenient checklist format, which readily allows them to assess the skills of individual children.

Cecily and Dave read that gross and fine motor abilities show marked development over the preschool years but also that there is a great deal of normal variation among individual children. They decide to work on a list of observable skills commonly gained by 4-year-olds and remind themselves that the items describe abilities *most* children gradually acquire during this year.

1. Hops on one foot for 7 to 9 hops
2. Catches a large ball with two hands and extended arms
3. Dresses self
4. Grasps and controls small objects (e.g., puzzle pieces, Legos, tape dispensers)
5. Alternates feet while climbing up and down a flight of stairs
6. Fastens buttons
7. Uses pincer grip on writing tools
8. Jumps 8 to 10 inches from standing broad jump position and lands on feet
9. Runs with control from start to finish and around turns
10. Cuts with scissors with moderate precision
11. Takes a step forward when throwing a small ball

Dave and Cecily certainly like the simplicity of this list as well as the clarity of the items and anticipate that the data will not be difficult or time-consuming to collect. They decide to rearrange the items to clarify the distinction between gross and fine motor skills and omit the item about dressing because it would not be observed within natural contexts. In order to monitor children's development over time, they plan to use the checklist three times over the course of the year. After pilot testing the checklist and making some adjustments, they observe the children's physical skills over the course of a week, writing anecdotes on handy pocket notepads, and then fill out a checklist for each child. Figure 6.2 presents the checklist as completed for Gilberto. (They plan to expand their checklist in the future to include items for 3- and 5-year-olds so as to help in assessing 4-year-olds who are not "average." For example, they will add items about increasing kicking and ball-catching skills.)

Interpreting the Data   Gilberto performed every gross motor item on the checklist except alternating feet while climbing up and down a flight of stairs. Because Lomas Day Care is a single floor facility with no playground equipment for climbing, Dave and Cecily took the children on a walk to the neighborhood park to observe this skill. Very few of the children earned a check on this item. Afterward, the teachers asked them if they have stairs at home, and most, including Gilberto, reported that they do not. What an important revelation!

Cecily and Dave note Gilberto's strengths in fine motor development (items 8 and 9). Because Gilberto is a young 4-year-old, his teachers are not concerned that he has trouble fastening his jean snaps and cutting precisely with scissors (items 7 and 10).

Physical Development of 4-Year-Olds

Center/Age level: Lomas Day Care/4-Year-Olds

Date: 10/24

Date:

Date:

Observers: Cecily and Dave   Child/Age   Gilberto/4:2

☑ ❑ ❑   1. Runs with control from start to finish and around turns

❑ ❑ ❑   2. Alternates feet while climbing up and down steps and stairs

☑ ❑ ❑   3. Jumps 8 to 10 inches from a standing broad-jump position and lands on feet

☑ ❑ ❑   4. Hops on one foot for 7 to 9 hops

☑ ❑ ❑   5. Catches a large ball with two hands and extended arms

☑ ❑ ❑   6. Takes a step forward when throwing a small ball

❑ ❑ ❑   7. Fastens typical clothing closures (e.g., buttons, jean snaps, zippers, or belts)

☑ ❑ ❑   8. Grasps and controls small objects (e.g., puzzle pieces, Legos, tape dispensers)

☑ ❑ ❑   9. Uses pincer grip on writing tools

❑ ❑ ❑   10. Cuts with scissors with moderate precision (on or close to a line)

Comments:

Figure 6.2.   Preschool checklist example.

Follow-Through Plans   The checklist results stimulate Dave and Cecily to plan some walking trips to nearby places that have steps and stairs in order to provide a variety of opportunities for the children to climb up and down. Together, the teachers and children also build obstacle courses that include a few treads for practice.

Gilberto's checklist is filed in his portfolio with a reminder tab to check his progress after several months to allow time for the effects of maturation and practice.

Other 4-year-olds in Cecily and Dave's class demonstrate motor strengths and weaknesses different from those of Gilberto. The checklist assessments heighten the teachers' awareness of individuals and stimulate them to take advantage of opportunities to practice specific skills with specific children. For example, Sarvenez (who runs with arms wide and at an uneven pace) may enjoy trotting around the yard with the security of the teacher's hand to announce that it is time to go inside. Charlotte may be just the child to help cut out a new magazine picture of a freeway system to hang in the block area. And Hubie may be the perfect candidate to stand next to the ball bin and catch the balls to put away at the end of outside time.

Data from checklists may be used, as shown, to plan supportive activities for individual children; note that although specific children are targeted, others may benefit as well. The teacher trotting around the yard with Sarvenez may soon find they are accompanied by a whole herd of children becoming more proficient runners. The benefits to one often extend to many.

When the teachers study the results for all of the children in the class, the checklist might also yield information about the strengths and limitations of the program

The assessment of individual children's physical development leads to the planning of supportive follow-through activities.

and environment. Suppose almost none of the 4-year-olds can catch a ball. Dave and Cecily scratch their heads for a second before realizing that they hardly ever take the balls out of the storage closet! They need to correct this oversight. Or perhaps the teachers do not know if the children can manage their own fasteners because these tasks are usually done for them; after all, Cecily and Dave are so much more efficient at buttoning and snapping than the children are. This, too, can change. Checklists provide valuable information about how well curriculum goals are being met.

Primary Grade Example

Consider our Ethical Responsibilities to Families

NAEYC Ideal I-2.6

"To help family members improve their understanding of their children and to enhance their skills as parents" (Feeney & Kipnis, 1992, p.6).

Read on to see how parenting is supported and enhanced by careful planning of a parent workshop.

A kindergarten teacher wants to keep close track of his students' math development. The teacher, Aram, decides to use the detailed curriculum checklists supplied by the teacher's manual (Baratta-Lorton, 1995) to assess each child's progress; Aram is thoroughly familiar with the meaning of each item, assessment procedures, and appropriate math activities to support children's growth. The section on counting is adapted for Figure 6.3.

Interpreting the Data   Aram assesses his students' counting skills in mid-September and determines from the results that several children, including Blanca, are ready for practice in counting on.

> The skill of counting on is a useful problem-solving tool in solving addition problems. It involves the child being able to perceive the number of objects in one group and count from there to obtain the total. Children who have this skill solve addition problems more quickly. When faced with a group of four objects and a second group of three objects, for example, these children *know* there are four objects in the first group so they merely count from there: *four,* five, six, seven. Children without this skill must find the total by counting both groups: One, two, three, four, five, six, seven. A child who has this skill quickly discovers that the total can be found by counting on either group, which encourages flexibility and a concrete understanding of the associativity of addition. (Baratta-Lorton, 1995, p. 103)

Follow-Through Plans   After the September 13 assessment, Aram plans two activities from the math text (Baratta-Lorton, 1995) to give Blanca and several of her

Counting Checklist

School/Grade: Hidden Ridge Elementary/Kindergarten

Date: 9/13

Observer: Aram   Child/Age: Blanca/5;3

1. Memorizing the sequence of number names
   - ❏ From 1–5
   - ❏ 6–10
   - ☑ 11–20
   - ❏ 20+

2. Counting objects (1:1 correspondence)
   - ❏ Groups of from 1–5
   - ☑ 6–10
   - ❏ 11–20
   - ❏ 20+

3. Invariance or conservation of number
   - ☑ With the numbers from 1–5
   - ❏ 6–10

4. Instant recognition of small groups
   - ❏ 2
   - ❏ 3
   - ☑ 4
   - ❏ 5

5. Counting on

   Verbally
   - ❏ Starting with any number between 1–10 and counting to 10
   - ❏ 11–20 and counting to 20

   To solve a problem using objects
   - ❏ Starting with any number between 1–10 and counting to 10
   - ❏ 11–20 and counting to 20

Figure 6.3. Primary grade checklist example from a teacher's math manual.
Source: From *Mathematics Their Way* (pp. A-4 and A-5) by M. Baratta-Lorton, 1995, Menlo
Park, CA: Addison-Wesley. Copyright © 1995 by Addison-Wesley. Adapted with
permission.

6. Counting backward (to 1)

Verbally

❑   Starting at any number from 1–10

❑   11–20

To solve a problem using objects

❑   Starting at any number from 1–10

❑   11–20

Figure 6.3.   *(Continued).*

classmates the opportunity to discover and practice counting on. The first, "Bite Your Tongue," provides a gross motor experience of counting on.

> Ask the children to bend to one side two times, counting silently, then bend to the other side, counting aloud from three to six. This cycle is repeated over and over again with the children "biting their tongue" so the first two beats are silent. (p. 105)

The second activity, "Cover Up," provides practice counting on with objects after a teacher demonstration. Aram, pleased with the usefulness of the checklist, plans to reuse it again in 2 or 3 weeks after introducing counting on and counting backwards.

Furthermore, Aram recalls his participation in a math curriculum workshop; he learned new methods of using manipulative materials and new activities to support children's mathematical understanding. As a result, he feels equipped to create a learning environment that encourages flexible thinking in math. He would like to share his information with parents, so he begins to plan an evening workshop in which parents can actively learn some skills to help their children. His goals are to improve the parents' understanding of his classroom math program and broaden their skills as parent tutors.

Applications

Strengths and Limitations

The checklist is valued for its simplicity. In the evaluation of a child or a classroom, observers sometimes simply want to assess whether a skill, behavior, or program characteristic is present. Checklists provide this kind of information. Think about preparing for parent conferences: teachers may want to be able to tell the parents

When teachers accurately assess children's current abilities, they can respond appropriately to individual needs.

if their children can run, hop, throw and catch a ball, and the like. A checklist is a useful tool of evaluation and is frequently used to record developing skills (e.g., writing, language, counting). The examination of checklist results can also promote teaching strategies and activities aimed at supporting specific areas of children's development and provide feedback about curriculum success.

Guard against the tendency to see skills or other characteristics as simply as they are portrayed on the checklist. The checklist only notes whether a characteristic is present; it does not indicate gradations of development within an item. Think about two children who cannot hop on one foot for seven to nine hops. An observer cannot use a checklist to document that one child has almost mastered the coordination whereas another hasn't the slightest notion of how to hop. The checklist only marks the mastery. Consider an added complication. Suppose a child who fails to hop nine times does so easily the next day. Is one demonstration sufficient for a check? Checklists are often lax about specifying criteria for a check (e.g., "counts" versus "counts five objects"). This limitation can cause serious confusion among checklist users.

In addition, reliance on checklists does not help educators figure out how to encourage the development of the characteristics not checked. A good teacher will evaluate data from checklists and other observational methods to maximize understanding of the characteristics of individual children or programs. The well-trained and conscientious teacher will then design activities to promote the unique growth of each developing child and make adjustments to increase program effectiveness.

Each checklist is only as good as its items and cannot make accommodations for exceptional cases; an item is either present or absent. Suppose a teacher uses an age-appropriate physical development checklist to observe Sarah (5;9), the youngest of four close-knit sisters, and discovers that Sarah does not know how to gallop. The teacher knows, however, that Sarah is a superb rope jumper and is capable of some fancy footwork. The teacher suspects that Sarah has the physical capabilities to gallop but perhaps has never been taught or bothered to learn because of lack of interest. As an observer, the teacher may not check the galloping item but regrets that the checklist does not accurately reflect Sarah's gross motor skills.

Action Project 6.1
Checklist Exercise

Imagine you are a preschool or kindergarten teacher planning a field trip. You have parent volunteers who will accompany groups of four children, and you want to be sure that all children benefit from the varied learning experiences available. Decide on an interesting field trip, and construct a checklist that would allow the parent volunteers to assess whether the individual children in their groups experience all components of the field trip. In your pre-field trip meeting with the parent volunteers, you clarify that although you want each child to participate as fully as possible in the field trip activities, children's refusals (e.g., refusal to pet a pig) are to be respected

Points to Remember

A checklist is an efficient, usually convenient, observational method to assess the presence of specific behaviors, skills, or characteristics. The observer may focus on individuals, curricula, or environments and collect useful information, which is preferably augmented by data collected by running and anecdotal records. Not only do checklists provide the observer with the opportunity to learn more about the subject, but the data should also help lay the foundation for responsive teaching strategies and activities as well as program fine-tuning.

Take a Moment to Reflect

Review the final paragraph under the section Strengths and Limitations about Sarah (5;9) who failed the checklist item of galloping even though she is a highly skilled rope jumper. Imagine that her teacher shares the checklist results at a parent conference with you, one of Sarah's parents. Like most people, you find yourself focusing on the unchecked items rather than noting Sarah's progress represented by the checked items. Reflect on the following:

1. How might you feel about the quality and comprehensiveness of your daughter's physical development evaluation?

2. Explore one of your own lingering or recurring feelings about an evaluation you considered unfair because you were not allowed to explain your incorrect answer.

3. What "red flags" do your reflections raise about writing checklist items? How can we best avoid children's and parents' feelings of unjust evaluations in early childhood education?

CHAPTER 7

Observing the Development of Individual Children by Using Rating Scales

September is a time of rededication and fervor in America as most children and teachers return to school. The mood at South Gate School was energetic. Committed to increasing parental involvement, the staff launched an exciting new parent-involvement component. There was much enthusiasm for the development of parent partnerships. Joint projects were undertaken, parent–teacher committees were formed, and new ideas blazed.

Now it is May, time to evaluate and formulate next year's goals. A new committee is formed to evaluate the home–school connection and propose changes. Members of the committee begin writing a checklist for parents' feedback but quickly become dissatisfied with the quality of the information they expect they would gather. Think about some of the committee's initial checklist items listed below.

During the current school year, did you

- ❑ Receive school newsletters?

- ❑ Attend parent seminars?

- ❑ Volunteer at school?

- ❑ Participate in the home study program?

How would the committee's information be limited by the checklist method?

In the South Gate School vignette, the committee members soon realize they do not simply want to know if the parents received newsletters, attended parent seminars, volunteered at school, or participated in the home study program (those would be appropriate items for a checklist). Rather, the committee wants the parents to assess the effectiveness of each of these home–school communication projects. The committee chooses to develop a rating scale, the method examined in this chapter.

Each of us has had opportunities to experience rating scales; restaurants, hotels, movies, child centers, and children's academic progress on report cards are frequently rated. Consider, even, our own unconscious ways of rating desserts, the neighborhoods in our communities, or the behavior of people around us.

This chapter addresses the use of rating scales in observing and recording the development of young children. First a note of caution. Early childhood teachers are tempted to rely heavily on itemized assessment methods (e.g., checklists or rating scales) because of their familiarity and ease in use. Thus, an important lesson in this chapter is learning when the rating scale method is appropriate.

Overview of Observing Using Rating Scales

Description

Rating scales are observational "instruments used to assess the quality of a particular trait, characteristic, or attribute with assessment usually based on pre-determined criteria (scale)" (Kapel et al., 1991, p. 467). In the early childhood classroom, rating scales can be used to evaluate children, teachers, programs, or environments. Although this chapter concentrates on the observation of individual children, a few examples of rating teachers and programs demonstrate the versatility of this observational method.

When using a rating scale, the observer is asked to make an appraisal of the listed characteristics by assigning a value to each along a continuum; the observer estimates the frequency of occurrence or degree of intensity for each item. Judgments can be based on direct observations, past observations (preferably documented observations, such as anecdotes or running records), or over all impressions. Kerlinger (1986) referred to this latter type of observation as "remembered behavior or perceived behavior" (p. 494).

Rating scales and checklists both are assessment tools that are easy to use in the early childhood classroom (Diffely & Fleege, 1993). In addition, both tools use predesigned forms that are simple to mark, provide opportunities to observe either all or selected areas of development, and may be based on direct observation or memory. They differ in one primary way—purpose. "Whereas checklists are used to indicate whether a behavior is present or absent, rating scales require the rater to make a qualitative judgment about the extent to which a behavior is present" (Worthham, 1995, p. 139). When the observer desires value-based data, rating scales are the most appropriate choice.

There are several types of rating scales, each using different organizational designs. Our study is limited to three specific forms popularly used in early childhood classrooms: numerical, graphic, and category.

The first type, the *numerical rating scale,* offers choices designated by assigned number values. The observer simply circles the number that indicates the best choice for each item. Those preschools applying for accreditation through the National Academy of Early Childhood Programs are already familiar with this type of rating scale. The self-study program for teachers, directors, and parents utilizes this type of observational tool. Figure 7.1 presents three examples from the *Guide to Accreditation* (National Academy of Early Childhood Programs, 1991a).

A-8b Staff help children deal with anger, sadness, and frustrations by comforting, identifying, reflecting feelings, and helping children use words to solve their problems. (p. 25)	1	2	3
B-7c (Staff) Encourage children to think, reason, question, and experiment. (p. 29)	1	2	3
J-3 Individual descriptions of children's development and learning are written and compiled as a basis for planning appropriate activities, as a means of facilitating optimal development of each child, and as records for use in communications with parents. (p. 62)	1	2	3

Note: Marking 1 indicates *not met,* marking 2 indicates *partially met*, and marking 3 indicates *fully met.*

Figure 7.1. Numerical rating scale Example 1.
Source: From the *Guide to Accreditation*, rev. ed., by the National Academy of Early Childhood Programs, 1991, Washington, DC: National Association for the Education of Young Children. Copyright © 1991 by the National Association for the Education of Young Children. Reprinted by permission.

Those who work in school-age programs may be familiar with the well-constructed numerical rating scale—*School-Age Care Environment Rating Scale* (Harms, Jacobs, & White, 1996). As shown in Figure 7.2, by assigning specific characteristics to every other number, all observers base their judgments on the same criteria and bias is minimized.

The second type of rating scale, the *graphic rating scale,* provides "a line containing different positions and anchored at least on extreme ends. By checking some point on the line, the raters indicate their evaluation of a trait along a continuum" (Sax, 1989, p. 590). In this type, the observer makes an overall assessment by marking the quality of each item using the descriptive words on the continuum. Typical sets of descriptors are these: never, sometimes, frequently, always—not yet, occasionally, often—never, sporadically, regularly—poor, average, excellent. Figure 7.3 assesses fine motor development based on the growth indicators from Chapter 2. Can you see that this type of rating scale got its name from the repeated visual arrangement of the descriptors?

	Inadequate		Minimal		Good		Excellent
	1	2	3	4	5	6	7
Arts and Crafts*	• Art materials not accessible for children to use as a free choice activity. • Regimented use of materials (Ex: mostly teacher-directed projects).		• Some materials accessible for free choice daily. • Materials are in good condition (Ex: felt pens not dried out, clay soft enough to work). • Staff help available when needed.		• Variety of materials accessible for free choice daily. • Individual expressions and free choice encouraged. • Very few activities require following an example.		• Opportunity to learn new skills and complete long-range projects (Ex. sculpting, pottery, embroidery).

*Materials: felt pens, crayons and pencils for drawing, tempera and watercolor paints, glue, scissors, clay, play dough, and materials for collage, embroidery, weaving, origami, jewelry making.

Figure 7.2. Numerical rating scale Example 2.

When using the graphic rating scale design, be aware of one potential problem—personal interpretations. Imagine how different observers may translate the meaning of these descriptors in Figure 7.3: never, occasionally, frequently, always.

The third type of rating scale, the *category rating scale,* "presents the observer or judge with several categories from which he picks the one that best characterizes the behavior or characteristic of the object being rated" (Kerlinger, 1986, p. 494). Characteristics rated are ordered from no signs of development to maximum development or vice versa, and the observer chooses the one that best represents the child's growth. The example of a category rating scale   (Figure 7.4) asks the observer to rate a child's behavior during group

Demonstrates the ability to use the pincer grip and/or pick up small objects with finger tips	Never	Occasionally	Frequently	Always
Demonstrates the ability to fasten and unfasten	Never	Occasionally	Frequently	Always
Demonstrates the ability to effectively cut paper with scissors	Never	Occasionally	Frequently	Always
Demonstrates the ability to insert and remove small pieces	Never	Occasionally	Frequently	Always
Demonstrates the ability to string or lace items	Never	Occasionally	Frequently	Always

Figure 7.3.   Graphic rating scale example.

At group time, the child

_____ Squirms or fidgets and is distracted by or distracts others

_____ Attends when being held by or touching an adult

_____ Attends most of the time but loses interest

_____ Attends carefully by listening and interacting with ideas that relate to the topic

Figure 7.4.   Category rating scale example.

time. Note that this example is arranged in a descending order on a vertical continuum.

We have briefly surveyed three types of rating scale designs. When constructing your own instrument or choosing an existing instrument, check that the format yields clear results. The next activity provides just such practice.

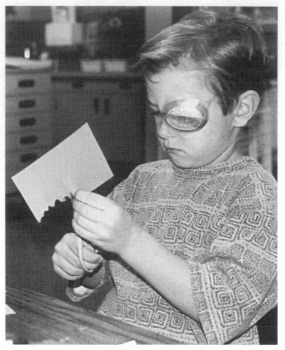

Understanding of children's growth can be bolstered by the appropriate use of rating scales.

Practice Activity 7.1
Examination of Rating Scale Design

Select one item from the following list of prosocial characteristics (Beaty, 1994, p. 137) and construct numerical, graphic, and category rating scales for that item. Write clear descriptors.

Prosocial Characteristics:

- Shows concern for someone in distress
- Shows delight for someone experiencing pleasure
- Shares something with another
- Gives something of his or her own to another
- Takes turns without a fuss
- Complies with requests without a fuss
- Helps another do a task
- Helps (cares for) another in need

The following is an example of a numerical, a graphic, and a category rating scale for the first item in the list (i.e., "shows concern for someone in distress").

Numerical

1	2	3	4
No attention given to a distressed person	Consoles a distressed friend	Consoles a distressed person who is nearby	Consoles a distressed person no matter where she/he is in the room

Graphic

Shows concern for someone in distress	Never	Sporadically	Regularly	Always

Category

_____ Does not console other children in distress
_____ Consoles a selected friend in distress
_____ Consoles a distressed child who is close by
_____ Consoles unselected (any) children in distress

After you have constructed the rating scales for Practice Activity 7.1, evaluate each type of rating scale design for clarity, ease in use, and personal preference.

Purpose

Rating scales are used to evaluate children, teachers, environments, or programs in a specified area(s) by positioning the items to be observed on a horizontal or vertical continuum. This method can best be used for assessing individuals once or on repeated occasions throughout the year.

"Assessment provides teachers with useful information to successfully fulfill their responsibilities: to support children's learning and development, to plan for individuals and groups, and to communicate with parents" (National Association for the Education of Young Children and the National Association of Early Childhood Specialists in State Departments of Education, 1991, p. 32). Repeated use of rating scales for individual children can provide information about developmental change over time. For instance, rating scales can be used throughout the year to assess the advancement of fine and gross motor skills, a child's degree of social maturity, the growth of language, the recurrence of aggressive behaviors, or a child's reading stages. The same rating scale administered more than once a year can provide pre/post growth comparisons, often on one rating scale using color-coded marks.

The most authentic results are obtained when assessments are based on several observed incidents that occur naturally within the classroom over a period of time; this is in contrast to a testing process in which children are pulled aside and asked to perform. These naturally occurring incidents are best remembered when they have been preserved as running records or anecdotes.

Individual rating scales may compile large amounts of information, usually categorized by developmental areas. Discerning practitioners do not simply file those completed forms in the child's portfolio and wait for the end of the year to reassess. Instead, when evaluations are complete, they analyze each form, look for patterns, compare it with other records, and plan follow-up observations or experiences as the year progresses.

Guidelines for Constructing Rating Scales

Although well-designed rating scales are available, a teacher may not be able to find an existing scale for a selected area of concern or one that the teacher can use to observe specific developmental goals. For example, Figure 7.3 illustrated a teacher-developed scale based on growth indicators.

The Practice Activity gave a first-hand opportunity to construct at least one item of a rating scale. Was the task deceptive? The rating scale form appears simple, but the process of writing items and choosing descriptors that are clear, as objective as possible, comprehensive, and as free of observer bias as possible can be a tedious and often complex task, even for a seasoned researcher. Construction of a rating scale is, indeed, not a task to embark upon halfheartedly. Allow plenty of time for designing and pilot testing. To develop productive rating scales follow the guidelines given in Box 7.1.

Rating scales may provide one method of assessing stages of creative development.

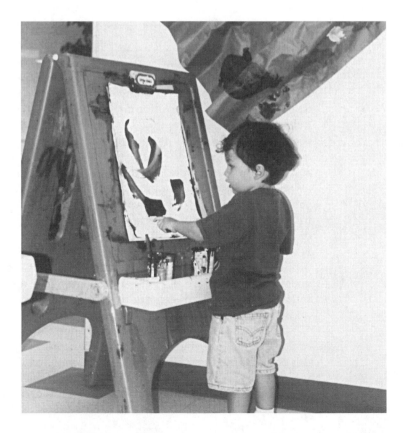

Box 7.1
Designing a Rating Scale

1. Select an appropriate topic.
2. Research the topic in libraries and classrooms.
3. Identify clear and distinct items to be rated. Reject ambiguous terms. Select terms that can be interpreted the same way by all observers.
4. Design a recording form.
   - Choose the rating scale that best suits your needs, preferences, and subject matter: numerical, graphic, or category.
   - Use a heading similar to that of a running record.
     Center or School/Age level or Grade:

     Date:

     Observer: Child/Age:

     Add instructions if needed.
   - Assign clear meanings to the scale descriptors. Be careful that the descriptors do not overlap.
   - Choose the number of descriptors that gives an accurate picture of each item.
   - Be aware of the error of central tendency. If an odd number of descriptors is chosen, observers may tend to rate in the middle "to avoid making difficult decisions" (Borg & Gall, 1989, p. 493). Exercise caution or use an even number.
5. Pilot test the first-draft rating scale, and make any necessary corrections.

If, as a classroom teacher, you choose to use a ready-made instrument, be sure to check it against the given guidelines. Many available rating scales are poorly constructed. Using such an instrument could produce faulty judgments and conclusions.

Integration of Developmental Theory and Observation

Preschool Example

During the preschool years, good programs assist children in mastering such self-help skills as dressing, toileting, cleaning up materials, and the like. A child's sense of autonomy is developed through the young child's acts of independence, self-assertion, and decision making (Hendrick, 1996). Let's explore how the teacher uses observations in assessment and planning to facilitate children's developing autonomy.

Organized classroom materials foster autonomy.

Treasured Times Preschool has established a policy that all parents must attend four parent education sessions per year. One session covers Erikson's stages of emotional development with an emphasis on the preschool years. Another session trains the parents in anecdotal record keeping. Consequently, the parent volunteers in Billy Ray's 3-year-old classroom are well equipped to help him gather anecdotal records in the area of autonomy. He assigns different children to each of the volunteers on the days they help. Before long many anecdotes are logged for all of the children.

Billy Ray also contributes anecdotes and running records to each child's portfolio. Using this observational data bank and his memory of perceived behavior, Billy Ray is able to fill out an autonomy rating scale for each of the 12 children in his class. Figure 7.5 offers the results for a child named Rosey. How can this rating-scale information help Billy Ray promote Rosey's optimal growth? What suggestions for follow-up plans are in order?

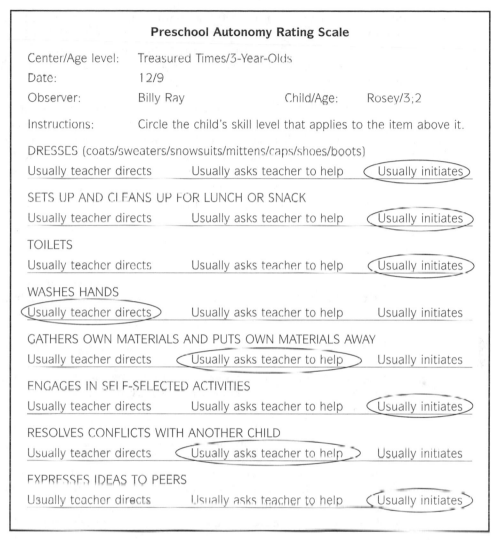

Figure 7.5. Preschool rating scale for Rosey.

Interpreting the Data Bill Ray begins by checking each rating scale for any possible error of central tendency. Finding none, he compares the children's rating scales, looking for threads of similarity. His group, overall, is quite capable and acts with autonomy. On occasion, boots or new jackets require assistance; that's understandable. From the rating scales Billy Ray can see that all of the children appeared to have difficulty remembering hand washing. He will investigate that tomorrow!

Billy Ray singles out Rosey's rating scale (Figure 7.5) for further study. He notices that Rosey "engages in self-selected activities" but "asks for assistance in gathering and putting away materials." He asks himself, "Why the dichotomy?" Billy Ray would like to encourage Rosey's full autonomy. The next item reads "asks for assistance in conflict resolution." This behavior, suitable for a child of Rosey's age, will continue to develop. Billy Ray plans to keep ongoing anecdotes to ensure that conflict resolution remains an observational priority. In particular, he will watch for times when Rosey is successful on her own.

Follow-Through Plans   Billy Ray surveys the classroom environment and keeps Rosey in mind as he thinks about 3-year-olds' abilities. He immediately spots a possible deterrent to individual autonomy. Although Billy Ray has organized and labeled the block center and a parent helper recently arranged the housekeeping center methodically, Rosey's favorite centers (the art and reading areas) are not so serviceable. Billy Ray resolves to add a labeled help-yourself art shelf so that Rosey and others can independently select and put away materials of their choice.

Billy Ray assembles a low shelf to hold materials that need minimal supervision, such as crayons, markers, paper, scissors, paste, paper punch, yarn, and magazines. He invites Rosey to help him arrange the beginnings of the newly assembled help-yourself art shelf; for better success, they start out with only a few items on the shelf. Rosey eagerly points out the best place for the markers and the paper. A few weeks later as Billy Ray expands the number of materials on the shelf, he puts each item in a marked storage container with its picture and invites Rosey to arrange and help label them. He can see that she has no hesitations. As time passes, Rosey popularizes the usage of the help-yourself art shelf and seems to adopt a personal interest in cleaning up this area.

In the reading corner Billy Ray's class has an extraordinary number of books; unfortunately, they are shelved in disarray. To promote autonomy in this area, Billy Ray classifies many of the books into a few popular topics. For instance, all animal books get a piece of red tape on the binding and are filed in the red-painted section of the bookshelf. Billy Ray puts an animal picture on the front of the red section and so on, until the color/picture coding is complete. Now finding and returning books are much easier. Billy Ray puts another child who also had difficulty initiating cleanup in charge of this center. Using the information drawn from a rating-scale evaluation, this teacher improved the classroom environment so that several children were able to become more autonomous over the course of the year.

Primary Grade Example

Consider Our Ethical Responsibilities to Children

NAEYC Ideal I-1.4

"To appreciate the special vulnerability of children" (Feeney & Kipnis, 1992, p. 4).

Read on to see how Melana fulfills this ethical responsibility.

Rating scales can be used at any time throughout the year. Some teachers prefer to use the same scale at several different intervals, dating each mark. Melana first used her teacher-designed graphic rating scale during the third week of school (Figure 7.6). She wanted to assess current work habits so that she could begin to form a comprehensive picture of each child, thus enabling her to plan and meet individual needs better. Figure 7.6 is a completed rating scale for a child named Andrew. As you read this figure, be aware of your initial interpretations. Do you think this teacher is sensitive to the error of central tendency?

Primary Grade Work Habits Rating Scale

School/Grade: Meadowbrook Elementary/Third Grade

Date: 10/7

Observer: Melana   Name/Age: Andrew/8;2

Instructions: Put an *X* under the rating that applies on each line.

KEY: Always =   10 out of 10 times
        Usually =   At least 8 out of 10 times
        Sometimes = At least 5 out of 10 times
        Rarely =   At least 2 out of 10 times
        Never =   0 out of 10 times

	Always	Usually	Sometimes	Rarely	Never
Listens attentively				X	
Follows oral directions			X		
Stays on task		X			
Does assignments neatly			X		
Completes work		X			
Shows self-confidence in work	X				
Uses time productively			X		
Works cooperatively with others	X				
Successfully works independently				X	

Figure 7.6.   Primary grade rating scale example.

Interpreting the Data   After analyzing the ratings of Andrew's work habits, what did you infer about his classroom behavior? Did you picture a child who is out of his seat often or constantly talking with other children? Or perhaps you saw him as being confused and needing to ask other classmates what to do on assigned work. Might Andrew be a typical example of a "problem kid"?

When Andrew's teacher, Melana, sits down to interpret the ratings on the scale that used an uneven number of descriptors, her first task is to check that her ratings in the middle category (sometimes) are not compromised ratings because she was unsure. Melana takes time to recheck her evaluations for each of the three categories she rated down the middle. Satisfied that she has made sound choices, she continues on.

Being a trained teacher in observational methods, Melana is also aware of the serious danger of labeling, which is inherent in using rating scales as a final evaluation of children. Melana's approach is to use the rating scale as a beginning point in assessing, understanding, and planning. Now she looks closely at the results. Andrew's inconsistent ratings raise immediate questions. How could Andrew usually complete his work yet have trouble listening to directions and working independently? Melana had based her ratings on her grade book and her memory of his classroom behavior. She is aware of Andrew's inattention and excessive talking, but he seems to complete most of his work satisfactorily. What was going on?

Melana checks the anecdotes in Andrew's portfolio; several record Andrew's eagerness to contribute terrific ideas to class discussions. Melana also notes that he is often a leader in group projects. He is well liked by his classmates and is frequently chosen first in team games. He shows a definite strength in social development. To gain a more accurate picture, Melana pulls together all the information she has recorded during the first 3 weeks. She reviews her grade book once again. It documents another strength—finishes work and excellent understandings. Included in Andrew's portfolio is a recent profile (this is the first chance Melana has had to review the results) that shows Andrew's learning style as visual/kinesthetic. That means his best channels for processing information are through his eyes and body. The profile also reveals that Andrew's ears are his weakest processing channel. No wonder he rarely appears to listen and has trouble following oral directions! The rating scale marks began to make sense to Melana.

Follow-Through Plans   The teacher-constructed rating scale helps Melana gain a more precise image of Andrew's work habits, but it also leads her to explore other pertinent observations. She is now ready to plan teaching/learning strategies based on Andrew's individual needs. Melana's makes the following immediate plans:

- *Direction Giving:* Stand by Andrew or have eye contact when giving short oral directions for a kinesthetic connection. Capitalize on his visual mode of learning and write lengthy directions on the board. Have a student read the written directions a second time aloud. Underline the key words in the directions.

- *Work Improvement:* Label assignments in grade book OD or WD (oral or written directions). In those two columns keep a tally of times Andrew's papers were neat and not neat. See if there is a relationship between written direction-giving and neat work. Perhaps he hurries after he has had to spend time figuring out what to do (when oral directions are given), usually by asking others.

The issue of Andrew's productivity and independent work is difficult for Melana. She does not want to squelch Andrew's gregarious personality and his natural leadership skills. She wants to encourage this strength as she helps him develop the weak area—independent work. How to do that is the task at hand. After much thought, Melana comes to the conclusion that her teaching strategies seldom allow for partner learning. From her past experience she thought that interpersonally adept children are more comfortable when they are able to share new insights with other children.

Melana prides herself on having a quiet classroom despite all of the times she has to remind Andrew to quit talking. Looking back in Andrew's portfolio, she finds some anecdotes of incidents when Andrew seems so excited from reading about science in his self-chosen books that he shares newfound information with the child next to him. Perhaps if she gave Andrew a specific time he could count on each day to have conversations, he would grow toward using independent work time appropriately. Melana develops her plans further as follows:

- *Group Work:* Set up daily cooperative reading experiences. Using small groups, plan activities in which the children can read favorite stories to each other, share stories they have written, or discuss story characters they are reading about. Suggest that the shared reading groups, especially ones whose members are kinesthetic learners, develop skits or puppet shows together.

Oh yes, the whole picture is becoming very clear to her. She has not allowed the children enough social exchange; Andrew is trying to meet his own need. She feels fortunate that it is early in the year and that she has uncovered a necessary adjustment in her teaching strategies by observing and studying Andrew's portfolio. So, where else can she adjust?

- *Math Tasks:* Andrew shows a special interest in math. Melana does not want to miss the opportunity to reinforce Andrew's critical-thinking skills. In addition to the present small group instruction and independent work in math, Melana decides to add a box full of "brain teasers." At first, the activity will be part of the group math work. Eventually, the teasers will be made available for children to work on in pairs when they have finished their independent work. Melana will reserve a portion of one bulletin board wall for children to share their analytical projects.

Melana sees a definite change in Andrew's work habits almost immediately when he is given written instructions and more time to work cooperatively. Melana confers with Andrew, and they discuss the new plan before its inauguration. Andrew likes the idea of written directions and suggests that the paired reading experience follow the independent reading time. He tells Melana that occasionally he writes stories or has an idea that he just has to tell someone during independent work time.

After another 6 weeks Melana repeats the rating scale. All of Andrew's marks are in the *always* or *usually* columns. Melana is satisfied with Andrew's progress and with the new learning environment. Not only are Andrew's strong social needs supported, but according to her latest class rating scales, children who were somewhat withdrawn are beginning to take a more active part in cooperative or paired work times.

What other ideas can be added to Melana's beginning plans? There rarely is just one right way! The sky is the limit as long as the plans effectively fit the child's needs and are integrated with the teacher's style.

Applications

Strengths and Limitations

Rating scales and checklists share many strengths. Like checklists, rating scales require less time to complete than do other observational methods. With high classroom demands and hectic schedules, teachers appreciate the simplicity of these two methods. Rating scales and checklists can be based on prerecorded anecdotes and running records and can therefore be completed at the teacher's convenience. Both methods are relatively easy to mark and require no special training. These orderly forms also offer a developmental summary for parent conferences.

In the early childhood classroom, rating scales are especially useful to assess multiple characteristics within a given area or multiple areas. Unlike the checklist, which records only the presence or the absence of a characteristic, the rating scale allows the observer to measure the degree or frequency of behavioral characteristics (Diffily & Fleege, 1993). We have already looked at how an instrument assessing autonomy can quickly give a detailed picture, thus allowing the teacher to compare children within the classroom or to evaluate one child. "Convenience and efficiency are primary reasons for the widespread use of rating scales" (Witt, Hefter, & Pheiffer, 1990, p. 368).

The many advantages of rating scales, however, are often overshadowed by the disadvantages. One limitation is the possible subjectivity of ratings. If the descriptors are ambiguous, "a summary of the observer's opinion is produced rather than actual observed events" (Stallings & Mohlmar, 1990, p. 640). In the section on graphic rating scales, the difficulty of descriptor interpretation when assigning ratings has already been mentioned. Practice Activity 7.1 illustrates the flip side of that limitation; constructing any of the three rating scale designs with clearly defined items and descriptors that represent the observer's true assessment is challenging but achievable. Once again, caution is needed.

A second limitation is present in the process of assessment because the observer, unless she or he has constructed the scale, is asked to pigeonhole the evaluation by using limited, preselected choices on the rating scale continuum, perhaps restricting a response. This forced choice limitation is a common frustration and reminds me of the recent discussion at my house following the "eggplant soup dinner." I love to experiment making new kinds of soup once a week. We've enjoyed my adventurous culinary practices—until I made the eggplant soup. That soup was certainly memorable! I asked my husband how he would rate it. "On a scale of what?" he asked, having been highly schooled in research. "Oh, 1 to 3," I answered, trying to decide if I'd ever make it again. "I'd prefer more choices; I'll use 1 to 7," he countered as he continued to develop the following scale:

1. Would cause sickness
2. Wouldn't eat it unless starving
3. Was tolerable
4. Just average
5. Would choose to have it occasionally
6. Would enjoy having it several times a month
7. Wow! I'd tell everyone about it. A true culinary pleasure.

I listened with delight and thought of the abbreviated rating scale I use on all my recipes.

1. No clean bowls
2. No comments
3. Crowd pleaser

I refer to the shortened scale to decide whether the dish is worth making again. I would find the seven-point system time-consuming and cumbersome. (Just in case you are curious, my husband rated the eggplant soup a 4 on his scale. I gave it a 1 on my scale; I wouldn't make it again!) So you see, each rater can have a preferred scale. If you don't construct your own scale, however, you are asked to make a choice that may not be as representative of your evaluation as you would like. To counteract this restriction, many teachers use spaces between the items for written comments.

In addition, when assigning ratings another caution must be kept in mind. It is important for the observer to know the child's abilities well and refrain from judgments based on only one observation. Medinnus (1976) delivered the following warning:

> Since rating scales are attempts to quantify observation, the validity of such ratings depends largely on the adequacy of observations that the ratings are based on. The adequacy is determined by the amount of time spent observing the child as well as by the number of different settings and situations in which he is observed (p. 25)

A third limitation is the influence of observer bias. For instance, observers may rate a child who has well-developed language skills as a leader or observers may rate a child as uncooperative because the child's older sibling was. Thus, the ratings are based on an impression. "If this impression is favorable, they tend to rate every item high; if it is unfavorable, to rate every item low." (Alkin with Linden, Noel, & Ray, 1992, p. 1348). This bias, which is known as the halo effect, was discussed in Chapter 5. Please note, if the characteristics being rated are unclear or too complex, the halo effect may be unavoidable, rendering the validity of the ratings questionable.

The fourth and final limitation is that rating scales, like checklists, do not tell the conditions that surround the evaluation. The skills, behaviors, or conditions being rated are lifted out of their context, thus leaving an overall evaluation of isolated items. If rating scale assessments are coordinated with running records or anecdotal records, however, they become a useful summary for planning and conferences.

Action Project 7.1
Practice in Using a Rating Scale

Design a rating scale that evaluates impulse control in the early childhood classroom.

- Review the guidelines for construction.
- Refer to Chapter 2 or a child-development textbook for background information.
- Select your rating scale design and construct your instrument.
- Guard against observer bias.
- Pilot test the rating scale.

With the newly constructed rating scale in hand, locate a preschool or K–3 teacher who will work with you in trying out your observational instrument in the classroom. To ensure that all items are clearly written, ask a friend to accompany you and try out your newly constructed instrument, too. Observe the same child. After the observation, discuss your first attempt at designing an instrument. Did either of you have any problems using the rating scale? Were your results the same? If not, why not? Share your results in class.

Points to Remember

Because they are fast and easy to use, rating scales are popular with teachers. Rating scales are also versatile; the basis for marking rating scales can be direct observations or impressions of perceived behavior. To use rating scales accurately, however, teachers must be watchful to avoid the error of central tendency and the halo effect. Use caution!

Many rating scales come ready-made for the early childhood classroom; however, some teachers prefer to construct their own. This chapter reviews design alternatives and offers guidelines for success for teachers who wish to create their own scales.

When used with children, rating scales can be helpful in making overall assessments for diagnosing individual needs, facilitating conferences, and charting growth over time.

Take a Moment to Reflect

In this chapter the preschool example showed a teacher, Billy Ray, using rating scale information to further children's autonomy. If we probe further, we find that Billy Ray's developmental view of the nature of a child is that each child is a growing plant. Using that metaphor, his job is to provide the unfolding plant with the proper amount of water and food, the right soil conditions, and of course daily nurturing. He determined the necessary prescription by using observation. Do you share Billy Ray's view of the nature of a child? What if a teacher views boys and girls as miniature adults, competent children, blank tablets, or investments in the future (Morrison, 1995)? Reflect on your interpretation of each view, then consider either of the following questions.

1. How would observation, recording, and planning be utilized in each view?

2. As a challenge, choose two of the views and compare how autonomy would be facilitated in each view?

CHAPTER 8

Observing the Development of Individual Children by Using ABC Narrative Event Sampling

W hen Billy Ray evaluates the rating scales on preschool autonomy for all the children in his preschool class (see Figure 7.5 in Chapter 7), he becomes interested in yet another child, Kirby. He wonders why Kirby (4;1) usually requires a teacher's help to express ideas to others. Billy Ray wants to discover those circumstances that motivate Kirby to ask for help and those that are conducive to his autonomous communication. Billy Ray is also curious about how other children respond to Kirby's communication. Therefore, he wants to explore the antecedents and consequences of this particular rating scale item.

The review of rating scales can typically leave the observer interested in the dynamics behind particular items; Billy Ray is no exception. The observational method introduced in this chapter will allow him to learn about Kirby's communication abilities within their natural contexts.

Two forms of event sampling are studied in *Through the Looking Glass:* ABC narrative event sampling and tally event sampling; in addition, a close cousin, time sampling, is presented in Chapter 11. This chapter introduces the ABC narrative event sampling format for investigating the causes and consequences of an event. The study of causes will help Billy Ray identify the situations that prompt Kirby to request the teacher's help when expressing his ideas to others. The study of consequences focuses on what follows: how others respond to Kirby and what kinds of feedback his communications evoke from his peers. In other observational investigations, observers may wish to uncover the frequencies of events; in such cases, the tally event sampling format discussed in Chapter 10 can be used.

Overview of Observing Using ABC Narrative Event Sampling

Sampling

To record every instance of Kirby's peer communications, Billy Ray would have to be his shadow. In most busy classrooms, however, teachers do not have the luxury of observing one child exclusively for an indefinite period of time. As a compromise, a sample or subset of Kirby's communications is collected and allowed to represent his peer communications in general. Let's think about an analogy for a few minutes to explore the meanings of sampling and samples.

Imagine that the quality control manager of a cereal company wants to know what proportions of pretzels, peanuts, and cereal are in a mix it sells and therefore requests your careful assistance. Of course, you cannot count every piece in the thousands of boxes filled in the factory even in a single day. As an alternative, you place a 2½-lb empty coffee can under the filling chute on the packaging line and count all these pieces to calculate the percentages of pretzels, peanuts, and cereal. You allow the ingredients in the can (the sample) to represent the ingredients in all boxes of this product (the population).

Consider a few potential problems. First, you are concerned about the size of the sample, in this case the coffee can. You want to collect enough of the mixture to feel confident that your sample is representative of the bin. You know the coffee can would fill about one box of the mixture, whereas a smaller sample, say a hand-ful or even a cupful, might be unrepresentative just by chance. A coffee can is large enough that chance (random) conglomerates of ingredients (e.g., a bunch of peanuts) even out.

Because the can was filled from the same packaging line as the product boxes, you are confident that the ingredients in your sample have been as well mixed as those in the boxes. Suppose, instead, you had drawn your sample from the top of a large bin feeding into the filling chute. If the peanuts were poured into this bin first, the pretzels second, and the cereal last and the ingredients were not mixed at the top, your scoop would contain only cereal and would therefore be unrepresen-tative. You are reassured by knowing your sample comes straight from the filling chute.

You also evaluate possible subjectivity in your work for the cereal company. If you had allowed yourself to scoop out the sample yourself, your selection might have revealed your personal biases. Imagine these scenarios. You want the cereal company to put in more of your favorite ingredient, so you purposely look for a no-peanut place to scoop. This unrepresentative sample will help make your case for adding more peanuts. Or suppose you are a loyal employee of the company and are tired of hearing complaints that there aren't enough pretzels in the mixture—so you just happen to aim your scoop toward the bunch of pretzels in view. Your data will show them! Therefore, in the interest of accuracy and objectivity, you place your coffee can under the filling chute and let the machine pour in a random sam-ple of ingredients.

Now think back to observational projects in the early childhood classroom; the same problems apply. You must be careful to observe enough examples of the be-havior(s) under study to ensure that your sample is representative. You have to col-lect data from a well-stirred pot—consider time of day, activities, and the people in the classroom. Moreover, you must be careful that your own views, predictions, and wishes don't get in the way of collecting a truly *representative sample*. With this knowl-edge you can follow Kerlinger's (1986) definition: "a 'representative sample' means that the sample has approximately the characteristics of the population relevant to the research in question" (p. 11).

If you fail to collect a representative sample, the results may lead you to an incorrect conclusion. For example, the observation of Kirby's expressions of ideas to others pertains to the entire school day. If you observed Kirby only during outside time when he sticks close to his best friend, you might conclude that he usually is competent in his communications. Just as Kirby may be more comfortable talking with some people than others, he may also have more difficulty in large groups than small groups or vice versa. The data will tell. To draw a representative sample of Kirby's communications to others, you observe him during each time block over several days to ensure an accurate portrait.

Description

Boehm (1992) defined *event sampling* as "recording every time during an observation period a specified target behavior occurs such as 'child speaks to another child'" (p. 288). In Kirby's case, "expressing ideas to others" is the behavioral event of interest to his teacher. Through event sampling, the observer studies events in their everyday contexts and collects enough of them to draw conclusions.

Event sampling permits the observer to collect data about the targeted behavior in a time-efficient manner because it concentrates his or her attention on only that behavior. Although an observer is not able to see every targeted event of interest over an indefinite period of time, a sample of observations over a limited period should serve to represent the behavior. Billy Ray cannot observe all of Kirby's communications even for a day (he wouldn't get anything else done), but he can observe enough of Kirby's communications to feel comfortable in allowing his collection to represent the entirety. Thus, the collection of observed events is a sample of all Kirby's communications.

Observers using event sampling try to record an event whenever it naturally occurs over a limited and specified period. Think about the logistics of exploring children's participation during clean-up time. The observer must be ready to record when clean-up times naturally occur. In this case the observational period might be limited to 10 minutes during the day, and the teacher may choose to collect a sample of observations over a week or two. In contrast, to study a teacher's classroom-management methods, the observer must be watchful at various times throughout the day to attend to management events as they arise. If the events occur fairly frequently, an adequate sample might be accumulated in 4 or 5 days.

The preceding description is applicable to event sampling methods in general. Chapter 10 will introduce a tally event sampling method to study children, teachers, and interactions, but for now we return to the individual (child or teacher) as the focus of study. Bell and Low (1977) presented a straightforward method of observing naturally occurring events: *the ABC narrative method.* Although their method is not the only means of collecting narrative qualitative data for event sampling, its clear organization and ease of use make it worthy of special attention. The ABC method concentrates the observer's attention on the antecedent event (*A*), the behavior or event itself (*B*), and the consequence of the event (*C*). Therefore, the event is seen in the context of what came before and what followed. Think about how well this observational method will meet Billy Ray's needs in his exploration of Kirby's dependent communications.

Now consider two more examples. A preschool teacher concerned about a child who grabs toys organizes an ABC event sampling recording form around what preceded the grabbing (*A*), the event itself (*B*), and what immediately followed (*C*). A primary grade teacher who is concerned about a child's seemingly random cruel remarks (e.g., "I knew you'd get that one wrong!") plans to do an ABC narrative event sampling to investigate what prompts the remarks (*A*), each remark itself (*B*), and how the victim of the remark and others respond (*C*). ABC narrative event sampling can be used to examine a wide range of problems.

Take a few moments to suggest appropriate events to study through the ABC narrative event sampling approach. Choose behaviors or events within their naturally occurring contexts—items that you could follow from their roots to fruition.

Practice Activity 8.1
Topics for ABC Narrative Event Sampling

List three topics that may be appropriately studied by ABC narrative event sampling in the early childhood classroom. Remember that this method is useful when you want to observe an event carefully in context. You will be searching for what prompts the event and what follows.

Examples:

- Wandering and unoccupied behavior
- Fearful behavior

1.

2.

3.

Purpose

When the goal of observation is to uncover the contextual causes and effects of an individual's behavior, the ABC narrative approach to event sampling is an excellent method. Suppose a child consistently throws several temper tantrums over the course of the day, and the perplexed teacher wants to explore these events in search of a possible pattern or explanation. At this point, the teacher does not write an anecdotal record about one tantrum because the goal is to evaluate the processes of many tantrums. Nor does the teacher prepare items to observe (as in checklists and rating scales) because of uncertainty about the key elements in this child's process of temper tantrums. The narrative approach to event sampling is the observational method of choice because it allows the teacher to remain unrestricted by a prepared form with predetermined categories and free to observe the natural unfolding of the temper-tantrum events.

Let's step back for a moment and take a look at the forest rather than the trees. Why do we care about understanding the cause of an event? Many child guidance books offer creative and practical solutions to common behavior problems and are not concerned with their causes; however, if teachers assume, for example, that there is one best way to respond to a temper tantrum, they close the door on the opportunity to respond to children as individuals at their own developmental levels with their own strengths, interests, family and cultural histories, limitations, and personalities.

There are many possible causes of temper tantrums, and some will be easier to pinpoint than others. Temper tantrums might result from children's fatigue from long hours in day care or might serve as vents of frustration for young children whose language development does not yet adequately serve their needs to communicate. An observer might clearly see tantrums toward the end of the day or in response to communication difficulties. However, the observer may not be able to identify clear patterns, thus prompting a look beyond the classroom. Perhaps a child feels insecure upon the arrival of a new baby in the family or anxious over the recent separation of the parents. There are probably other situations that prompt young children to release their emotional tension—usually at the most inopportune times! Knowing what is behind individual children's temper tantrums allows teachers to reevaluate the 5:00 p.m. activities at a day care center, help verbalize the feelings of the 2½-year-old with little language, promote sociodramatic play with a child experiencing a new baby at home, or increase the emotional support of a child under stress. The point is that teachers explore causes of events within their natural contexts in order to devise appropriate and helpful responses for particular children.

Guidelines for ABC Narrative Event Sampling

After deciding on an appropriate event to study, the observer prepares a sheet of paper with the typical heading of information at the top and four columns below labeled *Time, Antecedent Event, Behavior,* and *Consequence*. This format is presented in Figure 8.1.

The observer keeps the recording sheet on a clipboard close at hand to record the event under scrutiny whenever it is observed during a specified time period or periods. Occasionally, an observer might miss seeing the antecedent event; if so, he or she continues to record the time, behavior, and consequences. This happened to Gabrielle, the observer in Figure 8.3, and she used an ellipsis (. . .) to indicate the gap of information. She hopes that the remaining information, in conjunction with the observations of many complete events, will still add up to the "big picture."

ABC Analysis Title

Center or School/Age level or Grade:

Date: Time:

Observer: Child/Age:

Behavior:

Time	Antecedent Event	Behavior	Consequence

Figure 8.1 ABC narrative event sampling recording form.

Integration of Developmental Theory and Observation

Preschool Example

Rachel is a quiet and shy 4-year-old girl who has posed no problems for her teachers, Sal and Pam. Several anecdotal observations focusing on Rachel during large- and small-group activities and directed outside games describe a cooperative group member. In November when the classroom of 24 children is running smoothly, however, the teachers begin to pay more attention to Rachel's behavior during free-choice times. She typically stays with an activity for no more than 10 minutes and wanders around the room until a new activity is suggested. Rachel rarely makes anything to take home; when she does, her artwork appears rather simple, like something a younger child could have accomplished. Sal, who is most familiar with Rachel, takes responsibility for observing Rachel's wandering behavior. The ABC form in Figure 8.2 is kept on a clipboard in the classroom for a 2-day sampling period; included in the figure is a *portion* of the data collected.

Interpreting the Data At the end of the second day of observation, Sal and Pam read over the event descriptions on their ABC event sampling form. They are disheartened to see that in Rachel's first hour of school on 11/8, she did virtually nothing. She was not intently involved with materials or people, and she did not initiate activities or interactions. She responded agreeably to suggestions from

The ABC narrative event sampling method is an effective means of understanding behaviors within their natural contexts.

ABC Analysis of Rachel's Unoccupied Behavior

Center/Age level: Peach Hill Nursery School/3- and 4-Year-Olds

Dates: 11/8   Time: 8:15–9:15 A.M.
                    11/9   8:15–9:15, 10:05–10:30 A.M.

Observer: Sal   Child/Age: Rachel (4;3)

Behavior: Wandering around the room, unoccupied

Time	Antecedent Event	Behavior	Consequence
11/8 8:15	Rachel arrives with Mom. Mom kisses her good-bye.	Wanders around room for 15 minutes, watching children.	Alex says, "Want to play cars with me?" Pushes cars on block area carpet for 6 minutes.
8:40	Watches the noisy arrival of the bus kids. Pam (teacher) says, "OK, free-choice time. Find something to do."	Watches Daisy and Chloe hang up jackets and rush off to house area.	Turns attention back to kids entering room.
8:46	Sal (teacher) says to Rachel, "You need to get started now."	Walks slowly around room with no expression on her face, looking carefully in each area.	Goes to art area and rolls play dough with rolling pin for 4 minutes. Looks around classroom more than at her play dough.
8:54	Puts play dough away.	Walks slowly to edge of manipulative area and watches Pam (teacher) and 3 kids.	Pam (teacher) says, "Would you like to join us? Here are some Bristle Blocks." Rachel focuses on stacking blocks for 5 minutes.
9:13	Pam leaves area.	Stops building and watches other kids. Smiles at Betsy.	Betsy smiles back and asks, "Want to play dough?" Rachel nods. They leave the blocks on the floor and head toward the art area.
11/9 8:15	Rachel arrives with Mom and hugs her good-bye.	Scans the room and walks toward art area where Betsy and Yiota are mixing paint. Watches from the edge of the area.	Betsy and Yiota don't appear to notice her.

Figure 8.2.   ABC narrative event sampling form: Preschool example.

8:24 Remains near the art area.	Looks through the color-labeled crayon containers on the shelf and re-sorts a few crayons that are out of place.	Sal (teacher) checks on the paint consistency, looks at Rachel, and says, "The paints are ready. Would you like to use them?" Rachel nods and goes to the easel next to Betsy.
8:51 Hangs painting of red and yellow lines up to dry.	Wanders around room until clean-up time.	Sal asks her to help him clean up in the manipulative area. She does not reply but helps efficiently.
10:10 Outside time begins.	Circles perimeter of yard twice in 10 minutes.	On second round Pam (teacher) calls out, "Rachel, do you want a push on the swing?" Rachel shakes head no and continues circling.
10:25 Children in sand box bring over two pails of water.	Stops slightly behind tree to observe.	Children do not notice her.

Figure 8.2.   (*Continued*).

Pam, Alex, and Betsy as if she had no plans or ideas of her own. The events recorded on 11/9 again show Rachel's willingness to go along with others' proposals. Sal and Pam worry that Peach Hill Nursery School is not optimizing this 4-year-old's development.

The 2-day sample of observations documents Rachel's wandering and unoccupied behavior during free-choice times both inside and outside the classroom. Sal and Pam reread the anecdotal records that describe Rachel's interest and willing participation in structured times, such as circle and story. They suspect that they did not notice her behavior during free-choice time during the first 2 months of school because she is such a cooperative group member.

Follow-Through Plans   Sal and Pam feel bad for having overlooked Rachel's consistent wandering and unoccupied behavior during free-choice times, but they concentrate their energies on the future. They put the data to use and develop several strategies for helping Rachel focus her attention and learn more from her encounters with materials and other people. The following four summaries are drawn from the ABC event sampling form along with the teaching strategies they prompted in Sal and Pam.

SUMMARY OF OBSERVATION   Sal and Pam realize that neither of them personally greeted Rachel and that she responded positively to friendly overtures from Alex and Betsy.

STRATEGY   Sal will come over to greet Rachel when she arrives and tell her about special materials out in the various areas.

SUMMARY OF OBSERVATION   Pam announced when it was free-choice time and said, "Find something to do"; Sal told Rachel that it was time to play and to get started. Perhaps Rachel has no clear understanding of her options or what is expected of her during free-choice time. Or perhaps she is overwhelmed by her options.

STRATEGY   When Sal greets Rachel, he will remind her that during free-choice time, she can choose her own materials and friends to play with. He will also stay with her until she gets started. He might walk around the classroom with her to help her make her choice.

SUMMARY OF OBSERVATION   The data show that Rachel worked superficially with materials (e.g., pushing cars, rolling play dough, painting only lines). Perhaps she is not comfortable enough with other children to concentrate on her activity, or perhaps she has not had much experience in working with many of the materials available at Peach Hill Nursery School. She did, however, respond positively to Betsy's initiative and observed Betsy mixing paint.

STRATEGY   Betsy will join Sal's small-group time so that a friendship between Rachel and Betsy can be fostered.

STRATEGY   Once during each free-choice time, Sal will work next to Rachel with the same materials to model new ideas. He will be careful to build from her initial activity. For example, when she chooses play dough, he might roll out lots of snakes and see if Rachel is interested in shaping them into objects like bowls, log houses, or other ideas she might have.

STRATEGY   Sal will use small-group times to explore many uses of familiar materials to widen Rachel's experience with objects. He suspects that he has overlooked the importance of exploration for other children as well. For example, he might plan an activity to explore print making with Bristle Blocks and other small manipulatives. Dipping the objects in paint to make prints on paper, pressing them into clay to form imprints, or making rubbings with crayons and paper are all options. Another day, the children might use Bristle Blocks for building. They might first stick them together flat on the table, then form a high tower, and next build enclosures. These activities might be done individually and then in a group so that one huge flat surface, tower, and enclosure are put together. Sal would offer the children a variety of small counting animals to go inside their building. He will plan many small-group times that encourage the children to explore materials, make things with them, and then pretend with them.

SUMMARY OF OBSERVATION   Rachel's wandering and unoccupied behavior continued during outside time as she circled the yard and watched others.

STRATEGY   Outside, the teachers will plan optional group games to provide some enticing structure for Rachel and encourage her to play with other children.

STRATEGY   Sal and Pam will reuse their ABC event sampling form on Rachel in 2 weeks to observe her progress. They expect to see more focused behavior during free-choice and outside times.

The ABC event sampling method proved to be productive for Sal and Pam. It allowed them to observe in detail a problem of which they had only vaguely been aware. Sal's recordings of the event in context evidenced noteworthy consistencies in the child's behavior. Instead of limiting the observer's attention to the wandering and unoccupied behavior, the ABC method provided a means of observing which classroom situations prompted Rachel's wandering and what followed. The teachers took advantage of the data collected to plan strategies to enhance Rachel's development. Data collected on a different child's unfocused behavior during free-choice time might well have shown different patterns, thereby suggesting the trial of different teaching strategies.

Primary Grade Example

Consider Our Ethical Responsibilities to Children

NAEYC Ideal I-1.3

"To recognize and respect the uniqueness and the potential of each child" (Feeney & Kipnis, 1992, p. 4).

Read on to see how Gabrielle fulfills this ethical responsibility.

Gabrielle teaches first grade and is nearly fed up with Adam's off-task behavior that consistently disturbs other children's work and activities. Although she knows that she has an ample reserve of surface patience, she is wearing thin inside. Some mornings, she notices herself dreading to face Adam again.

At the end of a dismal week, Gabrielle promises herself to keep an ABC narrative event sampling form close at hand beginning on Monday. She worries that she will neglect the observation once she is involved in teaching, but she is motivated to try. Her reprimands, pleas, and light punishments have been to no avail. Figure 8.3 contains a *portion* of the data Gabrielle collected over the next week. (Recall that Gabrielle uses an ellipsis [. . .] to indicate a gap in the information collected).

ABC Analysis of Adam's Off-Task Behaviors

School/Grade: Jefferson Elementary/First Grade
Dates: 10/16 to 10/20   Time: Various
Observer: Gabrielle   Child/Age: Adam/6;7
Behavior: Off-task behavior

Time	Antecedent Event	Behavior	Consequence
10;17 8:20	. . . I had just started math activity with 6 children.	Pokes neighbor (Marcus) with pencil.	Marcus squirms, then laughs aloud. I say, "Excuse me, Adam."
8:22	. . . Math activity.	Pretends to draw on back of Marcus' shirt (uses eraser).	Marcus yells, "Hey!" I say, "Please, Adam, pay attention."
8:25	. . . Math activity.	Grabs Marcus' eraser.	Marcus wrestles his eraser back. I ignore.
8:27	I demonstrate a subtraction problem on the board.	Is under his desk when I turn around.	I send Adam to the time-out desk isolated at the side of the classroom.
11:45	I regretfully close *Matilda* by R. Dahl and say we are out of reading time for today.	Groans loudly and argues, "Oh come on Mrs. Ambleson. Just a little more, please. We can be late for lunch; come on, *please*. The lines are too long anyway."	I say, "I'm sorry; we'll read more tomorrow," and dismiss the class for lunch.
12:40	. . . Sustained silent reading time; OK for 5 minutes. Reads *Frog and Toad* for umpteenth time.	Puts head and arms down on desk and rolls into Marcus.	Marcus rolls back. I say, "Sit up please, boys."
12:43	. . . Sustained silent reading time continues.	Cups chin in hands and stares across at Rayme.	Rayme glares and whispers harshly, "Stop it, Adam." Sianna and Noriko join in the scolding. I send Adam to the time-out seat.

Figure 8.3. ABC narrative event sampling form: Primary grade example.

1:30	Adam is cooperative in "7-up." I announce "Around the World" (math game) and ask for a volunteer.	Throws eraser in air and goes on floor to retrieve it.	I say, "You won't get a turn, Adam, with that kind of behavior."

Figure 8.3. (*Continued*).

Interpreting the Data   By Friday lunchtime, Gabrielle can stand the suspense no longer. Anxious to confirm her growing suspicions nourished by her data collection, she eats at her desk and rereads the seven pages of event descriptions (remember Figure 8.3 reproduces a portion). The data are voluminous, and she tries to think of some ways to make them manageable.

Gabrielle experiments with sorting Adam's off-task behaviors into categories to look for possible patterns. She finds four times during the school day that account for the bulk of the problems: math time, the end of story time, sustained silent reading time, and group math games. Then she begins to do some figuring. First she counts up all of Adam's observed off-task behaviors over the course of the 4½ days of observation and finds the sum to be 38. She tallies his off-task behaviors in each category and lumps the remaining six into an *other* category. Finally, she divides each category sum by the total number of off-task behaviors (38) to find its percentage of total off-task behaviors. For example, she divides the 17 math-time incidents by the total 38 to get .45 or 45% of the total off-task behaviors. (Notice that Gabrielle is doing some quantitative analysis with the qualitative narrative data, an option possible with lengthy samplings.) The results, displayed in Figure 8.4, would have surprised Gabrielle on Monday before she began her data collection.

Adam's Off-Task Behaviors (10/16 to 10/20)		
Time	**Number**	**Percent of Total Off-Task Behaviors**
Math activity	17	45
End of story time	5	13
Sustained silent reading	6	16
Group math games	4	10
Other	6	16
	38	100

Figure 8.4.   Understanding ABC event sampling data.

Careful study of the data
leads to appropriate follow-
through plans.

Before Gabrielle systematically began to gather data on Adam's off-task behaviors, she would have predicted that they occurred at an even pace throughout the day. She is excited because this is not the case and feels rewarded for her week-long observation efforts. Now it is time to study the contexts of Adam's off-task behaviors and search for the meaning behind the data.

Follow-Through Plans   Gabrielle's observations cluster around three major areas: math activities, sustained silent reading, and classroom control. In the privacy of her classroom, this thoughtful, reflective teacher lays aside her pride and wrestles with the data staring her in the face.

SUMMARY OF OBSERVATION   Gabrielle considers the high proportion of off-task behaviors during math activities and realizes that problems during math time or group math games account for 55% of the total; she wonders if this is an important clue. Had Adam's off-task behaviors commenced and accelerated as math became more difficult? The grade book documents his initial average and then declining grades, and two anecdotal records describe behavioral disruptions during math time. She forms an hypothesis that Adam's disruptions during math are connected to his tentative (at best) understanding of the subject matter; disturbances are Adam's ticket out of math.

STRATEGY   Gabrielle plans to do more spot checking of children's daily math assignments to be sure they are on the right track or clear up confusion before frustration and failure set in. She concludes that she got behind in this responsibility because she relied too heavily on parental help in correcting math assignments and tests. She rededicates herself to becoming familiar with her students' specific strengths and weaknesses.

STRATEGY   Suspecting that Adam's problems center around subtraction, Gabrielle begins to plan next week's math using manipulatives to allow the children to experience subtraction concretely. Gabrielle, confident in her ability to teach math, is certain she can effectively reduce Adam's errors.

SUMMARY OF OBSERVATION   The disturbances during story time and sustained silent reading time encourage Gabrielle to turn her attention to Adam's reading interests and abilities. Judging from his pleas for story time to continue, Adam relishes a compelling story. Unfortunately, this appreciation is not being satisfied by his choice to read the same book (however good) over and over.

STRATEGY   Gabrielle plans to build on Adam's interests and excellent reading ability and to decrease his disruptive behavior in the process. Knowing his love of Arnold Lobel's endearing characters Frog and Toad, she is convinced there are other literary characters who can also win Adam's heart. Edward Marshall's George and Martha are two who might fit the bill, as well as Elsie Fay from *Troll Country* a bit later. She will also browse through some of Steven Kellogg books to check the reading difficulty and keep *The Beast in Ms. Rooney's Room* series by Patricia Reilly Giff in mind for later in the year. She is excited by the superb store of authors just waiting for Adam's discovery.

SUMMARY OF OBSERVATION   Gabrielle admits that her reprimands of Adam's off-task behaviors are neither meant nor taken seriously; she has not acted like a teacher who expects her directions to be followed. She resolves to reevaluate her classroom control and to begin this process with Adam (hopefully a manageable task).

STRATEGY   Gabrielle will consider the reason behind an off-task behavior before criticizing a child. She appreciates the benefit provided by the ABC narrative event sampling method in helping her focus on the antecedents of Adam's off-task behaviors.

STRATEGY   On Monday's plan Gabrielle schedules time for a class discussion about classroom rules; it is obviously time to revisit this issue. Her goal is for the children to brainstorm suggestions for classroom rules. When they talk about why rules are important, Gabrielle will enlist their explanations of how the welfare of the classroom depends on the actions of the individuals. The children can imagine the resulting chaos if everyone talks at once or throws erasers in the air. The rules will be evaluated and a reasonable list posted in the classroom. Gabrielle anticipates that this group experience will help the children perceive the rules as less arbitrary and more compelling.

STRATEGY   Gabrielle also examines Adam's long complaint when story time had to end at 11:45 a.m. Whether or not she or Adam likes it, Jefferson Elementary School runs on a schedule. She realizes, however, that her abrupt dismissal did not acknowledge Adam's feelings of regret. She might have said that she understood his wishes to continue but that lunchtime was not something they could choose to skip or delay. On Monday she will ask Adam to keep an eye on the clock and let her know when she has to stop reading for lunch; sharing in the responsibility for keeping the class on schedule might be a productive experience for him. Gabrielle will continue to look for these types of opportunities to help children build self-control rather than relying on a time-out desk.

As Gabrielle relaxes during the last few moments of her lunch break and savors her feelings of accomplishment, she warmly remembers her college class on observation: time and study well spent.

Applications

Now let's move on to an activity that asks you to solve the puzzle of an event. In Practice Activity 8.2, you will identify the clues of a child's behavior in order to zero in on observations that generate responsive and appropriate teaching strategies.

Practice Activity 8.2
Narrative Event Sampling: Acquisition of a Second Language

You are the teacher of a preschool child who has recently arrived in the United States with her family from Hong Kong. During the first week, the child said nothing; thereafter, she began to speak occasionally in Chinese. Toward the end of her third week, you notice Lin speaking a word or two in English. You are very excited and resolve to keep an ABC narrative event sampling form to observe the situations that seem to promote Lin's attempts to speak English.

Examine the following brief ABC data to identify events or situations that seem conducive to Lin's learning and speaking English. Then write down specific summaries of observations that lead to specific strategies. For example, after observing that Lin smiled and quietly said "hi" to Marion, you plan to encourage that friendship by putting their snack placemats next to one another.

ABC Analysis of Lin's Attempts to Speak English

Center/Age level: Where the Kids Are/3-Year-Olds

Date: 4/26   Time: 8:30–9:00 A.M.
                                              (free-choice time)

Observer: Robbie   Child/Age: Lin/3;10

Behavior: Lin attempts to speak English

Time	Antecedent Event	Behavior	Consequence
8:30	Marion arrives with her mother and is holding a stuffed bear. Lin stares at the bear.	Smiles and says "hi" softly and without eye contact.	Marion smiles back and goes to the house area.
8:40	Stands near the house area, watching Marion and Carlota feed their bears at the table.	When noticed by the girls, raises her arms and asks a question (it sounds like "Bear?").	Carlota says, "Lin, what?" Lin does not answer. All look confused, and Lin moves away.
8:55	Max (teacher) is mixing sand and water with children in the sand area to make molds. Lin wanders to the outskirts.	Max says, "Lin, would you like to play with us?" Smiles broadly and says "yes" in a loud, clear voice.	Hesitantly approaches a vacant space next to Damon, a quiet 3-year-old. Works with the sand molds with silent enjoyment and concentration.

Summary of observation:

Strategy:

Summary of observation:

Strategy:

Summary of observation:

Strategy:

Strengths and Limitations

The primary value of the ABC narrative event sampling method is to study a behavior in the context of its antecedents and consequences. Observers use this method to explore an event as it naturally unfolds from its causes through its outcomes. The ABC method promotes the exploration and understanding of the relevant features surrounding an event.

The ABC method also heightens awareness of children as individuals. It focuses attention on a unique person in the midst of often complex circumstances. The ABC method looks at events with a video- rather than with a still-camera lens; there is no stop-action photography here. A problem is viewed as a process with prompting conditions and results. Such scrutiny allows observers to respond with individualized strategies.

The care with which an event is analyzed can also be a drawback because the ABC method requires time and commitment. It can be a burden for overextended teachers or for those who lack support in the classroom. The observer requires time to observe the event in progress and record data. This is true of all observational methods and is not so much a limitation as an admonition to teachers to work observational time into their daily schedules.

The ABC method is best used by observers with keen eyes and who strive toward objectivity. Observers with predrawn conclusions will easily shade their observations from the truth. The ABC method will illuminate an event for those who have the skills and vigilance to look.

Action Project 8.1
ABC Narrative Event Sampling

Return to the list of appropriate ABC narrative event sampling topics in Practice Activity 8.1. If you teach, try out one of the topics in your classroom. If you do not teach, arrange a visit to a preschool or elementary school to practice the ABC method. After collecting a reasonable sample narrative data, analyze them and write down appropriate follow-through plans. Remember, to gain more than a superficial understanding of the method, you must try it out.

Points to Remember

The ABC narrative event sampling format allows the observer to explore specific behaviors of individual children; these behaviors may (e.g., Adam's off-task behaviors) or may not (e.g., Lin's preliminary attempts to speak English) be problematic. The purpose of this observational method is to reveal behaviors within the contexts of their antecedents and consequences. The observer using the ABC format yearns for enlightenment; the goal is not to document or assess individual children's development but to understand patterns of behavior. Responding to the unique yield of qualitative data, the observer plans supportive teaching strategies.

Take a Moment to Reflect

Observation projects are due in a child-development practicum class, and two graduating seniors compare experiences. Pat volunteered in an ethnically diverse elementary school and was asked by a teacher to observe a 3rd-grader, Danny. Usually cooperative and competent in all subjects, Danny recently began to display antagonistic behavior toward his classmates and an overall lack of attention and cooperation. Over an entire school day, Pat employed the ABC narrative event sampling method and then examined the data for patterns. She found Danny was inattentive when attention of the class was on the front of the room (e.g., on the chalkboard or a book), but when he was moved from his rear seat to the front, he worked productively. Discussion with the teacher provided the information that a recently broken copy machine had necessitated math problems being written on the board and that Danny had complained of headaches. You guessed it: Danny needs glasses! The teacher responded to Pat's report with guilt that was fortunately overshadowed by a sense of relief, gratitude to Pat, and plans for a vision check.

Shannon chose to do her internship in the child life specialist department of a children's hospital. One of her responsibilities involved working in the children's playroom that should serve as a safe haven from medical procedures (e.g., checks of vital signs and delivery of medications). Shannon was frustrated, however, by the frequent interruptions of medical staff that intruded on the children's play. She created a tally event sampling instrument (see Chapter 10) to study the agents of the interruptions. Shannon found 17% of the interruptions were committed by registered nurses, 24% by licensed vocational nurses, and 57% by clinical assistants; the more highly trained nursing staff better protected the sanctuary of the playroom. Shannon's final meeting with her Child Life Specialist supervisor is tomorrow, and she has begun to plan how she will present her findings.

Reflect on strategies to present information to your supervisor:

1. Fortunately for Pat, Danny's teacher requested the observation and was receptive to the results. How might she have handled the situation if the teacher had been defensive about or resistant to the information about Danny?

2. How might Shannon and her supervisor convince their nursing coworkers that supportive changes should be made?

3. Sometimes you might have to give negative feedback to your supervisor. Recall a few supervisors you have had. How might they have responded to unfavorable information? Did you ever have to give your supervisor negative information? What are some productive communication strategies?

CHAPTER 9

Classroom Portfolios and Parent Conferences

As we end with Part II of *Through the Looking Glass,* recall with affection some of the children you've met so far in this book:

- Annie, who seized the red tractor for reasons unknown, in Chapter 1
- Taki, who played a listening lotto game, in Chapter 4
- Song, whose teacher confronted the insensitivity of a few classmates, in Chapter 5
- Gilberto, as yet unable to alternate feet when climbing up and down stairs, in Chapter 6
- Andrew, whose work habits were unproductive, in Chapter 7
- Rachel, who spent most of free-choice time wandering, in Chapter 8

Each of these children sparkles with individuality; each is unique and multifaceted in development. They will all blossom in supportive early childhood classrooms, and most have at least one parent or guardian who wants and needs to know how they are progressing in school. How can their teachers organize their observations and retrieve necessary information for planning and effectively communicating the results to these children's parents?

As we have studied, the trained early childhood professional keeps comprehensive observational records for all children. These observational treasures will have limited value unless the records are easily accessed for classroom and conference use. There is, yet, another aspect of observation to explore.

The goal of this chapter is to answer the question posed at the end of the preceding vignette: how can teachers organize observations and retrieve information for classroom planning and parent conferences? You will become acquainted with options in organizing bountiful classroom observational records and sow the seeds for successful family–teacher partnerships. The first part of this chapter discusses designing and personalizing portfolios and record-keeping procedures for ease in usability, as well as identifying opportunities to collect and maintain records. The second part of the chapter presents the topic of parent–teacher conferences—preparation, content, and leadership. Although the teacher-in-training cannot apply this information immediately and comprehensively, this chapter develops tools that guide professional growth.

Overview of Classroom Portfolios

Throughout the year early childhood teachers may complete running records, anecdotal records, checklists, rating scales, and ABC narrative event samplings for each of their students. Occasionally, a tally event sampling or time sampling (Chapters 10 and 11), usually recorded for groups, is kept for a single child. As a result, early childhood educators gather a great deal of observational documentation over the course of a year. Some of these records note specific developmental milestones. Some records are used immediately to plan activities and teaching strategies. Other records are saved to illustrate points during parent conferences or develop Individual Education Plans (IEP) and Individual Family Service Plans (IFSP). All records are used to understand the overall developmental progress of each child (Feeney, Christensen, & Moravcik, 1996).

In addition to an abundance of teacher observations, selected samples of children's work are kept throughout the year to illustrate growth and learning over time. For the preschool child, samples may include artwork; dictated stories; photographs of block structures, science activities, and dramatic play episodes; and any other examples that show the child's most outstanding strengths or unique capabilities (Benjamin, 1994; McAfee & Leong, 1994). For the primary grade child, samples may include the student's selected examples of classroom assignments/projects that are of special interest or show skill mastery, an assignment that was revised, a favorite piece of creative writing and/or artwork, a register of books read, language audiotapes, and written reflections of growth assessments made by the child (Crosswhite & Rosmann, 1995; McAfee & Leong, 1994; Mindes, Ireton, & Mardell-Czudnowski, 1996). These multidimensional concrete examples augment teacher observations and provide for the child's involvement in the record-keeping process.

It is easy to visualize the organizational challenge presented by these mounds of observational records and work samples. This challenge can be as overwhelming as filing income taxes is to some people. Organizing, however, does not have to produce anxiety if the teacher uses a workable record-keeping system. Remember, the point is to organize early childhood records for simple access, not to store the records away as we do with our tax records for once-a-year retrieval.

Let's look at the payoffs from using systematized observational records. First, an efficient record-keeping system retains and orders documents of each child's developmental growth; it is a priceless memory bank, easily accessed by the teacher. In contrast, unorganized observations become an explosion of papers piled high or tossed into a file folder or desk drawer. Consequently, shuffling through these records to understand individual development becomes time consuming, difficult, and often frustrating. Second, an organized storehouse of observations allows for smooth, consistent planning of classroom activities that respond to individual needs. Masses of unorganized observations often result in abandonment of planning to meet individual needs; curricula become haphazard or uniformly prescribed for all children. And third, with systematic record keeping, teachers have abundant information at their fingertips and can prepare for conferences expediently and confidently. In summary, organizing observations is essential for first-rate teaching!

Description

A record-keeping system for portfolios is a specified procedure used to organize the selected samples of children's work and the many observations written by the teacher throughout the year. An organized system acts as a frame within which to assemble the developmental puzzle pieces for each child. Once the teacher has chosen or created an arrangement for keeping observational records, all of the children's records are stored in like fashion. The system allows the teacher to collect as much individual observational information as is wanted; the system also allows the teacher to arrange this information in logical order and to protect the child's privacy.

Two designs for record-keeping systems are described in the following discussion. The farsighted teacher-in-training will explore and compare the systems, noting the advantages and disadvantages of each. Time spent in examining workable systems provides the foundation for determining a preference and, eventually, a confident choice once the teacher is inside the classroom. On the other hand, experienced teachers may have other ideas that have worked for them. There is much room for additions, improvements, and diversity.

Notebook or File Box System

Observational records for 12 or 15 children can be housed in a 3-inch, three-ring binder or three large 5-by-8-inch file boxes. In this chapter these two systems are treated together because their internal organizations are the same; they differ only in the teacher's preference for the outer container (notebook or file box). Using either the notebook or the file box system, the teacher arranges classroom observations using the major developmental areas discussed in Chapters 2 and 3: *physical, cognitive, psychosocial,* and *creative.* (The order of the areas makes no difference as long as they are consistent within the system.) The notebook or file box is sectioned off by index tabs into the traditional developmental areas for each child. (Valuable space is saved if the child's name and birth date are placed on the first tab with the title of the first developmental area. In this example it is *Cognitive.*)

First index tab:	Child's Name and Birth Date
	Cognitive
Second index tab, indented:	Psychosocial
Third index tab, indented:	Physical
Fourth index tab, indented:	Creative

Not all teachers choose to use the traditional developmental areas listed above. Because of the monumental importance of language during the preschool years, many preschool teachers prefer to have a separate index for it. Other teachers choose to include language development under the cognitive index. Some teachers

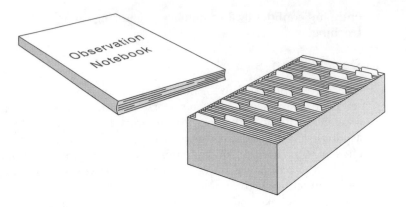

To conserve space, instead of using a blank page or index card for each
section, put an index tab on the first observation page or card you put in each
section. This advice will help when managing 60 or more index tabs! In
addition, color coding the index tabs proves to be time efficient.

prefer to have a separate index for perceptual development; others cover this aspect of development under *cognitive* and *physical*. The primary grade teacher may
want to subcategorize cognitive development by using color-coded pages or cards
for reading, math, and other subjects.

Regardless of how the categories are selected, all observations can be filed behind the corresponding developmental index tab in notebooks or file boxes. In fact
some observations may be duplicated and filed behind more than one section (e.g.,
an anecdote about a child's easel painting that shows creative, cognitive, and/or
fine motor advances). Each separately filed observation is dated and filed in
chronological order. This method of organization simplifies filing and retrieval.

Some teachers think the file box system is more convenient than the notebook
system because file boxes kept on the desk top are always within reach. One teacher,
a proponent of the file box system, sought to facilitate collecting and filing of observations. She made a simple ¾-length smock with two big pockets just the size of the

file cards she was using; that way, she could keep a pen and several empty file cards handy for writing her daily observations. Using the handy pockets, she could quickly slip the completed cards away and file them when she had a few extra moments.

In primary grades, teachers may also use smock pockets to keep handy cards with checklists of skills in math and reading. The file box system is simple to use because all of the cards are the same size and fit behind the index dividers.

The notebook system would be the best choice for teachers who prefer to write observations on a clipboard, a pad of paper, or on large peel-off labels. In addition, notebooks are often the choice if the school uses developmental checklists, assessments, or inventories that fit nicely in a notebook but are too bulky for a file box. Teachers who use these forms have high regard for the versatility of notebooks.

File Folder System

An alternative record-keeping system is the use of individual file folders. For each child in the class, the teacher labels a file with the child's name and birth date. (Alphabetizing the folders permits quick reference.) Inside each file are four recording sheets (Figures 9.1 or 9.2) that contain the following headings: *Cognitive, Psychosocial, Physical,* and *Creative.* Take a minute to familiarize yourself with these samples of preschool and primary grade recording sheets. Each of the four boxes represents one entire page in each child's file folder. Color-coding the recording sheets is an effective organizational strategy.

Within each child's file, anecdotes are written on these sheets (or stuck on if the teacher uses peel-off labels). Other observational records and relevant information available to the teacher (e.g., running records, checklists, rating scales, ABC narrative event samplings, other observations, primary grade reading and writing inventories, and cross-references for photographs and videotapes—more on this later in the chapter) are filed behind the appropriate developmental sheets. Please note that licensing regulations and educational standards in many states require each child's medical forms and personal information to be filed separately in a central office. If permitted, however, the competent teacher takes time to review these files, summarizing pertinent information for classroom records, and stores this information in each child's folder. A recording sheet with this information, labeled *General Data,* can be added as a first page.

The recording sheets in Figures 9.1 and 9.2 provide a flexible, expandable organizational framework. For teachers who prefer a more detailed and thorough system, the subcategories listed under each of the four developmental areas can be used. (Many of the subcategories are the growth indicators described in Chapters 2 and 3.) The system may be personalized by adding or deleting categories based on the classroom goals. Teachers using specific systems can modify the recording sheets. For example, those using the *High/Scope Child Observation Record—(COR)* (High/Scope Educational Research Foundation, 1992a) may want to coordinate their record keeping by substituting the *COR's* six developmental areas for the traditional ones shown in Figure 9.1 and using its letter items for subcategories.

Page 1

Cognitive Development

Representational abilities

Language   Number development

Reasoning   Seriation

Theory of mind   Classification

Memory   Other

Entry 1—Date. Anecdote

Entry 2—Date. Anecdote

. . . and so forth with each entry on the 8½- by 11-inch pages

Page 2

Psychosocial Development

Self-concept

Play   Fears

Aggression   Impulse control

Expanding relationships with adults and peers

Other

Entry 1—Date. Anecdote

Entry 2—Date. Anecdote

. . . and so forth with each entry on the 8½- by 11-inch pages

Page 3

Physical Development

FINE   GROSS
MOTOR SKILLS: MOTOR SKILLS:

Grasp/control   Run
Fasten/unfasten   Jump
Insert/remove   Hop
String/lace   Gallop
Use scissors   Skip
Other   Climb
                      Balance
                      Catch
                      Throw
                      Kick

Entry 1—Date. Anecdote

Entry 2—Date. Anecdote

. . . and so forth with each entry on the 8½- by 11-inch pages

Page 4

Creative Development

Flexibility   Risk taking

Sensitivity   Imagination

Resourcefulness

Expressive experiences and skills in using creative materials (two-dimensional and three-dimensional art, music, dramatic play, writing, blocks)

Entry 1—Date. Anecdote

Entry 2—Date. Anecdote

. . . and so forth with each entry on the 8½- by 11-inch pages

Figure 9.1.   Preschool anecdotal recording sheets using subcategories.

Page 1	Page 2
Cognitive Development	**Psychosocial Development**
Representational abilities	Self-concept and self-esteem
Metacognition — Number development	Prosocial — Moral development
Logical thought — Memory	Play
Language — Classification	Relationships with peers
Subject areas — Other	Stress management Other
Entry 1—Date. Anecdote	Entry 1—Date. Anecdote
Entry 2—Date. Anecdote	Entry 2—Date. Anecdote
. . . and so forth with each entry on the 8½- by 11-inch pages	. . . and so forth with each entry on the 8½- by 11-inch pages

Page 3	Page 4
Physical Development	**Creative Development**
FINE — GROSS	Flexibility — Risk taking
MOTOR SKILLS: — MOTOR SKILLS:	Sensitivity — Imagination
Use of tools — Arm/leg strength	Resourcefulness
Uniformity of — Speed	Expressive experiences and skills in using creative materials (two-dimensional and three dimensional music, creative dramatics, writing, block play)
letters and — Coordination	
numbers — Agility	
Eye–hand —	
coordination — Endurance	
Other — Specialized	
skills in sports	
Entry 1—Date. Anecdote	Entry 1—Date. Anecdote
Entry 2—Date. Anecdote	Entry 2—Date. Anecdote
. . . and so forth with each entry on the 8½- by 11-inch pages	. . . and so forth with each entry on the 8½- by 11-inch pages

Figure 9.2. Primary grade anecdotal recording sheets using subcategories.

The purpose of the subcategories is to present the teacher with a quick check-off system to ensure that records have been gathered in all domains of development, thus giving an expansive picture of the child's developmental progress. As the teacher records an entry for one of the major developmental areas, a check is made next to the appropriate subcategory on the top of the sheet. For example, if the teacher observed a child who was fearful when the fire fighter visited the class, the anecdote would be recorded on the sheet headed *Psychosocial Development* and one check made before the subcategory of fears. Because of their own interests and strengths, teachers may find themselves collecting observations that concentrate on certain areas and subcategories of a child's development and neglect others.

> Do you have a tendency to be drawn to the most verbal children in your group, the children who help others solve problems, or the children who never break program rules? Observational assessment will point out to you on a day-by-day basis how much or how little you know about all the children in your program. (High/Scope Educational Research Foundation, 1992b, p. 4)

By adopting a detailed system that provides check-offs for observational entries, a teacher can merely glance at the sheets to see if the total picture for each child has been captured.

Practicing teachers report that using the anecdotal recording sheets with subcategories is a major support to the teaching process. The built-in organization of recording sheets (with other observations appropriately filed behind one of the four developmental headings) saves precious hours when studying growth patterns, planning activities, and preparing for conferences.

When using the file folder system, choose the appropriate size of file to ease the potential storage problem. Large file folders are recommended if unwieldy representations, like easel paintings, are to be included in the teacher-kept portfolios. The file folders, regardless of size, can be conveniently stored and transported, if necessary, in a plastic carrying case obtained from the local stationery shop.

Child-Created Portfolios

Another important decision to make when choosing a system is to determine where children's work samples will be kept. They might be housed in the teacher's system or in their own portfolios—"a purposeful collection of children's work that illustrates their efforts, progress, and achievements and potentially provides a rich documentation for each child's experience throughout the year" (Meisels, 1993, p. 34).

Over-size work samples (e.g., easel paintings) and child access are two reasons that many teachers prefer to house the children's work samples separately from the teacher-made observational records, thus creating child portfolios. These expandable files can hold all subject matter examples including math. "Children as early as preschool can help prepare their own portfolios by choosing which materials they want to present to their parents" (Billman & Sherman, 1996, p. 37). These concrete examples may be stored in large (18 × 24 inches) construction paper or newspaper envelopes (usually put together by the teacher and decorated by the child), legal-size file folders, roll-away racks for hanging files, or scrap books (McAfee & Leong, 1994; Mindes et al., 1996). In choosing a separate child portfolio system, explore the following questions:

- Is there easy child access? Consider the storage location within the room and the procedure children will use to independently file samples.

- How will various-size work samples be accommodated? Are group projects to be included?

- Can the child personalize the cover?

- How will photographs of child work samples be protected if they are included in this system rather than housed with the teacher's observations?

Again, there is no one right way to organize record-keeping systems. Whether the teacher uses a system separate from the children's or keeps all the observations and work samples in one folder is a personal choice. Proponents of the separate systems, however, profess that when children are given the opportunity to choose and contribute to the record-keeping process, ownership in the learning process is strengthened and self-esteem is enhanced (Freeman & Freeman, 1991).

Comparison of Record-Keeping Systems

Three different management schemes for organizing and storing observations within teacher portfolios have been shown: notebooks, file boxes, and file folders. In addition, methods for creating child-kept portfolios were discussed. A system tailored to meet personal teaching needs will be concise, orderly, and workable; study the advantages and disadvantages of the three systems compared in Figure 9.3. As you read through this figure, you may also want to keep a mental tally of the strengths and limitations of keeping children's work samples separate.

What system initially strikes your fancy? Ask experienced teachers what type of portfolio system works best for them and why. Perhaps the school you work in already has a system in place; if so, you may need only to experiment with modifications to suit

| | Advantages | |
Notebook	File Box	File Folders
Expandable	Expandable	Expandable
Closed cover keeps observations confidential	Closed cover can keep observations confidential	Keeps observations confidential
Easy to transport	Durable	Easy to transport when placed in case
Durable	Ease in planning	Planning at a glance using recording sheets
Quick-reference indexes	Quick filing on desktop	Least amount of storage space
Easy storage	Cards fit in pockets for classroom mobility	Compact and comprehensive recording sheets
Versatile		Large files hold over-size student papers
Held in place with rings		
	Disadvantages	
Takes more time to file using rings	One box per 4 to 6 children	Papers are loose in file
Difficult to sort for planning	Cannot fit all records in file box	
Cannot store children's work within notebook	Cannot store children's work in file box	
	Cumbersome to transport	

Figure 9.3.   Advantages/disadvantages of record-keeping systems.

your individual preferences. If you are selecting the system, however, you may want to try out several types of systems and then base your decision on your own needs. You may want to mix components of two systems. For example, if you prefer the notebook system but like the recording sheets from the file folder system—simply replace the four development index tabs in the notebook with the recording sheets. There are endless possibilities. Don't be in a hurry. Use the first 6 months to create a serviceable system; remember that it must work for you or you won't use it. A functional record-keeping system is one of the early childhood educator's most prized possessions!

Guidelines for Designing a Classroom System

At this point you may have some ideas of your own for keeping your records organized. Some helpful hints follow.

There are many ways to
systematize records; here are
two.

- Choose a system that accommodates all methods of observation used in the
  classroom (e.g., running records, anecdotes, checklists, rating scales, ABC
  narrative event sampling).
- Check the format for ease in filing and planning.
- Label one index tab for each child. Arrange sections behind each name using
  major developmental areas. To save tabs, write the first area label on the child's
  name tab.

- Use color coding whenever advantageous. Color coding the recording sheets saves time when filing (e.g., all physical recording sheets are printed on red paper; all cognitive recording sheets are printed on green paper, etc.)

- If the system does not include space for samples of children's work, determine how those will be filed and stored.

- Ensure that your system protects confidentiality.

- Understand that parents have legal access to all school records on their children. This law promotes an open-door policy and facilitates parental involvement in informed decision making.

There are many ways to organize and store observations rather than haphazardly collecting them in one big file folder for the entire class. Without a filing system, those valuable observations will serve little use in planning and conducting conferences.

Finding the Time

Inexperienced teachers most often ask, "When do classroom teachers find the time to do record keeping? Isn't it terribly time-consuming?" Do not be thrown off by initial perceptions. Compare the teacher who saves priceless time when developmental records are stored systematically with the college student who saves time in studying for exams when all the class notes are organized, easy to read, and pertinent. Tailor-made record-keeping systems are time efficient.

A careful look at a program may reveal time-saving modifications and identify moments that can be used for record keeping. Moving away from curricula that rely heavily on planning product art frees time needed to file observations and make plans based on emerging individual needs. Teachers are also freed up in class when product art gives way to creative art; teachers do not have to spend time ensuring that children correctly duplicate the product. Many K–3 teachers report that when less time is devoted to direct teaching and more time is devoted to experiential learning (employing developmentally appropriate curricula), observational/recording intervals are plentiful. In addition, many preschool programs compensate their teachers for an additional planning hour each day so they can record, file, and plan, and teachers working at day care centers can use nap time for record keeping. Primary grade teachers have planning time built into their contracts. And don't forget, we live in the age of technology. A voice-activated computer may eventually become the record-keeping system of choice because it will write, file, and organize, thus saving valuable time.

Flexibility and commitment are the cornerstones of effective daily observations. Teachers rely on their own rhythm and class happenings when gathering observations on children's growth in the areas of cognitive, psychosocial, physical, and creative development. From day to day new observational opportunities surge, rarely at the same time each day. Most teachers (depending on class size) strive to collect an average of one or two anecdotes a week for each child, along with the use of other observational methods. An average means that there will be times when more growth is occurring for one child and the teacher will want to capture many incidents for that particular child for several days. Perhaps 6 or 7 days may go by before another significant happening is recorded for that same child. Systematic observation enables teachers to tune into the unique ebb and flow within their classrooms while documenting each child's development clearly and totally.

Novice teachers, however, may need to establish a daily rhythm. To avoid the "I tried it once and it didn't work" syndrome, consider an observational routine using a specific focus.

> We realize the process may seem a bit overwhelming to busy caregivers at first; but by beginning with spontaneous observations and gradually introducing regular planned observations, by focusing observations on only a few children at a time, and by scheduling time—to interpret the observations, the assessment process can be manageable. (Leavitt & Eheart, 1991, p. 9)

Figure 9.4 describes specific observational and recording times that teachers have reported as successful. These examples are offered as possibilities, not rigid schedules.

Times to Observe	Times to Record and File
As children first arrive (see Jeffrey's and Thienkim's running records in Chapter 4, Lin's ABC event sampling in Chapter 8)	As children arrive
During center time, free-choice time, or independent work time (see Taki's running record in Chapter 4, anecdotes in Chapter 5, Rachel's ABC event sampling in Chapter 8)	During center time, free-choice, or independent work time if others are present to assist the children
At snack time and lunch time (especially good for psychosocial anecdotes)	During lunchtime
During outdoor time (see Evan's running record in Chapter 5)	While children are at recess
When trained parent helpers are in the classroom (see Rosey's rating scale in Chapter 7)	After children depart

Figure 9.4.   Examples of observing and recording/filing opportunities.

Overview of Parent Conferences

Parent conferences are scheduled appointments for teachers and family members to share their support of and concerns about the growth of these families' children. Whether the conference is the traditional fall/spring event or has been specially called to discuss a child's specific problem, the attitude of partnership prevails (Berger, 1995).

> Schools must recognize and applaud the home as the foundation of the child's learning. Teachers must make every effort to bridge the gap between home and school. Effective communication between teachers and parents can and will bridge the gap. (Lawler, 1991, p. 89)

The teacher plays a key role in the development of the partnership. A positive tone is maintained and leadership is provided by a teacher who is prepared and trained. Read on to see how the teacher who has made comprehensive observations, filed them in a usable manner, and periodically reviewed them can plan for a conference confidently and proficiently.

Conference Preparation and Content

The child's developmental level and the educational program guide the conference content. For example, the content of a conference with a day care toddler's family is very different from that of a conference with a primary grade child's family. Likewise, the conference content for various programs within the same age-range may be based on different overall goals, thus influencing the content (e.g., the emphasis of the conference content for a child in a Montessori program may differ from that for a child in a Head Start program).

Regardless of the program type, the teacher begins to prepare for the conference by filling out a conference form for each child (see examples in Figures 9.5 and 9.6). This form is based on the running records, anecdotes, checklists, rating scales, other observations, and work samples systematically stored in the observation portfolio. The prepared form establishes a focus for the conference.

The next two figures supply a structure for compiling the developmental information to be shared at the conference. The first one, Figure 9.5, is an example of a half-day preschool conference form emphasizing the developmental summary. Most families of children in half-day programs are familiar with the typical day. Many parents stay and observe on various occasions. Several have the luxury of helping out in their children's classroom. However, all-day child development programs for children 2½ to 5 years of age will want to include a description of the typical day in their conference reports because most all-day children have full-time working parents. In this fall preschool form (spring conference form excludes goals), the teacher provides developmental information based on classroom observations and fills out the teacher's portion before the conference.

Primary grade conferences traditionally have centered around a report card concentrating on the child's subject matter proficiency and school behavior. De-

Preschool Conference Form

School's Name   **Fall Conference**

Our Fall Conference is for sharing information, concerns, and goals.

Child's Name: Age: Date:

Physical

    Teacher—

    Family—

    Goals—

Socio-Emotional

    Teacher—

    Family—

    Goals—

Cognitive

    Teacher—

    Family—

    Goals—

Creative

    Teacher—

    Family—

    Goals—

Teacher's Signature _____ _____

Family Member's Signature _____

Figure 9.5. Sample preschool conference form (condensed in size).
Source: Courtesy of L. Way, Pacific Preschool, Laguna Niguel, California. Copyright © 1997 by L. Way. Reprinted with permission.

velopmentally appropriate curricula have, however, become increasingly imple-mented in K–3 classrooms. In these classrooms teachers and family members are concerned with the child's comprehensive growth and development. At confer-ences the graded report card is replaced or augmented with a more expansive re-

School's Name

Primary Grade Conference Form

Name: Age: Grade: Date:

Cognitive: Covers the academic areas of reading, writing, math, science, social studies, health, language, listening/speaking. Also includes problem-solving abilities, logical thought, classification, seriation, memory, and perspective taking.

Psychosocial: Includes personal and social development, such as peer and adult relationships, impulse control, motivation, self-concept, self-esteem, and moral reasoning.

Physical: Discusses both gross and fine motor development. Includes child's abilities in physical skill development.

Creative: Includes music, art, writing, block play, and dramatics.

Goals:

Figure 9.6.   Sample primary grade conference form (condensed in size).

porting form (see Figure 9.6). The National Association for the Education of Young Children guidelines for developmentally appropriate practices for 6- through 8-year-olds (Bredekamp & Copple, 1997) make the following suggestions for evaluations:

> Teachers and parents share useful, specific feedback about individual children's learning and developmental strengths and needs. Children's progress is shared with parents in the form of narrative comments following an outline of topics and in language that parents understand. A child's progress is reported in comparison to his or her own previous performance, and parents are given general information about how the child compares to age-related expectations. Letter or numerical grades are considered inadequate reflections of children's ongoing learning. (p. 176)

Figure 9.6 suggests a developmentally appropriate conference form for the primary grade years. The teacher summarizes the child's development in all four areas, drawing on the teacher's records and the child's work samples. A well-designed record-keeping system pays high dividends when you are preparing conference forms!

In addition to preparing a conference summary form, some teachers send home a short questionnaire (4 or 5 open-ended questions) to help the families begin to think about their children's school experiences, topics to discuss, and goals to formulate. Two sample questions are offered by Mindes et al. (1996): "When you think about it, what excited Willard most about second grade? Were there assignments or activities that he seemed excited to do and couldn't wait to go to school that day?" (p. 153).

Recognizing that most families have terrifically busy lives, some speak English as a second language, and others may have negative school memories, short preconference questionnaires can encourage focused thinking time and help parents to confidently participate in a productive discussion.

Getting Started

Even though "a conference provides you and family members with time to share information and perceptions" (Feeney et al., 1996, p. 490), it is the teacher's responsibility to facilitate productive communications from start to finish. How is that done? It is accomplished by understanding the main purposes of a conference: listening, sharing, and strengthening the family–teacher partnership as it relates to the children's growth and development.

Now let's look at how a conference is generally carried out. First, the teacher welcomes the family members and sees that everyone is comfortably seated. (Be sure there are enough adult chairs!) Hendricks (1996) suggested that the time limit be mentioned in a conversational manner early on. An example would be, "Time to talk together never seems long enough; I'm so pleased we were able to arrange this 30-minute meeting." Then the teacher begins the discussion by setting a positive tone—sharing about an outstanding strength the child possesses or a recent accomplishment. Here are two examples:

Family partnerships are enriched through scheduled conferences.

- It's a real joy to see how Keara has grown in her ability to use words to solve problems independently. We've worked very hard on this. She seems so much more confident in this area at school. What do you see at home?
- Omar has such well-developed motor skills. I often observe his agility and coordination when he runs, hops, and skips. He's a great skipper. I've noticed recently that he doesn't seem to have the interest in the trikes that he used to. I think he's ready to try a two-wheeler; what do you think?

The opening positive statement does not have to detail a monumental achievement. For the child who seems "lacking in strengths," the teacher looks for the small positives, such as attendance, a special interest, a hobby, or a family trip or excursion that the child talked about. The discussion of the child's overall development can begin in any area as long as it is positive.

After the teacher breaks the ice by setting a positive tone and inviting interaction with the family member(s), the discussion continues via the content of the conference form (see Figures 9.5 and 9.6). The teacher, well prepared with examples of pertinent anecdotes and samples of the child's work, leads the family members through an informal conversation on all areas of the child's development summarized on the form. This process is enhanced when both the teacher and the family members have a copy of the written conference summary form in front of them.

Throughout the conference the teacher asks the family members if they've noticed similar or the same developmental strengths or weaknesses that may need to be addressed. Many times, family members relate stories that correlate with what the teacher has seen at school. Sometimes family members are surprised and report that their child is different at home. The teacher listens attentively and jots down this important input on the form. The teacher can then summarize joint concerns. During the fall conference, the teacher and family members can then establish specific goals for the child.

The teacher and the family bring their own perspectives to the conference table, interpreting the child's growth through their own observational prisms. Together they peer through the looking glass, often doubling the visibility. The conference is a collaboration; it sets in place the desired family–school partnership.

Supporting Documentation

Effective conferences require sharing of selected observations (often anecdotes) to augment the summaries. The trained teacher also selects samples of the child's work (e.g., drawings, stories, primary grade math or writing papers) to illustrate various topics on the conference form. For example, the teacher may present a painting or a collage that shows the child's ability to represent or a child's unfinished math assignments as evidence of weak work habits. Families appreciate documentation in the form of children's work samples and can more clearly understand their children's developmental advances or impediments when samples accompany the written summaries.

Another way to widen the perspective and document written comments is to present audiotape, videotape, or videodisc records and photographs (Billman & Sherman, 1996). The use of instant photographs is demonstrated by a teacher who tells about Juanita, a child who always responded with, "I don't know," when her parents asked her what she did at preschool:

> During the parent conference I brought out some photos of Juanita's science discoveries using magnets and balances along with photos of her block-building feats and her favorite dramatic play scenario—the office. Her parents were delighted to see her emerging science interest and her active classroom participation. Those pictures were worth a thousand words!

The use of videotapes is becoming increasingly common in parent conferences. The use of the video camera to film children at work in the classroom can offer parents an enlightening and rewarding view of their child. A videotape can be useful in clarifying a child's strengths and weaknesses or portraying developmental progress. For example, video clips can be chosen to show a young preschooler's growing ability to interact with other children. As the children progress in years, video clips can highlight leadership skills. Let's look at how one teacher integrated videotapes into a conference.

I once taught a 4-year-old, Bethany, who was precocious in her artwork. By the second or third month, Bethany ventured out into the block area, where she became as interested in pursuing social contacts as in building. Her time in the art area declined, and she took less time and care with her projects. Unfortunately (from my perspective), her parents grew increasingly dissatisfied with the "quality" of work Bethany brought home from preschool!

My verbal explanations of Bethany's change in pursuits were not as effective as a videotape of Bethany during free-choice time in persuading her parents that her time was being well spent. Once they recovered from their initial surprise and disappointment (remember, their expectations were not being met), they began to appreciate how hard Bethany was working to expand her social networks. In the short term the videotape lessened the parents' anxieties about unproductive time in preschool and, in the long run, helped to allow Bethany the needed time to achieve a balanced life at school.

"Photographs and audio or video recording provide concrete evidence of young children's performance in the classroom. . . . [They] document performances with an accuracy and competence not possible with written records" (Smith, Kuhs, & Ryan, 1993, p. 12). These selected pieces of media can provide valuable insights during the family–teacher conference. Family members value the opportunity to see their children on their own and leave the conference with a broadened understanding of the educational program.

Guidelines for Parent Conferences

1. *Frequency.* Both preschools and primary grades typically offer two yearly conferences for each child. To strengthen the family partnership and develop joint goals for the child, a fall conference is offered about a month after school has begun. To discuss the child's growth, goal realizations, and next year's educational plans, a springtime conference is offered at the end of the year. Conferences offered only on a volunteer basis that are left up to the parents' request place total responsibility on the parents and miss the intended goal of partnership, thus robbing the child of an optimal developmental environment.

2. *Preparation.* Treat each child individually. Carefully review portfolios of teachers' observational records and children's work samples. Write each child's developmental summary on a conference form. Write with your mind and your heart. Remember to be tactful and gentle, gentle, gentle with your words. Choose items to discuss, such as children's work, photos, and anecdotes. Organize.

3. *Planning.* Set a time that is convenient for the teacher and the family. Aim for a 30-minute session. Invite the family or guardian.

4. *Setup.* Arrange a comfortable place for the family or guardian to wait. Provide adult-size chairs and a table with reading materials. Early childhood magazines, class photo albums, or stories children have dictated or written help early arrivals pass the time. A pitcher of ice water or a pot of coffee is always appreciated.

5. *Appointment.* Start the conference on time! Keep track of the time so that others are not inconvenienced. During the conference be friendly, positive, and open.

Photographs of children at work in the early childhood classroom strengthen parent conferences.

Listen and exchange views. Keep your purpose in mind. Develop goals with the parent(s) on the basis of shared information. Send home a copy of the conference form with the family.

6. *Follow-up.* Make a phone call, send a note home with the child, or informally chat at departure time to keep the lines of communication open. Schedule another conference or make a home visit if a concern requires additional attention. Let your sincere interest be known; continue to build partnerships!

Guidelines for Using Videotapes During Parent Conferences

1. *Know the equipment.* Valuable conference time will be wasted if the you cannot work the equipment efficiently.

2. *Plan the program.* Select which tape clips of each child to show and know where to find them. Carefully preview each tape and record the counter numbers of each clip.

3. *Utilize videotapes to make substantive points to the families.* Videotapes can illustrate how children work in groups, their interests, their strengths, and so forth. Think about each selection and how you want to use it during the conference. Planning time will be shortened if the video clips depicting more than one child are cross-referenced in each child's portfolio.

4. *Present a balanced view of each child.* Try to show families at least two clips of their child to document the variety of activities and experiences that are part of early childhood education. Remember that the clip may be short yet effective.

In summary, it is the process illustrated in the cycle of observing, recording, planning, evaluating, and communicating (see Chapter 1) that surrounds conferences. The child is the focus, and the intention is to build a partnership with the family to support the child's growth.

During a responsive and supportive conference, family members readily furnish additional information, offer new insights, ask questions, and make suggestions. Their family perspectives help give the teacher the broadest possible view of the child. As family members and the teacher share their own perspectives of the child's abilities and developing abilities, a valuable partnership is created. Throughout the year this partnership is developed by keeping the lines of communication open and staying in touch.

Applications

To exemplify the conference process, let's get acquainted with Toby (4;8). Before the conference day, Toby's teacher compiled the conference form summaries using the observations from Toby's portfolio; the documents in Toby's portfolio are displayed in Figure 9.7. (This portfolio is unusually large for the middle of October because of the teacher's present focus on Toby's pressing developmental needs.)

With the purpose of the conference in mind (to enhance the family–teacher team approach by listening, discussing, and sharing joys and concerns regarding

12 *anecdotes* representing physical, cognitive, psychosocial, and creative development dated as follows: 9/9, 9/14, 9/15, 9/17, 9/18, 9/25, 9/28, 10/1, 10/5, 10/8, 10/12, 10/13

2 *running records* (one inside and one outside) dated 9/11 and 9/16, each 5 minutes

ABC narrative event sampling on group entrance dated 9/21 to 9/24

COR (Child Observation Record) *rating scale* completed 10/14 based on preceding records

1 *video clip* of outside play
2 *dictated stories*

Figure 9.7. Portfolio documents.

Toby's developmental progress), read through the summary (Figure 9.8) and begin to answer the following questions. What topics would you, as a teacher, be sure to discuss with his parents at the conference? What would be your tentative plans and goals for Toby? Conference dialogue will ultimately determine joint goals; however, effective teachers come prepared with some possible goal suggestions. Practice Activity 9.1 will give you an opportunity to make some preconference goal suggestions based on the summary information.

Seaside Developmental Center

Fall Conference

Name: Toby   Age: 4;8   Date: 10/16

Physical
Teacher: In large motor skills Toby shows confidence and thoroughly enjoys running, jumping, and climbing   all executed with ease and coordination. His movements are smooth and controlled; he is an excellent ball handler. While executing the multiple movements of an obstacle course, he demonstrates strength and agility in all large motor activities.

   Toby's interest in small motor tasks is limited to working with manipulatives such as puzzles and occasionally visiting the art table. He has not yet established hand dominance; he picks up art tools (crayons, brushes, chalk) or puzzle pieces with either his right or left hand.

Parent:

Goals:

Figure 9.8. Completed preschool conference form.

Cognitive
Teacher: Toby has a large vocabulary and complex sentence structure; his language is rich. He likes relating what he knows to new information. When participating in a group, he asks thoughtful questions and has creative ideas.

Through language he demonstrates representation, classification, and seriation. He exhibits admirable recall abilities daily.

Toby loves books. He spends some of each morning's free-choice time in the language area.

If asked, Toby can print his name with either hand when a model is provided. He counts using 1;1 correspondence up to 12.

Parent:

Goals:

Psychosocial
Teacher: Toby shows no fears and is inquisitive, curious, and adventurous. Directing his exuberance when he is interacting with other children is his biggest challenge. He is often "out-of-bounds," engaging in rough play and frequent outbursts of anger when playing with other children. Children have already begun to avoid and reject him in their play. Guidance and close proximity to adults offer support as he learns to use his words to tell his friends when he doesn't like what is going on.

Entering a group poses a particular problem for Toby. During the first weeks of school Toby chose to enter groups by force—knocking down structures, throwing sand, etc. Toby and I have begun to work together in this area. As a first step, I have assured him that I can tell he wants to play with others, and when he wants help, he should come and tell me. As his trust grows, he seeks my help more often. He seems to be pleased with his few (at this point) successes.

Toby focuses the longest on solitary self-selected tasks. He is proud of his mastery of puzzles. He is interested in books and number games. He is very cooperative when engaged with an adult one-on-one or with a small group on a directed task.

Parent:

Goals:

Creative
Teacher: At this point Toby's creative ability is displayed primarily in his verbal skills and dramatic play. For limited periods of time he engages in positive role-play (e.g., pizza maker or daddy). As his psychosocial skills develop, his ability to display his creativity will blossom.

Parent:

Goals:

Figure 9.8.   *(Continued.)*
Source: Courtesy of I. Andrews, St. Margaret's Preschool, San Juan Capistrano, California. 1992 by I. Andrews. Adapted from personal class records with parents' permission.

Toby was chosen specifically to demonstrate how a teacher can use a positive tone throughout the conference to relate important and sensitive developmental information. This year, the last year before kindergarten, will be a critical year in Toby's growth. His parents are already aware of many of their child's abilities and talents as well as his limitations (remember that this child is 4;8). Toby's teacher knows that a collaborative parent–teacher effort to establish joint goals will serve Toby's best interest.

Consider Our Ethical Responsibilities to Families

NAEYC Ideal I-2.5

"To interpret each child's progress to parents within the framework of a developmental perspective and to help families understand and appreciate the value of developmentally appropriate early childhood programs" (Feeney & Kipnis, 1992, p. 6).

Read on to see how Toby's teacher fulfills this ethical responsibility.

Practice Activity 9.1
Suggestions for Teacher Goals

The goals recorded on each child's conference form are jointly set by the teacher and the parent(s) during the conference. The teacher, however, prepares for the conference by writing (on a separate piece of paper) some ideas for possible goals that address strengths and weaknesses.

After reviewing the conference form below, try your hand at writing some preconference goals as if you were Toby's teacher.

What are your initial preconference goals for Toby? Depending on the child, most teachers like to prepare 2 to 4 preconference goals in each developmental area.

Physical goals:

Example: To provide experiences in fine motor development based on Toby's interest, invite Toby to assist the teacher in putting out some manipulative activities for free-choice time.

Cognitive goals:

Psychosocial goals:

Creative goals:

To implement successful conferences, the teacher must be skilled in writing goals and summaries. Practice Activity 9.2 offers practice in writing summaries.

Practice Activity 9.2
Practice in Writing Summaries

It is time to prepare for fall conferences at Eighth Street Elementary. The teacher thoughtfully fills in the conference form to discuss Keo's (5;3) development. The teacher praises Keo's gregarious personality, which is loved by all. The teacher also applauds Keo's adeptness in large motor development. The teacher is concerned, however, about Keo's preoccupation with superhero figures; Keo's compelling interest interferes with other kindergarten activities. The teacher also discusses Keo's limited fine motor skills.

Using the form modeled by Toby's teacher, imagine that you are Keo's teacher preparing for a fall conference. Write the psychosocial paragraph addressing Keo's attraction to superheroes. Be positive, clear, and concise when conveying this information.

Eighth Street Elementary
Fall Conference

Name: Keo   Age: 5;3   Date:

Psychosocial:

Action Project 9.1
Evaluation of Record-Keeping Systems

Option 1

Choose three schools that serve the age group you are interested in (2½- to 8-year-olds). Call ahead and request *blank* copies of their observation sheets, record-keeping sheets, and conference forms. If each school can meet your need, stop by and pick up the forms.

(If a school cannot meet your request, choose another that can.) Upon examination of your collections from three schools, answer the following questions by writing down your findings.

- What information about each child do the various forms collect, and what information do they omit? How are they similar and different?
- Do the forms meet the guidelines given in this chapter for designing your own system? If not, what modifications would you suggest?

Option 2

Visit one school that serves children of the age you are interested in (2½- to 8-year-olds) and uses written observations. Obtain *blank* copies of the observation sheets, record-keeping sheets, and conference forms. Make an appointment and discuss them with a teacher or teachers at the school. Learn how the sheets and forms are used at that school. Find out what the teacher(s) considers the benefits and drawbacks of the samples you've collected. Write down your findings.

Points to Remember

A portfolio contains examples of the children's school performance (work samples) and teacher observations of the child's development (Gelfer & Perkins, 1996). A serviceable portfolio system will promote efficiency and confidentiality in filing observations and ease in retrieving information to tailor activities to individual needs and prepare for parent conferences. Successful systems are designed to meet the teacher's and program's needs. Teachers may create their own systems, modify others' systems, or use one presented in this chapter (file boxes, notebooks, or file folders). Portfolios may be either inclusive (the teacher keeps the observations and supporting information in one record-keeping system) or separate (teachers and children maintain exclusive systems; work samples are kept by the children in their own portfolios).

One of the main features of an effective system is that it expedites planning for parent conferences. Having prepared a conference summary form, the teacher provides the guiding hand in conducting conferences that are positive, supportive, and sharing. Together, family members and the teacher build a partnership that ensures optimal progress for the child.

The organization necessary for record keeping and conference preparation requires teachers to prioritize their use of time; record keeping may seem overwhelming at first. Using a record-keeping system, however, is much like following the directions to a new destination—at first the instructions appear complex, but once you're on the road, the path is clear and simple to follow. The going becomes smooth and direct when teachers utilize systematic organization.

Take a Moment to Reflect

As adults, we have the opportunity to collect and store documentation for a variety of documentations: checking and savings accounts, recipes, mileage, grades, car repairs, monthly bills, doctor and dentist visits, insurance claims—the list goes on and on. Reflect on how you systematize your personal records and answer the following questions.

1. What type(s) of record-keeping system(s) has been most successful in your personal life experiences?

2. Would that type be a usable form for classroom observations?

3. In what areas of your life is record keeping difficult? Can you identify any negative habits that could possibly creep into your classroom record-keeping process?

PART III

Observing Children, Teachers, Interactions, and Environments

Girded with the *why* and *what* keys of observation from Part I and five of the how keys of observation from Part II, the odyssey of *Through the Looking Glass* moves to Part III. In this section the last of the *how* keys is added as the focus of our observation shifts from individual children to groups and the environment itself.

In Part III there are four chapters to explore. Chapters 10 and 11 investigate the final two observational methods: tally event sampling and time sampling. As in the previous method chapters, a detailed explanation of the method is followed by practice and application opportunities. These methods expand observational possibilities when the subjects of the observation become teachers, children, and their interactions. The preschool and primary grade examples in each of these chapters give a detailed account of classroom procedures for observing, recording, analyzing, and then using the data results in teaching plans. Chapter 12 describes and illustrates the process for constructing instruments used to answer specific classroom questions. In this chapter, the process is illustrated through a classroom example in which teachers observe children's separations from their parents and use the data to adjust support strategies. The final chapter in Part III, Chapter 13, examines the characteristics of indoor and outdoor environments and suggests appropriate observational choices. Whether designing a new facility, setting up a classroom for the first time, or reorganizing throughout the year, this chapter shows how information gleaned from environmental observations can help teachers provide optimal learning conditions.

At the completion of Part III, you will hold all the observational keys—the *why, what, how,* and *communication* keys. Part IV is the concluding stop on our travels *Through the Looking Glass.*

CHAPTER 10

Observing Children and Teachers at Work by Using Tally Event Sampling

A t the end of each week, the teachers at Canyon Primary School set aside time for individual class evaluations and general planning for the next week. They record and file observations in well-used portfolios. On these Friday afternoons, they spend the bulk of their planning time rereading observations, identifying emerging patterns, and planning appropriate activities and teaching strategies.

Today in Room 3, one team of teachers is pondering how to stimulate more divergent thinking during class discussions. The teachers are disturbed because observational records in many of the children's portfolios describe quick, short answers during discussions of interesting and complex topics. As the teachers brainstorm further, attention turns to their own teaching techniques. They begin to suspect that the way they lead discussions, specifically the types of questions they ask, could contribute to the recorded responses. The teachers decide to observe how often they ask questions that promote divergent thinking and extend language as opposed to questions that elicit one-word responses. What observational method could these teachers use to explore their own question-asking patterns over a 2-week period?

Observations in the early childhood classroom usually focus on behaviors of *individual children*. In the preceding vignette, however, you are asked to elect a method to observe how *teachers* could explore their question-asking patterns. The time has come to broaden our observational scope by expanding the subject of our observations to include more than one person; the looking glass widens.

As you puzzle over the question posed in the vignette and search your current knowledge for an appropriate method, you may think about using a checklist to observe and examine whether the teachers ask more questions that promote divergent thinking than questions that elicit a one-word response. A checklist is a good choice if the observers want to document only the presence or absence of the two types of questions and if they are observing only one teacher at a time. The Canyon Primary teachers, however, wish to investigate, analyze, and compare several teachers' questioning patterns on more than one occasion. In essence these teachers want to evaluate one aspect of their teaching methodology—question asking. To obtain the information requested in the vignette, we will explore a new method—tally event sampling.

Overview of Observing Using Tally Event Sampling

Description

Event sampling—does it sound familiar? It certainly does. Chapter 8 introduced *ABC narrative event sampling*. This chapter presents another event sampling method: *tally event sampling*. These two methods are similar in two ways. First, they both observe specified events (identified behaviors or situations). Second, they both use an observational period known as a *sampling*, a "technique used to select a microcosm from a given population" (Kapel et al., 1991 p. 495). As stated in Chapter 8, the data gleaned from a sampling is generalized to represent the whole; thus the results are referred to as a representative sample.

ABC narrative event sampling and tally event sampling differ in purpose, form, and data. The ABC approach is used to study causes and effects of individual children's behaviors. The tally approach is used to determine how often a specified event occurs. "With a tally system, an observer puts down a tally or tick *every time* a particular event occurs, e.g., every time the teacher asks a question or gives praise" (Hopkins, 1993, p. 100). The subject of ABC narrative event sampling is always individuals, while the subject(s) of tally event sampling can be individuals but are generally groups. The ABC method uses an A-B-C form that records written episodes; the tally approach uses a form called a grid to collect the tally marks (see Figure 10.1). The ABC approach generally yields qualitative data, whereas the tally approach provides quantitative data.

Let's return to the opening vignette of this chapter. The two Canyon Primary teachers ultimately chose tally event sampling because they wanted to find out the number of times during group discussions each of them asked an *open question* (a question that has many possible answers) or a *closed question* (a question that elicits a single correct answer, usually a one-word response). Using this method, the observer at Canyon Primary inscribed one tally mark each time one of the two types of questions was asked by a teacher during a group discussion—the focus of this observation. The tally marks were recorded on a grid that organized and simplified the potentially cumbersome task of observing several subjects (teachers) and recording abundant data (questions asked). Figure 10.1 exhibits the tally event sampling instrument developed by the Canyon Primary teachers.

This form may be expanded vertically to include additional teachers and horizontally to include other subjects. When observing preschools, room areas or activities may be substituted for the subject categories. This tally form enables the teachers to summarize and compare their overall patterns of open or closed questioning throughout the day. The results will undoubtedly promote conversation among these teachers about the value and implications of open and closed questions during class discussions. In addition, the teachers may discuss how this same process could be used to observe different categories of questions, such as explanation, demonstration, comprehension, and evaluation questions.

The tally approach can be used to examine a wide range of topics and is versatile because of its flexibility in subject choice. The observer can measure the frequency of events involving *one person* (e.g., a teacher's repeated use of classroom

Tally Event Sampling of Teachers' Open/Closed Questions									
School/Grade:									
Date:						Time:			
Observer:						Teachers:			
						Children:			
Event:		Open questions (O)—have many possible answers that allow the child opportunity to expand and explain Closed questions (C)—have one correct answer.								
Instructions:		Make one tally mark in the appropriate column each time a teacher asks a question during specific discussion times.								
Discussion Time	Science		Social Studies		Math		Shared Reading		Small Group	
Question / Teacher	O	C	O	C	O	C	O	C	O	C
Xavier										
Nadia										

Figure 10 1   Tally event sampling: Teachers' questions.

management techniques or the number of times a child is out of her or his seat during work periods), events involving *groups* (e.g., teachers' questioning patterns or children's use of *power language*—profanity or other offensive words such as "shut up"), or events involving *interactions* (e.g., children's language exchanges). Let's look closer at an excellent example of using tally sampling to observe child–child interactions (see Figure 10.2). Watson, Omark, Grouell and Heller (1981) presented a system for recording "who spoke Spanish . . . to whom within a classroom" (p. 126).

Watson et al. (1981) noted that teachers and aides could be added to the list for a more comprehensive classroom picture of verbal interactions in Spanish. In-

Tally Event Sampling of Spanish Language Interactions

Center or School/Grade:

Date: Time:

Observer: Teachers:

Children: Juan, Mary, Tony, Alberto, Dan, Rosalia

	Receivers					
Child	Juan	Mary	Tony	Alberto	Dan	Rosalia
Juan						
Mary						
Tony						
Alberto						
Dan						
Rosalia						

(Senders)

Figure 10.2. Tally event sampling: Language interactions.
Source: From *Nondiscriminatory Assessment: Volume I—Practitioner's Guide* by D. L. Watson, D. Omark, S. L. Grouell, and B. Heller, 1981, San Diego, CA: Los Amigos Research Associates. Copyright © 1981 by Los Amigas Research Associates. Reprinted by permission.

formation from this tally event sampling might help teachers in a bilingual classroom to pair children for collaborative apprenticeship (peer teaching), thus promoting friendships, mutual respect, and language development.

In a multilingual classroom the grid would specify the senders and receivers of messages as in Figure 10.2 and also the language used; language codes (e.g., J for Japanese) would be substituted for tally marks. Perhaps the data would show that one child converses only in Japanese with other Japanese-speaking students. On the basis of this information, the teacher might want to pair this child with a buddy who comfortably speaks both Japanese and English (Watson et al., 1981). Both children will profit from this cooperative arrangement.

Keep in mind that tally event sampling can be used to record various overt (observable and apparent) behaviors occurring infrequently or with moderate frequency. What about events that occur rapidly, incessantly, or with very high frequency? Those require yet another method, which is explained in Chapter 11.

What recurring events or behaviors would teachers want to examine? Think about appropriate topics that can be observed using the tally event sampling method.

Practice Activity 10.1
Tally Event Sampling Topics

Identify four topics that could be studied using tally event sampling.

Examples:

- Frequency of children's use of selected classroom centers
- Frequency of teachers' use of direct method instruction
- Frequency of staff members sharing resources and information with co-workers during weekly staff meetings

1.

2.

3.

4.

Purpose

Tally event sampling is most useful for teachers when they want to know how frequently a specific event occurs. Employing this approach, teachers can quickly and easily obtain quantitative information to be used in analyzing classroom problems and then in planning or revising teaching strategies, activities, and materials (Hintze & Shapiro, 1995). For example, one teacher concerned with meeting individual needs was interested in exploring how often each child used various methods to gain teachers' attention. With these data the teacher could analyze possible age and cultural preferences and apply the findings to better meet individual needs. The tally approach would furnish the requisite data.

Teachers can use tally sampled data to monitor developmental changes and the effectiveness of teaching strategies. Suppose a preschool teacher, Noi, who is exasperated with a child's use of power language, uses tally event sampling to check the child's frequency of power language use before and after intervention strategies. (Note—the subject of this tally event sampling is one child as opposed to a group.) In the first tally sampling period of 1 week, this child used power language an average of 9 times a day. (Noi expected 50 times!) As Noi sets into practice a plan to help the child learn to control this behavior, she knows that a behavior change may be a long and difficult process. And because the use of power language particularly irritates Noi, it seems as if no progress is being made. Nevertheless, after 2 weeks of concerted effort, Noi uses a second sampling period of 1 week to record the child's use of power language and finds that it has diminished to an average of twice a day! Encouraged by the positive results, she continues the corrective practices and looks forward to additional progress. Another power language sampling is planned for 3 weeks later.

Teachers are often shocked at the findings of tally event sampling, especially in the area of teacher and child behaviors. Particularly in large classrooms, teachers' perceptions of classroom behaviors are easily distorted. With quantitative information procured from the samplings, however, teachers can analyze patterns and plan for adjustments. Responding to the recorded data can facilitate, enrich, and promote an exceptional early childhood program.

Recording Time

Two common concerns for observers using the tally approach are how to determine the sampling period and how to gather information throughout an extended span of time. After all, the early childhood classroom is bursting with activity. How can the teacher predetermine the length of time it will take to gather sufficient data? How can a teacher manage the collection of data on one topic over several days?

The length of the sampling period is determined by the event studied, specifically how long the teacher thinks it will take to gather sufficient data for a representative sample. For instance, the teacher may record tallies daily for a week when sampling aggression in the classroom but only a few days when sampling direct teaching methods. Remember, tally marks are made on the recording form only when the event occurs.

Kerlinger (1986) offered this advice about managing the collection of data: "The investigator who is pursuing events must either know when the events are going to occur and be present when they occur, as with classroom events, or wait until they occur, as with quarrels" (p. 492). The teacher keeps the form close at hand (a clipboard is a popular prop) for the duration of the sampling period and records marks whenever the event occurs. Classrooms equipped with video cameras allow the teacher another option. By recording the event during the day and using the replay button, the teacher can mark the tallies on the instrument at the teacher's time of choice.

Confidentiality

In Chapter 9 notations were made to heed the confidentiality of individual observational records and portfolios. The same important instruction applies to records kept for groups of children or teachers. The format and the size of observational instruments, such as tally event sampling or time sampling (studied in Chapter 11), can pose more of a problem. If you are using a clipboard, take special care to keep a cover sheet over the instrument; on the other hand, if you are using a notebook, keep it closed when not in use. Attention to confidentiality is a significant component of professionalism.

Guidelines for Constructing Tally Event Sampling Instruments

Tally event sampling users may design an instrument to suit their observational needs. To ensure that the resulting grid can be used as objectively as possible to collect the necessary quantitative data and produce sound information, certain steps must be taken.

Box 10.1 presents an overview to assist the process of devising a tally event sampling instrument; each point in the box is explained and illustrated in the preschool example.

To illustrate this process two examples follow. The preschool example demonstrates how to design an instrument to record the frequency of children's partici-

---

Box 10.1
Designing and Using a Tally Event Sampling Instrument

1. Select an appropriate topic, formulate an observational question, and define the event.
2. Research the topic in libraries and classrooms. Review what others have already done in the selected area.
3. Identify clear and distinct categories.
   - Generate sets of categories, vertical and horizontal.
   - Define each set of categories when necessary.
   - Select a sign or category system.
   - Decide if category codes are needed.
4. Design a recording form.
   - Use the traditional heading.
   - Use the categories to construct the grid.
   - Label a space for comments at the bottom of the form.
5. Pilot test the instrument. Revise, if necessary, and pilot test again.
6. Establish inter-rater reliability.

pation in circle time. The primary grade example asks you to participate in constructing an instrument to research the question "Do teachers call on boys more than girls?"

Integration of Classroom Situations and Observation

Preschool Example

The scene for the six-step process of designing a tally event sampling instrument unfolds as follows. Molly, a new ½ day preschool teacher, is about 10 minutes into her 3-month evaluation with her director, Camisha. Up to this point, Camisha has praised Molly for her eager participation at staff meetings; she certainly is a good team member! Camisha has also commented about Molly's effective room arrangement, supportive relationships with families, and well-planned daily activities. Camisha now shifts the focus of the discussion and asks for Molly's assessment of her first 3 months on the job.

Molly takes a few minutes and shares the positive happenings within her classroom. She mentions the trust and relationship she is building with the children, her feeling of acceptance with other staff members, and the joy and professional pride she experiences in working at an accredited school. Then she takes a deep breath and says that she is pleased to have an invitation to discuss a "troublesome area" that she has been thinking about for several weeks. As Molly tells Camisha about her concern for the acting-out behaviors at circle time, Camisha nods her head and concurs that this is an area she'd like Molly to work on. Camisha says, "I think you will better understand the dynamics of your circle times if you zero in on when children participate and when they don't." After discussion, Camisha and Molly agree on the following plan of action. Molly will design an instrument to record circle participation and ask a classmate from an early childhood class she is taking to observe her circle times for a week. Following the observation period, Molly and Camisha will meet to discuss the results.

Molly returns to her classroom and confidently begins work on her instrument. Having taken a college class in observation, she is armed with the appropriate know-how and soon realizes that she needs to collect data not only on who participates productively, but also on the frequency of the misbehaviors. Therefore, she identifies her question as, "How often does each child in this classroom participate productively and counterproductively during specific circle activities?" Molly reviews the possible observational methods, and because she wants to count frequencies, she chooses the most appropriate one—tally event sampling. The process of designing a tally event sampling instrument (based on Box 10.1) is set in motion.

Step 1   With her observational topic selected and her question clearly stated, Molly completes Step 1 by defining the event so that it is open to only one interpretation.

Circle time can be enhanced by observation.

Circle time participation—the child joins in teacher-planned group activities in a productive or counterproductive manner.

Step 2   Choosing the horizontal and vertical categories (components of the chosen event) is the next step and requires Molly to research the topic of circle time. She checks her child-development textbook, curriculum books, and current journal articles on the topic in the library. She also reflects on her own experiences in this area. This important step determines what data will actually be collected.

Step 3   Molly determines that one set of categories is the children's names and the other set (given on the next page) is the types of activities during circle time. Based on her research, she carefully selects categories that do not overlap.

- Calendar activities
- Discussions
- Fingerplays or action activities that are not sung
- Games (e.g., teacher-planned cognitive, movement, auditory discrimination activities)
- Sharing (e.g., item from home, information, an experience)
- Songs sung with or without actions
- Stories or poetry read from books, presented on flannel boards, or told by an adult

Molly chooses subcategories to indicate whether each child's participation is productive or counterproductive by dividing each of the above categories into two parts (see Figure 10.3).

Molly considers the use of a category or sign system while choosing categories.

Category System	*Sign System*
Categories must be mutually exclusive; each category is distinct and separate from the others.	Categories must be mutually exclusive; each category is distinct and separate from the others.
AND	BUT
Categories must be exhaustive; a category is listed for every possible observed behavior. Nothing is left out.	Categories do not have to be exhaustive. Allows the observer to select only pertinent categories.

For the first set of categories, Molly has selected specific circle activities typical of her classroom. This set is not exhaustive, so she uses a sign system. For the other set, Molly plans to list every child in her classroom; she uses a category system for this set.

Molly quickly sketches out the grid and notes that codes are in order. Some of the category descriptors contain many letters and will be difficult to fit in the small spaces on the grid. She could use abbreviations, letters, numbers, or symbols. She settles for the efficiency of letters; they will serve to jog her memory if necessary:

C   = Calendar activities
D   = Discussions
F   = Fingerplays or action activities that are not sung
G   = Games (e.g., teacher-planned cognitive, movement, auditory-discrimination activities)
Sh = Sharing (e.g., item from home, information, an experience).

So = Songs sung with or without actions

St/P = Stories or poetry read from books, presented on flannel boards, or told by an adult

p = Productive participation (e.g., asks questions or comments related to topic, takes part in movement or song activity)

cp = Counterproductive participation (e.g., impulsively jumps up, blurts out comments or questions off the subject, distracts another)

When codes are used, the observer tries to memorize them before going into the classroom to observe. In the construction of Molly's form, she has room to include the code meanings in her heading for quick reference. Code definitions ensure that others can use and understand the form; they may be printed in the heading or, if lengthy, on a separate sheet or on the back.

Step 4   Molly begins the construction of the tally event sampling form by filling in the traditional heading. She then uses some scratch paper to try out a grid-arrangement pattern. Taking the size of the paper into account, she places the longest set (children's names) down the left side of the recording sheet and the shortest set of categories (circle activities) along the top; she positions the subcategories (p and cp) below each circle activity. With this arrangement, all the categories can fit on one sheet.

The tally event sampling grid is complete with the matrix that displays the intersection of the two sets of categories. The grid is placed below the heading and definitions (shown in Figure 10.3 without data).

Step 5   To check that the form is efficient, is easy to use, and collects the desired information, Molly pilot tests her instrument while visiting an afternoon classroom.

Molly has no difficulty using her instrument. She is pleased with the organization of the instrument but adds the comment row she had forgotten (see Figure 10.4 for revision).

Step 6   The final step in instrument construction, the inter-rater reliability check, is executed using paired observers. Molly enlists the help of Al, a fellow student from her early childhood evening class. They look over the instrument together. Molly foresees a possible problem and takes the time to "train" her inter-rater partner. Molly points out the difference between a movement game and a song sung with action. For example, a record with movement instructions and music in the background would be recorded under the G category as a teacher-planned movement activity. In contrast, the Hokie Pokie is a song sung with actions; it would be recorded under the So category.

With confidence in the category definitions, Molly and Al observe the same classroom during circle time, each using the tally instrument (as in Figure 10.4). When the observation time is complete, they check for consistency in what they recorded.

Inter-rater reliability is a measure between two or more observers resulting in a percentage that indicates the amount of agreement; exact agreement is 100%

**Tally Event Sampling
of Preschoolers' Participation in
Selected Circle Time Activities**

Center/Age level:

Date: Time:

Observer: Teacher:

                                                         Children:

Event: Circle time participation—the child joins in teacher-planned
                group activities in a productive or a counterproductive
                manner.

Codes: C = calendar activities, D = discussions, F = fingerplays or
                action activities not sung, G = games, Sh = sharing, So = songs
                with or without actions, St/P = stories or poetry read from
                books, presented on flannel boards, or told by an adult.

                p = productive participation, cp = counterproductive
                participation.

Instructions: Mark one tally mark in the appropriate box each time a child
                joins in during one of the specified circle activities. Record the
                tally within each category under productive (p) or
                counterproductive (cp) participation.

Circle Activity / Child	C		D		F		G		Sh		So		St/P	
	p	cp	p	cp	p	cp	p	cp	p	cp	p	cp	p	cp
Child 1														
Child 2														
Child 3														
and so forth														

Figure 10.3.   Tally event sampling preschool example: Circle participation.

(Boehm, 1992). Molly and her partner compute 94% agreement. (Chapter 12 explains the process for computing inter-rater reliability.) The high percentage indicates that these two observers are likely to produce similar results in different situations. If inter-rater reliability were low, Molly would reevaluate the instrument to clarify categories or definitions or to provide the observers with additional training.

Interpreting the Data   Al agrees to observe and collect participation tallies in Molly's preschool classroom for 5 days, recording each day during circle time (10:00–10:20 A.M.). The results have been compiled onto one form (Figure 10.4) for manageable analysis.

Tally Event Sampling
of Preschoolers' Participation in
Selected Circle Time Activities

Center/Age level: University Heights Children's Center/4-year-olds

Date: 1/10 to 1/14   Time: About 10.00–10:20 A.M.

Observer: Al   Teacher: Molly

                                         Children: Twelve—7 boys and 5 girls

Event: Circle time participation—the child joins in teacher-planned group activities in a productive or counterproductive manner.

Codes: C = calendar activities, D = discussions, F = fingerplays or action activities not sung, G = games, Sh = sharing, So = songs with or without actions, St/P = stories or poetry read from books, presented on flannel boards, or told by an adult.

                 p = productive participation, cp = counterproductive participation.

Instructions: Mark one tally mark in the appropriate box each time a child joins in during one of the specified circle activities. Record the tally within each category under productive (p) or counterproductive (cp) participation.

Circle Activity / Child	C		D		F		G		Sh		So		St/P	
	p	cp	p	cp	p	cp	p	cp	p	cp	p	cp	p	cp
Roman		/	/		///		/		/	/	///			
Hasana	/		/		///		//			/	///		///	/
Bailey		///	//				/	/	///			//		///
Mora		/			//		//	/			///	/		/
Davey	/	///	//				/	/		/	///	/		/

Figure 10.4.   Tally event sampling preschool example: Circle participation (data).

Circle Activity / Child	C p	C cp	D p	D cp	F p	F cp	G p	G cp	Sh p	Sh cp	So p	So cp	St/P p	St/P cp
Vito		/			///	/	/		/		/	/		/
Dusty	/				///	/	/				///			///
Luella		//		/	///	/	/				/	/		///
Yong	/				///	/	/				///			//
Zane	/			/	///	/					///		/	/
Caren			/	/	//		/		/		///		/	/
Martha Sue					//		/				/		/	
	5	11	3	7	27	5	13	3	3	6	27	6	6	17

Comments:

Bailey and Davey never get to circle time until after the opening fingerplay because they slowly pick-up and, in the process, play with the blocks.

One child shares per day on M/W/F.

One designated helper does calendar each day.

Songs are sung on M/W/F, fingerplays on M/W/Th.

Stories are read on T/W/Th/F, flannelboard on M.

One auditory discrimination game is played on Monday; one movement game is played on Tuesday.

One play yard problem is discussed on Tuesday.

Figure 10.4.   (*Continued*).

As Molly studies the results that Al gives her on Friday (Figure 10.4), she quickly sees some concerns. Molly, however, has studied observation and knows the importance of patiently computing the results so that detailed conclusions can be drawn from the quantitative data.

Adding down the column tallies shows the amount of productive and counterproductive participation in each circle activity for the week of observation. For example, there were 5 productive participations and 11 counterproductive participations during calendar activities. Adding across the rows shows the number of times each child participates in circle activities. For example, Roman had 11 tallies: 9 were productive and 2 counterproductive.

When Molly adds all the counterproductive columns, the data reveal that 40% (55 of the total 139) of the participation is counterproductive. Molly knows that is high! She studies totals of each row and column, computing each child's balance of productive and counterproductive circle time participation, as well as productive and counterproductive participation during each specific activity. Then she surveys the results and forms the following initial conclusions:

1. There is more counterproductive than productive participation during calendar activities, discussion, sharing, and stories. Stories that take place at the end of the circle time had the most counterproductive participation. There are two activities out of the seven that only one child per day can participate in—calendar and sharing.

2. There is more productive than counterproductive participation during finger-plays, games, and songs—the activities that involve all the children.

3. The average number of times a child participated (either productively or counterproductively) over the week is 11 times. All children except one counterproductively participated at least once; the most counterproductive participation by one child is 14, the average is 4.

As planned, Molly takes her tallied instrument and initial conclusions to Camisha's office to discuss the results. Camisha greets her in the doorway and apologetically tells her that she's unavailable for about 3 days because of state reports but suggests that in the meantime Molly visit the college's lab school to observe a model circle time. Camisha adds that she would be glad to provide a substitute for 1 day. Molly is delighted and knows that this will give her the opportunity to use her instrument to gather further information for follow-through plans.

Follow-Through Plans   When Molly meets with Camisha, she enthusiastically shares her tallied data (Figure 10.4), initial conclusions, and the following insights from her observational visit to the lab school.

• Buck, the teacher of the 4-year-old group at the lab school, had two 10-minute circle times: one just before and one after outdoor time. Each began with action songs. Molly observed only 2% counterproductive participation.

• With the children sitting on the perimeter of a circle, the first circle time engaged all children in a unique sharing experience. The child whose name had been drawn the day before had taken home the class mascot (a stuffed animal) and dictated a story to one of his or her parents about the mascot's adventures. With the teacher's help the child "read/told" the story and the children seemed interested to hear every word about the mascot's evening; they asked questions and made comments. Then another child whose name had also been drawn the day before shared the surprise box. In this share activity, the child takes home a small box fitted with a handle and an old-fashioned library card pocket on the outside. The child chooses one object to put in the box to share at school and with the help of the parent writes three clues, each progressively easier, and puts them in the library pocket. For instance, if the object is a pencil, the three clues might be: 1) it's hard and soft, 2) it comes in all colors, and 3) you can write with it. When this child shares, he or she reads (with the teacher's help) one clue at a time and the attentive children try to guess what is in the surprise box.

- The second circle time was arranged to help the children transition from outdoors to indoors, as well as to develop language and social skills. Buck divided this circle time into two smaller groups using the teacher assistant to lead one of the groups; the children participated in various combinations of singing songs or participating in fingerplays, games, story time, or discussions.

- Buck told Molly that shortening the duration; preparing ahead of time and having all the needed materials gathered; varying the activities; personalizing and modifying the songs, games, and activities; giving the children props to use whenever possible; choosing activities based on the children's interests and need for active involvement; and asking the child(ren) who had counterproductive behaviors to help plan circle time helped him have productive circle times.

- Molly also noticed that Buck's wall calendar had the name of the helper-of-the-day printed on each square. Buck told Molly that he eliminated the traditional calendar activity during circle time because he had observed too many counterproductive behaviors while children were asked to sit and wait for this abstract experience.

Camisha smiles as she listens to Molly's insights and acknowledges that Molly has paired two important steps. First, she found out what the participation looked like in her room and analyzed what was and wasn't working. Then she took the opportunity to learn new ideas. Molly thanks Camisha for sending her to see Buck's successful circle times. She says that she has gotten so many worthwhile suggestions, and she would like to try out many of them. The children in Buck's class were developing the sense of togetherness that Molly hoped her group will develop from productive circle participation.

Molly and Camisha both agree that small changes are most effective for the children and the teacher. Camisha proposes that Molly begin her circle changes by decreasing the time to 10 minutes and planning some activities that include involving the children in movement. Molly agrees and adds that she thought she would enlist the help of Bailey, the child with the most counterproductive participation, to choose the games and/or book. Molly decides to have the circle time when the children come in from outside—offering a movement activity followed by a short story, flannelboard, or game. Camisha and Molly agree to meet again in 2 weeks to review the circle participation. Molly plans to eventually have two circles times as Buck modeled. Her 4-year-olds could benefit from more group activities.

As Molly walks back to her classroom, she feels empowered by Camisha. Right from the start, Camisha had let her disclose her area of concern and suggested she gather the data and visit another school for modeling. Camisha had put Molly in charge of her own learning, and now Molly is on her way to facilitating productive and successful circle times.

Primary Grade Example

Consider Our Ethical Responsibilities to Co-Workers

NAEYC Ideal I-3A.1

"To establish and maintain relationships of trust and cooperation with co-workers" (Feeney & Kipnis, 1992, p. 8).

Read on to see how the teachers at Fitzgerald School fulfill this ethical responsibility.

Lee, the principal of Fitzgerald School (grades K–3), provides dynamic leadership through effective use of staff meetings. In today's meeting, Lee uses an article from *Educational Leadership* entitled, "Shortchanging Girls and Boys" (Bailey, 1996) as a springboard for discussion. After many opinions regarding the article have been shared, the principal shows some prerecorded videotape clips of teachers in the classroom. Lee directs the teachers to look at whom the video teachers call on when questions are asked. He points out that even though teachers intend to be unbiased and perceive themselves to be unbiased when choosing either a girl or a boy to call on, gender fairness is an area that needs constant review. The teachers begin to wonder if unintended preferences can creep into their goal to choose children equitably.

Much discussion is generated by the teachers about their own personal experiences with gender fairness in their classrooms. One teacher, Dakota, suspects that the subject being taught may produce unconscious biases (e.g., subscribing to stereotypes of boys being better and more interested in math than girls). She suggests that a classroom study could help raise consciousness. Another teacher, Giancarlo, thinks that teachers may call on boys more often than girls as a way to manage the class; in his experiences, boys have often been the eager hand wavers. He is interested in finding out whether girls raise their hands as often as boys and if teachers call on children of one gender more often than those of the other.

Do teachers call on boys more than girls?

Practice Activity 10.2
Construction of a Tally Event Sampling Instrument

In this activity you will have the opportunity to apply your understanding of tally event sampling. Your task will be to design an effective grid to collect the requested information for the Fitzgerald School teachers.

Let's return to the teachers' meeting for more details. The team of teachers decides to gather data to analyze the gender distribution of student responses to teachers' questions in their school. (The principal is enlisted to collect the data on the instrument designed by the teachers. He will use the observation windows so that the teachers will not be aware the day they are being observed.) The teachers choose tally event sampling to determine how many times girls and boys raise their hands in response to teachers' questions and the relative frequency at which each teacher calls on boys or girls. In order to compare the results, the data will be collected during math time in each classroom over a period of a month, and each teacher will be observed four times.

Having agreed on the event and determining that no event terms need to be defined, the next step is to develop the categories. The following categories are chosen:

Hand raisers: girls/boys
Teacher calls on: girls/boys

Using the categories defined above, construct a grid and fill in the following skeleton form. Give thought to using two levels of horizontal or vertical categories (see Figure 10.3 for the use of subcategories to create a second horizontal level).

Tally Event Sampling of Boy/Girl Hand Raising and Teachers' Responses

School/Grade: Time:

Date: Teachers:

Observer: Children:

(Define the event.)

(Fill in codes and meanings, if any are used.)

Instructions:

(Fill in horizontal categories, and then add vertical lines between categories.)

Teacher 1

Teacher 2

Teacher 3

Teacher 4 and so on listing the primary grade teachers

Interpreting the Data   After the pilot test of the grid and measurement of inter-rater reliability, the data can be collected and examined to further the teachers' understanding of gender fairness in one subject area (math) at their school. The staff will have a precise picture of the gender-related question-and-answer patterns by asking the following types of questions.

- Given the boy/girl ratios, does one gender in an individual classroom account for a disproportionate share of hand raisers?
- What is the relationship between the gender of hand raisers and the gender of those who are chosen?
- Do individual teachers have gender-preference patterns?
- Are there changes that the entire staff wants to work on?
- Are there teachers who seem to be gender equitable and could act as role models for teachers who may want to improve in this area?

Suppose the data from a classroom with an even number of boys and girls show that the teacher called on girls 28 times during math but called on boys 46 times; thus, the girls answered questions 38% of the time and the boys answered questions 62% of the time. The hypothetical data also show that the girls raised their hands 10% less often than the boys did. This staff is astounded and disturbed by these typical results. As a group, they examine individual teacher scores and find that the boy-choice trend is fairly equally distributed throughout all the classrooms. The principal continues his investigation by sampling during other times of the day, using both small and total class groups. Comparing the responses during different curriculum times will provide information about consistency in gender response choices during the entire day. Additional data will help the teachers draw sound conclusions. With a broad understanding the teachers can then develop strategies to foster gender equity throughout the curriculum areas.

The results of this gender inquiry may also lead to additional teaching strategies beyond calling on boys and girls equally; the teachers may consider checking gender access to computers, providing girl and boy models of achievement in every area, balancing female–male language usage, and monitoring children's reactions to others' mistakes. Striving to reduce biases and audit gender equity adds another dimension, or perhaps for some a renewed awareness, to the teacher's role. In this instance the consciousness raising was generated from observations using tally event sampling.

Applications

Strengths and Limitations

The greatest strengths of tally event sampling are efficiency and simplicity. Once the instrument has been constructed, making tally marks takes little teacher time. The form can be kept nearby on a clipboard or condensed to fit on a 5- by 8-inch card and kept in a pocket until complete. Event sampling is time-saving because it allows the observer to continue classroom activities while waiting for the selected event to happen. Tally marks can easily be collected, even in the busiest of classrooms.

The quantitative data collected through tally event sampling can be compared and analyzed quickly and impartially. The preschool circle participation example afforded a beginning experience.

> Quantitative analysis involves converting information to numbers—the number of times a person spoke in a group, the number of correct responses to specific questions, or the number of words in a composition. (Brause & Mayher, 1991, p. 136)

Chapters 11 and 12 discuss quantitative analysis further.

Quantitative data allow the observer to compare changes over time when the systematic observation follows the process of initial observation, intervention strategies, and follow-up observation. When this process is used another advantage emerges—confirmation of effective teaching strategies (Hintze & Shapiro, 1995).

The versatility of this approach provides for observations of one teacher or child, but more often for groups of teachers, children, or their interactions. Tally event sampling can be used with a wide variety of moderate or infrequently occurring topics. Think back through this chapter's examples; this method can be used by teachers for individual classrooms or by entire staffs for identified events schoolwide. Using event sampling to improve teacher effectiveness or the school environment is a potent way to build teamwork.

The major limitation of tally event sampling is that recording frequencies generally takes the behavior out of context. The tally approach method does not record what takes place before or after the event. The cause of and conditions surrounding the event are not identified in tally event sampling. Its function is limited to recording how often an identified event occurs.

Action Project 10.1
Preschool/Kindergarten Tally Event Sampling: Motor Development

Many educators believe that children will develop gross motor skills on their own if the equipment is available (although it is usually available only outdoors). According to Miller's study of preschool children's motor development (as cited in Poest, Williams, Witt, & Atwood, 1990), however, "children allowed to play in well-equipped motor play areas scored significantly below normal in motor development compared to those provided with planned motor activity centers and guided movement experiences" (p. 4).

Suppose the teachers at Center X observe that children often use the climbing structures for dramatic play and the tire swing (with little motion) for socializing. As a preliminary step before designing a planned motor development program, the teachers need a detailed understanding of how the children are using the outside equipment so that the motor development program can be planned according to the children's needs. The teachers' task, then, is to determine how often the children in the center use the outside equipment for motor development or for other specified purposes unrelated to motor skills. The data collection will require specific information regarding what other uses the children have for the equipment. For this action project you are invited to construct a tally event sampling grid on which these teachers may record the requested information.

Points to Remember

Observers appropriately select the tally event sampling observational method when they want to determine how frequently an identified event occurs. This simple and orderly technique allows the observer not only to look at individuals (a child or a teacher) but also to move into another observational arena—observing groups (children, teachers, and interactions).

Tally event sampling data is collected with instruments that are either pre-designed or created by teachers to respond to their immediate concerns and questions. The chapter has enumerated the steps for devising appropriate instruments.

The quantitative data from the tally observations can easily be analyzed and appropriately used to examine chosen behaviors, classroom strategies, curricula, or environments.

Take a Moment to Reflect

After Sophie's (5;2) first few days in kindergarten, she was unhappy to go to school because she was teased by two boys that her father called "bullies." When Sophie's mother picked her up from school on the fourth day and Sophie was in tears, her mom knew Sophie needed help in learning how to handle this difficult situation. After arriving home, her mom said, "Sophie when those boys bother you again, you just walk up to them and yell NO right in their faces!" Then Sophie's mom role-played with her until Sophie felt confident in her new skill. When Sophie's mom picked her up from school the next day, Sophie beamed from ear to ear and reported, "Mom, it really worked. When I yelled NO, those boys took off running."

Sophie is fortunate to have a mom who understands how to support and empower children. This parenting scenario may be an extraordinary case, but not an isolated one. Children often experience empowerment in school; teachers are alert to such opportunities moment by moment. Think about empowerment in your life and reflect on the following questions.

1. Recall a childhood incident in which you felt empowered or wished you had felt empowered to stand up for yourself. What was the situation, the empowerment, and the skill learned in the situation you recalled?
2. Is this situation an example of a topic that could be used for a tally event sampling in an early childhood classroom? If so, sketch the grid.

CHAPTER 11

Observing Children and Teachers at Work by Using Time Sampling

Aimee, a student teacher in early childhood education, would like to observe what teachers do and say in the classroom. Her initial items include:

Teacher Verbalizations	Teacher Behaviors
Provides new information	Prepares materials
Gives directions	Adds materials
Comments	Models new ideas
Asks questions	Presents materials
Praises	Observes children
Encourages	Instructs by direct
Greets	method
Criticizes	Cleans up/picks up
Talks with other adults	Unoccupied

What problems might be encountered if Aimee uses tally event sampling to observe teacher verbalizations and behaviors in a busy classroom?

No doubt you can imagine Aimee's weary hand and frazzled mind as she tries to observe all the preceding categories simultaneously; tally event sampling is not a practical means of studying events that occur rapidly. Fortunately, there is a more feasible observational method to apply in this case, one "that appears to be indigenous to research in child development" (Wright, 1960, p. 93).

Overview of Observing Using Time Sampling

Description

The unique component of time sampling is the use of predetermined units of time (time samples) to guide the observer's attention throughout the observational period. The observer records "whether or not specified behaviors are observed during predetermined and fixed time periods such as every thirty seconds or every minute" (Bochm, 1992, p. 287). The time sampling observational method thus provides "data relative to the frequency of occurrence of behaviors of concern over time" (p. 288).

There are two major methods to specify the time sampling units. In the first, a single time unit stipulates how long the observer observes and records before moving on to the next object of concentration. For example, an observer might listen to and code one teacher's verbalizations for 30 seconds before moving on to the next teacher. In the second method of specifying time sampling units, there are two separate time units: the first to stipulate the observational period and the second to stipulate the coding time. Using this format, an observer might watch one child for 20 seconds to study social play and then use 10 seconds to code the behavior(s); the observer, following this system for all children in the classroom, rotates observations in a prearranged order.

To answer the observational question (e.g., What do teachers do and say in the classroom?), the time sampling observational method depends on an easy-to-use recording grid (introduced in Chapter 10) to collect information in clear sets of defined categories. Categories primarily list behaviors (e.g., teacher verbalizations, children's social play), but categories listing characteristics (e.g., age, gender, curriculum area) may also add useful information. Because the time sampling format allows the observer to systematically shift attention from individual to individual, the observer usually focuses on more than one child or teacher.

Time sampling typically yields quantitative data about the group as a whole and about individuals. Thus while observers may compile information about a group of children in general (e.g., the incidence of types of play in a preschool classroom), they may also learn specific information about individuals (e.g., the predominance of individuals' play types). Furthermore, through the examination of children's and teachers' behaviors, observers may also evaluate the effectiveness of the program and environment.

Purpose

Time sampling observations are used for the methodical investigation of behaviors that occur in rapid succession (e.g., teacher verbalizations). The procedures of time sampling help observers collect representative data. They may then draw conclusions from the time samplings and use these conclusions to learn more about children and to refine their teaching strategies, the program, or the environment. Time sampling can be a systematic and efficient observational method.

Guidelines for Constructing Time Sampling Instruments

The thoughtful construction of time sampling instruments can produce the means to study rapidly occurring behaviors. The steps discussed in this section are summarized in Box 11.1.

The selection of an appropriate topic to study is the first step in using time sampling. The topic should focus on overt behaviors that occur rapidly. For example, the types of children's play are *overt behaviors* because the observer can

---

Box 11.1
Designing a Time Sampling Instrument

1. Select an appropriate topic, formulate an observational question, and define the event.
2. Research the topic in libraries and classrooms.
3. Identify clear, distinct categories.
   - Generate sets of categories, vertical and horizontal.
   - Define the categories when necessary.
   - Select a sign or category system.
   - Decide if category codes are needed.
4. Design a recording form.
   - Use the traditional heading.
   - Use the categories to construct a grid.
   - Specify the time sampling units.
   - Plan to collect the data in the form of tallies or durations.
   - Label a space for comments at the bottom of the form.
5. Pilot test the instrument. Revise, if necessary, and pilot test again.
6. Establish inter-rater reliability.

---

easily see if children are playing alone or with others and, with a bit more attention, if they are merely playing next to one another or truly engaging in cooperative play. The causes of children's derogatory comments about other children on the playground are usually not apparent to an observer and are therefore inappropriate for time sampling (and other observational methods). Utilizing the time sampling method, observers may study such diverse topics as gross motor activity during recess, child–child interactions, and teacher responses to children.

Time sampling is appropriate for observing behaviors that occur too frequently for the tally event sampling method to be effectively implemented. For example, teachers may verbalize so frequently that only time sampling methods can manage such an incessant flow of data. If, however, an observer wants to learn more about teachers' introductions of new materials into the classroom, time sampling would waste a good deal of the observer's time. This behavior occurs infrequently enough that the topic would be better handled by tally event sampling. Now take a few moments to generate a short list of topics appropriate for the time sampling observational method.

Practice Activity 11.1 _____
Appropriate Topics for the Time Sampling Observational Method

List three topics that can best be studied through the time sampling observational method. Remember that the behaviors to be observed must be overt and occur rapidly. You may include topics focusing on children and/or teachers.

Examples:

- Child–child verbalizations
- Types of interactions among children in an inclusive classroom
- Primary grade teachers' verbalizations during math time

1.

2.

3.

_____

After choosing time sampling for the topic at hand, the observer formulates an observational question. A clear question specifies a manageable portion of the topic to observe. For example, a teacher committed to an anti-bias curriculum may ask, "What types of play do children engage in with culturally diverse materials during free-choice time?"

Library research time, classroom observation, and the application of previous experience help the constructor of a time sampling instrument to investigate the topic and identify the precise categories to be observed. The categories of behaviors or characteristics should be mutually exclusive, but they may represent either a sign or category system (see Chapter 10), whichever provides the most appropriate information. Once selected, the behaviors should be clearly defined so that any user of the instrument interprets them in the same way. Parten's (1932) clear definition of parallel play from a classic time sampling study provides a fine example:

> *Parallel activity*—The child plays independently, but the activity he chooses naturally brings him among other children. He plays with toys that are like those which the children around him are using, but he plays with the toy as he sees fit, and does not try to influence or modify the activity of the children near him. He plays *beside* rather than *with* the other children. There is no attempt to control the coming or going of children in the group. (p. 250)

If category definitions are lengthy, they are usually printed on a separate sheet or on the back of the recording form so as not to take up valuable space. Definitions are reviewed before the observation so that once in the classroom the observer will need to refer to them only for occasional reminders or clarifications. The observer decides to use and memorize codes for the categories to be observed if the labels are long or cumbersome and would take up needed space on the recording form.

Working with well-defined categories, the observer is ready to design a recording form; see Figure 11.1 for the format and an example. Space is provided at the top for the traditional heading. Then one set of categories is listed horizontally near the top of the grid (e.g., teachers), and the other set of categories is listed vertically down the left side of the page where there is more room (e.g., types of verbalizations). Lines are drawn horizontally and vertically to mark off the two sets of categories, and a grid is completed as in Chapter 10. In many studies observers employ more than two sets of categories, so additional organization and detailing may be necessary.

The most difficult task in constructing a time sampling instrument is specifying the time sampling units. To create a feasible observational schedule that produces the requisite information, the observer must do some pilot testing. Previous experience and best guesses may help, but the greatest aid will be trying out the time sampling schedule under real conditions. As described earlier, one method allows the observer to observe and record within a single time unit without overlooking data; the example in Figure 11.1 specifies 60-second observing/recording time sampling units. When a time sampling instrument contains numerous categories, however, separate time units to observe and code reduce the risk of missing behaviors while recording (Figures 11.2 and 11.3). For example, the pilot testing of a detailed instrument might provide the feedback that 30 seconds of recording time are needed after the 20 seconds of observation. There is no substitute for this hands-on experience.

The observer considers the type of time sampling data that will best answer the observational question. Theoretically, time sampling forms that generate checks or tallies or that record the duration of the observed behaviors may be constructed (Medley & Mitzel, 1963). In practice, however, most observers reject the checks option because they want to learn more about the behaviors under study than simply if they are present; if not, then a checklist is a more straightforward method of choice. Simple checks on a time sampling form yield a minimum of information, so this method is best discarded in favor of the richer yields of tallies and durations.

If the observer is interested in the frequency of behaviors, recording tallies is appropriate. For example, a teacher might be interested in how often culturally diverse materials are used in exploratory versus representational play; tallies would specify the frequencies for easy comparison. As an alternative, the observer may choose to monitor the durations of each observed behavior with a stopwatch to answer questions about the proportionate time of the behaviors (e.g., time of teacher talk versus student talk in a third grade classroom). Instructions may also be given to combine tally- and duration-recording as in Figure 11.2.

Once the observational and coding time units are in place, a judgment needs to be made about how long to observe and during which parts of the day. If a study focuses on teachers' behaviors, the observer will sample their behaviors during all parts of the day and an abundance of data may be collected within a week. Note, however, that the high mental concentration necessary for observation may urge the observer to visit the classroom at various times over the course of several weeks rather than a whole day per visit; the goal may be to observe each time period (free

Time Sampling of Teachers' Verbalizations

Center or School/Age level or Grade:

Date: Time:

Observer: Teacher:

                                               Children:

Event: Teacher verbalizations

Instructions: Observe each teacher for 60 seconds, and mark a tally for each
                verbalization demonstrated. Rotate 60-second observational
                and coding time units from teacher to teacher throughout
                observational period.

Teacher / Verbalization	Teacher	Teacher Assistant	Student Teacher
Provides new information			
Gives directions			
Comments			
Asks questions			
Praises			
Encourages			
Greets			
Criticizes			
Talks with other adults			
Other			

Figure 11.1. Time sampling recording form.

play, snack, outside time, etc.) three times. If, on the other hand, a primary grade teacher's math instruction techniques are examined, the observer would collect data only during math time but on several different occasions.

The instrument is now ready for pilot testing so that any weaknesses may be identified. After adjustments are complete and the pilot test is successful, the observer establishes inter-rater reliability (detailed in Chapter 12) in preparation for data collection in a real classroom.

Integration of Classroom Situations and Observation

Consider Our Ethical Responsibilities to Colleagues

NAEYC Ideal I-3A.3

"To support co-workers in meeting their professional needs and in their professional development" (Feeney & Kipnis, 1992, p. 8).

Read on to see how Kemlyn fulfills this ethical responsibility.

Preschool Example

Blocks and preschool go together like apple blossoms and spring, and of course, there are good reasons why blocks are a staple of early childhood centers (Hirsch, 1996). The mere presence of blocks in a classroom, however, does not guarantee that children use them and learn from them. Teachers are responsible for organizing blocks and making them accessible to children, providing additional interesting materials to use with blocks, and extending children's work with blocks. Blocks offer endless learning potentials, but skilled teachers are necessary to fulfill them.

A child care director attended a directors' workshop on designing observational instruments and worked in a small group on an instrument to observe specific ways teachers interact with children in the block area. The directors sketched out a time sampling instrument (Figure 11.2) to observe systematically the staff's teaching strategies in the block area, pilot tested the instrument in one of the host's classrooms, and then established inter-rater reliability. Why did the directors select time sampling as an observational method? You now know the answer; think about the frequency and types of behaviors to observe, and you will be on your way.

The directors decided to use a sign rather than a category system when selecting teacher behaviors to observe in the block area because they were not interested

Blocks offer children a wealth of learning experiences in the early childhood classroom.

in tallying every possible behavior they might see. Rather, the directors were motivated to record those behaviors that support and extend children's block activities.
They planned to rotate systematically their observations from one teacher to the
next, mark a tally for each target behavior they saw during a 30-second observational time unit, and provide a 30-second recording time unit to code observations
and move to the next teacher. Pilot testing and the inter-rater reliability check
proved this system to be productive.

To collect some information about the duration of time teachers spend in and
out of the block area, the directors elected to circle the tally marks in the "not present in the block area" category when the teacher was not in the block area for all
of the observational time unit. Thus, a circled tally mark would indicate that the
teacher was not present in the block area for all 30 seconds of a time unit. A simple
tally would indicate that the teacher was not present in the block area for part of a
30-second observational time unit.

Now that she has returned, the director tells her child care teachers and assistants that she wants to observe during free-choice time to collect information for
future staff discussions. She uses the same instrument to collect data during free-
choice periods in each classroom on three different days; Figure 11.2 presents the
results from the 4-year-olds' room.

Interpreting the Data   The director, Kemlyn, observes 1 hour of free-choice time for
3 days using the observational form in Figure 11.2. During each day, she rotates her
observations from teacher to teacher, observing for 30 seconds, then coding for 30
seconds. Thus, in 60 total minutes of daily observation, she concentrates her attention on each of the three teachers for 20 minutes; of those 20 minutes, she observes
for 10 minutes and codes for 10 minutes. Consequently, over the course of 3 days,
she collects 30 minutes of data on each teacher.

Kemlyn is stunned to discover how infrequently children had the pleasure of a
teacher's company in the well-used block area. During her 90 minutes of observation (30 minutes per teacher), she made circled tallies for 61 minutes. She is particularly dissatisfied with her observations of Evelyn, the head teacher, who was not
present in the block area for 26 minutes. Perhaps her teaching skills in the block
area are so severely limited that she tends to avoid this area. It is also possible that
as a head teacher she focuses on the children as a class rather than as individuals
with unique strengths and interests. Whatever the reasons, Kemlyn realizes that the
head teacher in the 4-year-olds' classroom is not modeling effective teaching strategies in the block area.

On the other hand, Kemlyn was delighted to see Dante frequently down on the
carpet building with the children. For example, on one day he was involved in planning and constructing an elaborate cityscape with two boys. He was generous with
his encouragement and asked two open questions ("What are you going to build
next?" and "Where should I build my trade center?"). Dante wrapped a block in aluminum foil to simulate reflective building materials, thus modeling a new idea, and
offered the roll of foil to the boys with the restriction that they could use it for only
one building. The time sampling observations led Kemlyn to conclude that Dante

Time Sampling of Teaching Strategies in the Block Area

Center/Age level: Mesa Office Park Child Care/4-Year-Olds

Dates: 11/18 to 11/20   Time: 9:30–10:30 A.M.

Observer: Kemlyn   Free choice (7 centers available)

                                               Teachers: Evelyn, Dante, Mari

                                               Children: Twenty 4-year-olds

Event: Teaching strategies in the block area—teacher behaviors that support and extend children's block activities.

Instructions: Observe one teacher for 30 seconds and code for 30 seconds; rotate observations of teachers, and repeat throughout free-choice time. Mark a tally for each behavior observed in the block area. Circle tally mark when teacher is "not present in block area" for an entire 30-second observational period.

Behavior \ Teacher	Evelyn	Dante	Mari
Builds with child		𝑁𝑁 𝑁𝑁 𝑁𝑁 𝑁𝑁 𝑁𝑁 //// 29	
Offers materials		// 2	𝑁𝑁 / 6
Encourages	// 2	𝑁𝑁 𝑁𝑁 𝑁𝑁 / 16	𝑁𝑁 𝑁𝑁 𝑁𝑁 𝑁𝑁 // 22
Asks open questions	/ 1	𝑁𝑁 /// 8	𝑁𝑁 𝑁𝑁 𝑁𝑁 // 17
Models new ideas		/ 1	
Observes	// 2		

Figure 11.2. Time sampling preschool example: Block area teaching strategies.

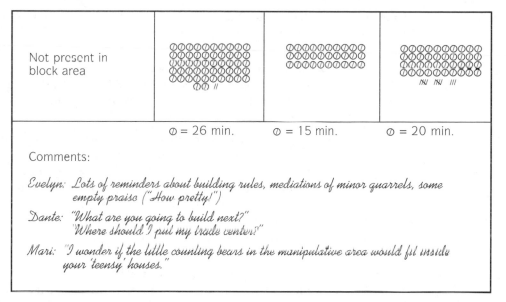

Figure 11.2.   (*Continued*).

enjoys playing with the children but that his methods of extending children's activities in the block area are minimal (he extended his own very well!). Kemlyn wants Dante to be able to step back from his involvement, observe the building in progress, and think about how he can best support the children's ideas. At present, the children are only following his lead.

Mari floated in and out of the block area during all three of Kemlyn's visits. Although she never stopped to build with a child or take a few moments for observation, she did ask open questions to inquire about what the children were doing, encourage their constructions, and offer additional materials (e.g., "I wonder if the little counting teddy bears in the manipulative area would fit inside your 'teensy' houses"). Mari seems to support children in their activities, and Kemlyn hopes that her teaching skills will blossom with information and guidance.

Kemlyn is glad she included the "not present in block area" category; her idea of circling tally marks to specify 30-second periods not in the block area allows her to document the durations of teachers' absences from the area. In the "Comments" section, she recorded verbatim quotes and other specifics she wanted to recall. For example, she noted that most of Evelyn's attention was on reminding children of the rules (e.g., height limits on building), mediating minor disputes about materials, and giving evaluative praise.

Follow-Through Plans   The data from the 4-year-olds' classroom are fairly typical of the data Kemlyn collected in the other classrooms. Kemlyn speculates that there are two major factors behind teachers' inability to work effectively in the block areas at Mesa Children's Center:

1. *Teachers do not have the requisite knowledge to identify children's growth in the block area.* They do not know how building skills progress and what children might learn in the block area. Further, the teachers do not know how to interact with children in order to promote this growth.

2. *Teachers lack observational skills.* Sound observational skills should enable teachers to assess individual children's building interests and skills and then aid the formation of supportive strategies. In her center, however, Kemlyn observes that there are no systematic approaches to collecting information about children's growth in the block area. Kemlyn is pleased to observe all of the classrooms functioning rather smoothly. The lack of teacher time in the block area is not due to pressing management or supervisory concerns elsewhere.

Kemlyn decides to tackle the two parts of the block area problem through her biweekly staff meetings and continued education. She calls a friend on the Board of the county chapter of the National Association for the Education of Young Children to ask for a speaker recommendation. She requests a person who is knowledgeable about stages of block building and learning opportunities in the block area and who will be able to guide teachers in planning supportive teaching strategies. This meeting will provide much needed information for the teachers. Two weeks later, Kemlyn will follow up with a workshop on anecdotal record keeping to begin the observational process. She makes plans to videotape children working in the block area in each classroom; clips will provide the basis for integrating the speaker's information about block building into the classrooms and for practicing anecdotal records. Finally, Kemlyn contacts the early childhood education department at the local college for course information and begins to consider how best to encourage her staff to continue professional training. Kemlyn enthusiastically anticipates collecting "new and improved" data on her time sampling instrument in 2 or 3 months.

Practice Activity 11.2
Block Area Teaching Strategies in a Kindergarten, First-Grade, or Second-Grade Classroom

Pilot test a copy of the time sampling instrument on block area teaching strategies in a kindergarten, first-grade, or second-grade classroom. Write down any modifications you would make. Remember that blocks are not the exclusive domain of children under age 5; their qualities extend far beyond.

Primary Grade Example

A second-grade teacher, Jorge, was intrigued by his summer reading, *The Art of Teaching Writing* (Calkins, 1994), which sent his mind spinning with questions and ideas. He found the book well-stocked with thought-provoking commentary on the nourishment of children's writing, research and experience to back up the author's conclusions, and marvelous anecdotes selected from a wide diversity of children. Jorge found validation in his zeal to read to his students on a daily basis because Calkins, too, believed that touching children with fabulous literature is a critical key to their own writing futures.

> When our children pull close around a shared text, when we read until our eyes shine with tears and we are silenced in the presence of the deepest parts of our lives, it shakes the ground that we and our students stand on as writers and as people. (p. 252)

Jorge also gained encouragement to set aside predictable and generous time for his class to write three afternoons a week: Tuesdays, Wednesdays, and Fridays. Finally, Jorge welcomed Calkins' understanding of the mix of writing levels within his single classroom; she is familiar with the real world.

> Many second graders can just barely read their names; others are devouring the entire works of Roald Dahl and Patricia MacLachlan. Some write only captions underneath drawings; others write long chapter books and research reports. Some children write with big, wobbly letters; others write with tiny, neat rows of cursive. (p. 109)

Once school is underway in September, Jorge wants to satisfy his curiosity about the types of feedback he gives to his second graders as the first step to expanding his skills as a writing teacher. He formulates the observational question, "What types of input do I give to children during the writing process?" Jorge begins to work on an observational instrument to evaluate his responses to students' writing.

First Jorge considers possible behaviors to observe during writing periods. Drawing both on his reading and experience, he categorizes the "teacher's strategies" as follows:

Teacher's Strategy

- *Listens*—Teacher listens attentively to a child to help the child become a more critical reader of her or his own writing. *Example:* "Mr. Mendoza, listen to the end of my story: 'Aren't you glad an ankylosaurus won't bother your plants?'"

- *Encourages or praises descriptively*—Teacher is descriptive in his or her encouragement or praise so that the child understands the value of the writing. *Example:* "Your question at the end of your story gives the reader a connection to you. As your reader, I felt as if you were talking just to me."

- *Gives information*—Teacher builds on a child's piece to help the child learn more about writing. *Example:* "I can see you had your reader in mind when you asked this question at the end of your story. Question-asking really gives the reader something to think about. A question can grab the reader's attention."

- *Asks question*—Teacher asks a child a question. *Example:* "What have you said so far in your piece?"

- *Answers question*—Teacher answers a child's question. *Example:* "Yes, it's fine to end a story with a question."

- *Suggests*—Teacher suggests a change or addition to the child's writing. *Example:* "Sometimes authors end their piece with a question to give the reader something to think about. Why don't you try it?"

- *Gives opinionated approval without substance*—Teacher praises a child's writing while focusing on its worth, not its substance. *Example:* "What a neat idea!"

- *Directs*—Teacher directs a change or addition to the child's writing. *Example:* "This question at the end doesn't have much to do with your story. Either take it out or show more of a connection."

- *Corrects*—Teacher corrects a child's writing. *Example:* "This question at the end of your story needs a question mark."

- *Criticizes*—Teacher criticizes a child's writing. *Example:* "Oh my, you forgot something at the very end of your story."

Jorge's reading also encourages him to specify the categories of writing components on which a teacher might focus. A teacher's input might center around the content of the writing, the design of the piece, the writing process, self-evaluation, or editing (Calkins, 1994). Jorge wants his observational instrument to reflect these "focuses of teacher's attention" so he can evaluate his priorities. Thus he generates a second set of categories and defines them as follows:

Focuses of Teacher's Attention
- *Content*—Teacher focuses on the subject matter of the child's writing. *Example:* "Your description of the frog on the ferris wheel makes me laugh!"

- *Design*—Teacher focuses on how the child has organized and shaped the piece (e.g., chronologically, thematically, snapshots), what the child emphasizes, and the pace of the piece. *Example:* "You told me so much about your dog by writing lots of little stories about her."

- *Writing process*—Teacher focuses on the child's strategies for writing. *Example:* "You planned to work on some different beginnings for your story. Tell me how that worked out."

- *Self-evaluation*—Teacher focuses on furthering child's assessment of his or her own writing. *Example:* "Let's look at the first and last drafts of your story. How do you think they are different?"

- *Editing*—Teacher focuses on the child's use of paragraphs, sentence structure, word choice, grammar, punctuation, or spelling. *Example:* "Listen to the suspenscful first sentence of your story: 'My most vived memore of my childhood was when I saw the misterys Zorf here is where my story begins.' I needed to pause and take a breath after 'Zorf.' A period there will show your reader where the next sentence begins."

Next, Jorge begins to think about how to put his observational instrument together. Knowing that teachers may speak continuously for short periods of time and realizing that an observer cannot record or remember every statement, Jorge decides to construct a time sampling instrument to deal with these rapidly occurring behaviors. He specifies the time sampling units as 20 seconds for observation and 30 seconds for coding. The 20 seconds for observation will provide time to observe the content of the teacher's comments, and the 30 seconds for coding will allow time for accurate coding and movement around the classroom when there is difficulty in hearing.

To obtain a comprehensive view of the writing instruction methods in place within his classroom, Jorge plans to collect data during four writing lessons on different days. He designates the use of tallies on the recording sheet to document the frequency of each targeted teacher behavior. He rejects checks because he wants to know more than if he just demonstrates a behavior once. He also rejects duration recording because of the impracticality of trying to record the duration of each statement; furthermore, he is confident that the content of his messages to children, not their length, will be the key to his skills.

Jorge constructs the grid shown in Figure 11.3. He puts the smaller set of categories (focuses of teacher's attention) along the top and the more numerous set (teacher input) down the side. Because there are many targeted behaviors, Jorge prints their definitions on an attached sheet for reference. He pilot tests the instrument in a colleague's class when his students are in music and finds it to be satisfactory.

An immediate problem for Jorge is that he will not be able to observe himself. He rejects using a tape recorder because he feels self-conscious on tape. Fortunately, Jorge is resourceful. He contacts the teacher-credentialing program at the area college and enlists the help of a student, Faranak. During a recess, they observe a fourth-grade writing lesson and easily establish inter-rater reliability. Faranak visits Jorge during four writing lessons and collects the data in Figure 11.3. He obviously knows what Faranak is observing because he constructed the instrument and undoubtedly tries to demonstrate his best teaching strategies; this inherent limitation of self-evaluation, however, should not dissuade teachers from the process. Jorge still gains valuable information from the experience.

Interpreting the Data   Together, Jorge and Faranak compile the data from the four observations and total the rows and columns. Jorge is immediately critical of his emphasis on children's editing (42 inputs) rather than on the content of their writing (41), the design of their pieces (3), their writing processes (31), or their self-evaluations of their writing (2). He is also struck by how little he seemed to help

Time Sampling of Teacher's Behaviors During Writing Time

School/Grade: Longfellow Elementary/Second Grade

Dates: 9/17, 9/18, 9/20, 9/24   Time: 1:00–1:40 P.M.

Observer: Faranak   Teacher: Jorge

                                                 Children: 19

Event: Teaching strategies during writing time—behaviors demonstrating type of teacher verbalization and focus of attention.

Instructions: Observe teacher for 20 seconds and code for 30 seconds; repeat throughout writing period. Mark each teacher input with a tally in the appropriate box.

Teacher's Strategy ╲ Focus of Teacher's Attention	Content	Design	Writing Process	Self-Evaluation	Editing	
Listens	///					3
Encourages/ praises descriptively	ⅣⅠ ///	///	ⅣⅠ //		ⅣⅠ ////	27
Gives information	ⅣⅠ ⅣⅠ ///				ⅣⅠ ⅣⅠ ⅣⅠ /	29
Asks question	////		ⅣⅠ ///	//	ⅣⅠ	19
Answers question	ⅣⅠ //					7
Suggests			////			4
Gives opinionated approval without substance	ⅣⅠ /		ⅣⅠ ⅣⅠ		////	20

Figure 11.3.   Time sampling primary grade example: Teaching writing.

Directs			//		~~M~~ ///	10
Corrects						0
Criticizes						0
	41	3	31	2	42	

Comments:

Figure 11.3.   (*Continued*).

The observational method of time sampling can collect data on rapidly occurring behaviors—for example, a teacher's behaviors during a child's writing conference.

children think about the way they wanted to design their pieces or to encourage them to appraise their own writing, and by how rarely he made a suggestion. Surely he has resources to share and can scaffold children's learning about writing. Although he is pleased to see that his encouragement outweighed his opinionated approval without substance statements, he plans to reduce the latter even further. He can just hear himself murmuring, "Oh, good; that's very nice." Such empty praise gives children nothing to hold on to, nothing to help them appreciate the substantive qualities of their writing.

Follow-Through Plans   Jorge's first plan is to have children read their stories to him and to each other in peer conferences. Thus, he will listen to children's stories and hear their underlying messages, hidden in intonation, expression, and hesitation.

Frankly, Jorge needs to learn more about design issues. His students tend to write their stories chronologically, never varying from this pattern. At least Jorge wants to open their eyes to other possibilities: poems, letters, memoirs, and journalistic articles. A child can write about an idea in many different formats; awareness of one's choices is a first step.

Jorge plans to use handy note cards to collect explicit questions to ask and points to make. Jorge looks forward to inviting Faranak to check his progress in several months.

It's your turn! Study the data in Figure 11.3 and plan some specifics in Jorge's quest to improve his teaching of writing. Remember that observational instruments are good only if they increase knowledge about teachers and children and lead the way toward developmental practices.

Practice Activity 11.3
Follow-Through Plans Based on a Time Sampling Instrument

Using the data in Figure 11.3, think about precise ways Jorge can improve his teaching of writing. Record your favorite three follow-through plans in the following space. You may wish to study box, row, or column totals.

Example: Encourage children to read their stories more frequently to Jorge and other children.

1.

2.

3.

Applications

Strengths and Limitations

The time sampling observational method is adaptable to various subjects (e.g., teachers or children, one or more) and can be an efficient and systematic means of observing rapidly occurring behaviors. A large number of observations can be collected in a short period of time with reasonable confidence that the samples are representative. The data collected are quantitative and are therefore useful for computing, studying, and comparing frequencies and percentages (more information in Chapter 12). The observer can remain unobtrusive and limit interference with the natural flow of events.

The limitations of time sampling revolve around the collection of quantitative data within predetermined units of time. The observer records frequencies but not qualities of events; therefore, the behaviors are not observed in context. Researchers further caution that time sampling may overestimate frequencies of behaviors and inaccurately record durations (Mann, Ten Have, Plunkett, & Meisels, 1991). The observer, as always, needs to match the information required with the most appropriate observational method.

Action Project 11.1
Constructing a Time Sampling Form to Observe Stages of Children's Block Play

Study the following summary of stages of block building (Hirsch, 1996):

Stage 1:   Blocks are carried around, not used for construction. This stage applies to the very young child.

Stage 2:   Building begins. Children make mostly rows, either horizontal (on the floor) or vertical (stacking). There is much repetition in this early block building.

Stage 3:   Bridging—two blocks with a space between them, connected by a third block—is used.

Stage 4:   Enclosures—blocks placed in such a way that they enclose a space—are made. Bridging and enclosures are among the earliest technical building problems that children have to solve. They occur soon after a child begins to use blocks regularly.

Stage 5:   With age, children become steadily more facile and imaginative in their block building. They use more blocks and create more elaborate designs, using pattern and balance.

Stage 6:   Naming of structures for dramatic play begins. Before this stage, children also may have named their structures, but the names were not necessarily related to the function of the building.

Stage 7:   Block buildings often reproduce or symbolize actual structures the children know, and there is a strong impulse toward dramatic play around the block structures. (pp. 142–148)*

Construct a time sampling instrument to observe stages of children's block building. The tasks are as follows:

- State your specific observational question, and define the event.
- Decide on labels or codes for each stage.
- Specify the observational and coding time units in your time sampling schedule.
- Elect to use tallies or observe the durations of the behaviors. Consider the advantages and disadvantages of each.
- Determine how long you will observe during which portions of the day and over what period of time.
- Construct a recording instrument; the following will get you started.

Stages of Block Building

Center/Age level:

Date: Time:

Observer: Teacher:

Definitions and Codes:

Event:

Instructions:

Stage / Child	Stage 1	Stage 2	Stage 3	Stage 4	Stage 5	Stage 6	Stage 7
Simon							

---

* From *The Block Book* (pp. 142–148) edited by Elisabeth S. Hirsch, 1996. Washington D.C.: National Association for the Education of Young Children. Copyright © 1984 by the National Association for the Education of Young Children. Adapted by permission.

Stage / Child	Stage 1	Stage 2	Stage 3	Stage 4	Stage 5	Stage 6	Stage 7
Andre							
Mitzi							
And so on							
Comments:							

Arrange to observe a preschool when children can use the block area. Pilot test your instrument, and then answer the following questions:

- Were your definitions and codes clear, or were you unsure of how to code some behaviors?
- How did your specification of observational and coding time units work out?
- Do you need to make some adjustments? If so, describe.

Next, choose the data from two children to discuss. Begin by responding to the following questions:

- What stages of block building did each child demonstrate? Was one stage most descriptive of her or his play?
- If you were each child's teacher, how could you support his or her block play?

Points to Remember

In this chapter the observational method of time sampling was introduced as a means of collecting representative samples of data on rapidly occurring behaviors. Examples demonstrated that time sampling is an appropriate means of investigating teachers' behaviors (e.g., interactions with preschool block builders and primary grade writers), and the preceding action project applied time sampling to the study of children's behaviors (e.g., stages of block building). Through the examination of children, teachers, and their interactions, observers can learn more about children's development, teachers' effectiveness, and the quality of the curriculum and the classroom environment. Time sampling lends itself to a quantitative analysis of data and is therefore best suited to topics in which the observer wants to compare frequencies.

Take a Moment to Reflect

Evelyn, Dante, and Mari are fortunate to have a director who will plan for and support their professional development. Kemlyn's organization of workshops to present information about developmental growth in the block area and anecdotal record keeping will promote learning on the job. Reflect on your own similar experiences.

1. Recall those colleagues or supervisors who have stimulated your professional development. Specifically, what did you learn from them? If you have not had practical work experience, describe one or two teachers who have tangibly contributed to your knowledge bank and personal growth.

2. What relationship do you see between professional development and job burnout?

CHAPTER **12**

Designing Observational Instruments to Use in the Early Childhood Classroom

Students in an observation class are asked to think of a variety of classroom topics that hold personal interest. Recall in the last chapter, for example, that a child care director was concerned about teachers' interactions with children in the block area and that a second-grade teacher wanted to evaluate his strategies of teaching writing. Some students consider topics regarding children's physical, cognitive, psychosocial, and creative development in the classroom. Other students consider topics regarding teachers' strategies, roles, and management approaches. Still other students have questions about the effectiveness of a curriculum or environment. What one topic holds substantial interest for you?

As an active reader of the previous chapters, you have probably raised some of your own questions about children and classroom processes—even without the prompt in the preceding vignette. Because appropriate previously constructed instruments will not always be available, you will need the observational tools and skills to respond to questions and problems that arise for you. This chapter is devoted to the process of designing and using an observational instrument to find answers to specific questions. Box 12.1 lists the critical steps in designing and using observational instruments.

Although the steps in Box 12.1 are presented in a sequential order, observers may need to backtrack several times during the design process. For example, after specifying an observational question and doing some pilot testing, an observer may discover that the question is unclear and requires refinement. Later, after pilot testing the first draft of an instrument, the observer may need to rework some confusing definitions and pilot test again. Such backtracking is a valuable component of the design process; thoughtful observers frequently reevaluate previous work and remain open to productive adjustments.

The steps for designing an observational instrument are described in this chapter, and an instrument to study parent and child separations at child care is constructed as the classroom example to illustrate each step. Most terms are not defined because very little of the information is new. This chapter, rather, serves to synthesize the information presented in previous chapters. The steps may be applied to the design of a checklist, rating scale, tally event sampling instrument, or time sampling instrument, but of course, an observer beginning with an observational question considers the workability of a greater variety of methods (i.e., running records, anecdotal records, and ABC narrative event sampling).

Box 12.1
Steps in Designing and Using Observational Instruments

1. Select an appropriate topic, and formulate an observational question.
2. Select an appropriate method of observation. If using the tally event sampling or time sampling method, define the event.
3. Research the topic in libraries and classrooms.
4. Identify clear, distinct categories.
5. Design a recording form.
6. Pilot test the instrument. Revise, if necessary, and pilot test again.
7. Establish inter-rater reliability.
8. Collect data.
9. Analyze and present the data.
10. Interpret the data.
11. Formulate follow-through plans.

Observational questions may focus on children, teachers, programs, and environments. Each observer has unique questions and concerns.

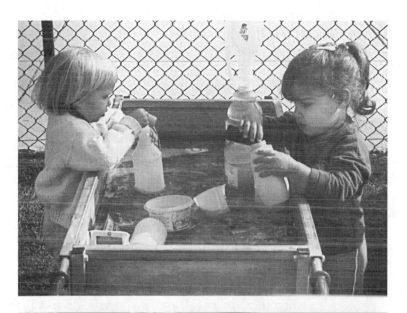

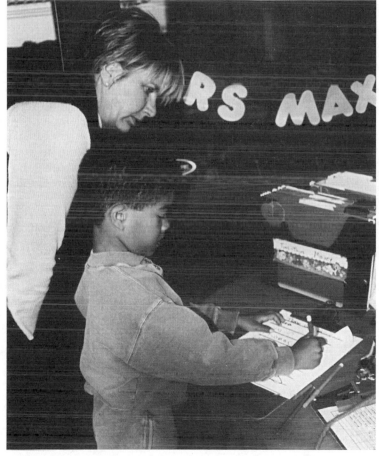

Select an Appropriate Topic, and Formulate an Observational Question

A useful observational topic is explicit and manageable rather than general and vague; as a result, the topic suggests specific categories to observe. For example, studying how parents and children separate at child care adequately suggests observable categories, whereas studying *imagination* does not. A productive technique of further narrowing the topic is to form a question to study. One question represents a workable initial focus and leads to a precise delineation of the specifics to be observed.

Classroom Example

At the conclusion of the staff meeting at High Street Child Care Center, Winona, a first year teacher, quietly asks her mentor, Bessie, if she can spare a few minutes. In the privacy of Bessie's room, Winona's lower lip trembles as she explains how the children in her class don't seem to like her. Her evidence is that most of the children don't want to stay at school, cling to their parents in the morning, and cry when their parents leave. She pleadingly asks Bessie if she will observe her to see what she is doing wrong.

Bessie puts an arm around Winona's shoulders and reminds her that it is only the third week of school and that many young children find separating from their parents difficult. However, Bessie acknowledges Winona's assessment that most of the children are having separation problems and suspects there are strategies that Winona and the parents could employ to effectively help children feel comfortable and welcome when they first arrive at school. Bessie tells Winona she needs a few days to work on an observation instrument but that she will be ready the next week.

Bessie sets to work, eager to help the new teacher placed under her mentoring wing. She devises the following observational question: How frequently do Winona and the parents demonstrate strategies to help children successfully separate from their parents and transition to school?

Select an Appropriate Method of Observation

After formulating an observational question, the appropriate method of observation may be quickly apparent to observers, or they may need to evaluate the potential effectiveness of each method. This book presents the following methods:

- Running records
- Anecdotal records
- Checklists
- Rating scales
- ABC narrative event sampling

- Tally event sampling
- Time sampling

After a review of each method's strengths and limitations (Cozby, 1997), the choice is made on the basis of which method will best answer the observational question (Evertson & Green, 1986).

Classroom Example

As Bessie reviews the observational methods familiar to her, she quickly rules out the methods of running records, anecdotal records, and ABC narrative event sampling because these will not accommodate group data nor yield the quantitative data needed to answer the observational question. She also rejects checklists and rating scales; these methods will not produce the frequency data Bessie wants for a fair evaluation of Winona over several days. The list of methods is effectively narrowed to tally event sampling and time sampling. A reassessment of her question helps Bessie make the final choice (How frequently do Winona and the parents demonstrate strategies to help children successfully separate from their parents and transition to school?) She knows parents bring their children to school individually over a 15-minute period, so she anticipates she can record data for each arrival; tally event sampling is the observational method to choose.

Bessie specifies parent–child separation as the event to observe and defines it as the process of children separating from their parents upon arrival at school.

Research the Topic in Libraries and Classrooms

Library research, classroom observation, and previous experience help identify the behaviors and characteristics that effectively answer an observational question.

Classroom Example

Over the next 2 days, Bessie consciously studies the separation processes in her own classroom and reflects on her past experiences with children reluctant to have their parents leave them. She jots down ideas of behaviors to observe. While searching the literature, Bessie is reminded of how important successful separations are to communicate confidence in children's abilities to handle their school experiences (Kettman, 1994). She finds Brazelton's advice (1992) particularly helpful in identifying effective parent strategies.

Identify Clear, Distinct Categories

Categories are clear and unambiguous, and they often must be defined. Depending on the scope of the focus, observers may choose a sign or a category system (see Chapter 10 for definitions), but in either case the categories must not overlap. Codes for categories may be specified to save space on the recording form.

Classroom Example

After reading and thinking about her topic, Bessie decides to focus on teacher strategies to help children separate from their parents and transition to school, parent strategies to help children separate from their parents and transition to school, and children's successful and unsuccessful separations. As a result, she identifies and defines two sets of categories to observe: children and strategies/separations. The set of children includes the names of all children in the class. Then she lists the following categories (with codes and definitions) under the strategies/separation set. She uses category codes to save space on the recording form and prints their definitions on the reverse side.

Teacher Strategies

- *T-G*—Teacher greets child verbally and/or physically.

- *T-CEH*—Teacher comments about the room, activities, or other children; encourages the child to begin an activity; or helps the child to do so.

- *T-P*—Teacher establishes physical proximity to the child.

- *T-D*—Teacher acknowledges parent's departure (says good-bye and/or encourages child to do so), reminds child of parents' return, expresses confidence in child, or suggests that the child look at concrete keepsake of parents (e.g., photo).

Although Bessie hopes her list is comprehensive, she adds an "other" category to provide the means to record additional unanticipated strategies. She therefore uses a category system for the set of teacher categories.

- *T-O*—Teacher uses a different strategy.

Parent Strategies

- *P-W*—Parent expresses warmth toward child verbally and/or by physical contact (e.g., holds a hand).

- *P-CEH*—Parent comments about the room, activities, or other children; encourages the child to put belongings in cubby or begin an activity; or helps the child to do so.

- *P-D*—Parent acknowledges own departure verbally (e.g., says good-bye) or physically (e.g., gives a farewell hug and kiss).

- *P-O*—Parent uses a different strategy.

Children's Successful/Unsuccessful Separations

- *C-SS*—Child successfully separates from parent.
- *C-US*—Child does not successfully separate from parent within 10 minutes.

Note Bessie uses category systems for the sets of parent strategies and child separations.

Design a Recording Form

Instrument recording forms begin with the heading used throughout this book, which includes the name of the center or school, the age level or grade, the dates and times of observation, the observer, and the person(s) being observed. Some forms require the definitions of the event observed, definitions of the categories and/or codes, and clear instructions to the observer; in addition, observers appreciate space at the bottom for relevant comments. The specific format of the remainder of the form must be compatible with the method used. A checklist, for example, would contain items preceded by check boxes, whereas a time sampling instrument would be based on a grid recording sheet.

Classroom Example

Bessie designs the recording form presented in Figure 12.1 and defines the codes as just discussed on the reverse side.

Pilot Test the Instrument

Although an observational instrument may appear adequate on paper, the process of trying it out in a classroom is essential to assessing its workability. Taking time to make adjustments in and additions to an instrument streamlines the future collection of useful information.

Classroom Example

Because High Street Child Care Center provides both preschool and day-care services, Bessie is able to leave her napping day-care children with her assistant teacher and observe an incoming class of 4-year-olds who arrive at 1:00 P.M. Her pilot testing raises two problems with her instrument. First, she discovers that her category of unsuccessful separation within 10 minutes is too limited. She observed one child–mother pair who spent 15 leisurely minutes together putting belongings away, walking around the classroom, and chatting with children and parents. The child's transition to school was happy, but Bessie's first draft of her instrument requires that the transition be tallied "unsuccessful." She removes the time restriction from the category description and rewrites the category definition as follows:

- *C-US*—Child does not successfully separate from parent.

Parent–Child Separations

Center/Age level:

Dates: Time:

Observer: Teacher:

                                                     Children:

Event: Parent–child separation—the process of children separating
                    from their parents upon arrival at school.

Codes: See reverse side.

Instructions: Mark one tally in the appropriate box for each teacher strategy,
                    parent strategy, and child separation observed.

Strategy and Separation / Child	Teacher Strategies					Parent Strategies				Child Separations	
	T-G	T-CEH	T-P	T-D	T-O	P-W	P-CEH	P-D	P-O	C-SS	C-US
Child 1											
Child 2											
Child 3											
Child 4											
Child 5											
Child 6											
Child 7											
Child 8											
Child 9											
Child 10											
Child 11											
Comments											

Figure 12.1.   Sample recording form design: Parent–child separations.

The second problem is simply visual. Bessie found all the small grid boxes visually uncomfortable and enlarges them. She pilot tests the revised instrument the next morning and is satisfied. Her revised form (with data) may be seen in Figure 12.3.

Establish Inter-Rater Reliability

Observers and designers of instruments want to have confidence that observers agree about how to use the instrument; all observers collecting data with an instrument should produce consistent, accurate, dependable—in short, reliable—data (Kerlinger, 1986). To explore the agreement between observers when they observe the same setting at the same time, the percentage of agreement may be calculated to represent the level of *inter-rater reliability* (Wheeler & Haertel, 1993). If the observers can demonstrate that their collected data are very similar, then they are ready to go out into various classrooms to observe on their own.

Agreement of 80% or higher (Cozby, 1997) provides confidence in the data collected. If the instrument is not reliable between raters, the instrument itself may need adjustments or the observers may need further training. Typical causes of low inter-rater reliability are unclear categories or instructions and insufficient training of observers. Although there are a few cautions about using percentage of agreement among observers as a measure of inter-rater reliability (see Dooley, 1990), this calculation is sufficient for an initial evaluation of the clarity and effectiveness of observational instruments.

A straightforward formula to compute rate of agreement between two observers ascertains their reliability (Boehm & Weinberg, 1997). The computational procedure is given in Figure 12.2 (always rounding numbers off to the nearest hundredth) along with an analysis of Bessie's and the director's data. Columns for additional observers may be added on the right-hand side in order to compute the agreement among more than two observers, and rechecking inter-rater reliability from time to time reevaluates the observers' consistency over time.

Classroom Example

To establish inter-rater reliability, Bessie asks her director to read the instrument and category code definitions and then observe the arrival of the children in an afternoon class with her. The data (column totals) collected by Bessie and the director demonstrate the process of computing observers' rate of agreement (see Figure 12.2). If desired, the rate (.76) may be multiplied by 100 to yield a percentage of agreement between observers (76%).

The observers' .76 rate of agreement is unsatisfactory, and Bessie and the director discuss their use of the observation instrument to identify possible problems. Two are immediately obvious. First, there are glaring discrepancies between their observations in the T-CEH and P-CEH categories; the director observed many more demonstrations of commenting, encouraging, and helping behaviors than Bessie. For each teacher–child and parent–child pair, Bessie put one tally in the appropriate box regardless of the number of such behaviors whereas the director tallied every one she saw.

Step	Category	Observer A (Bessie)	Observer B (Director)
1. Count the number of instances in each category for observers A and B.	T-G	12	10
	T-CEH	7	22
	T-P	9	10
	T-D	5	4
	T-O	0	5
	P-W	9	9
	P-CEH	6	17
	P-D	10	10
	P-O	0	6
	C-SS	10	10
	C-US	2	2
2. Total the number of observations for A and B.	Total	70 +	105 = 175
3. Count the number of agreements in each category and over categories for both observers.	T-G	10	
	T-CEH	7	
	T-P	9	
	T-D	4	
	T-O	0	
	P-W	9	
	P-CEH	6	
	P-D	10	
	P-O	0	
	C-SS	10	
	C-US	2	
	Total	67	

Figure 12.2.   Inter-rater reliability formula and computation.

Source: Adapted by permission of the publisher from Boehm, A. E. and Weinberg, R. A., *The Classroom Observer: A Guide for Developing Observation Skills*. (3rd ed.) (New York: Teachers College Press, © 1997 by Teachers College, Columbia University. All rights reserved.) p. 80 (Figure 7.2).

Step			
4. Divide the number of agreements by the total number of observations.	67	÷	175 = .38
5. Multiply the quotient by the number of observers; in this example there are two.	.38	×	2 = .76
Rate of agreement = .76			

Figure 12.2. (*Continued*).

Bessie realizes her directions are unclear, and she and the director review these categories in detail. If a mother says to her child, "Oh look, honey, there's Randy already busy with the trucks in the block area. Would you like to play with him?" and then walks with the child toward the blocks, how many tallies should be marked? Bessie would have marked one. The director, however, would have marked one tally for the comment about Randy, a second for the encouraging question, and a third for walking to the block area with the child; then she muses that she also could have marked a fourth tally for the comment about the blocks. The director then concludes that trying to mark every comment, encouragement, or help for 10 parent–child separations would render the instrument unworkable. Given overlapping arrivals, the observer cannot observe each child's experience in such detail. A time sampling instrument would have addressed this event frequency issue, but Bessie would not want the restrictions imposed by the time sampling units. She prefers the tally event sampling method that allows her to consistently gather data on which teacher and parent strategies are used. Bessie changes the instructions to eliminate the confusion (see Figure 12.3).

The second problem revolves around the *other* categories, T-O and P-O, with Bessie recording 0 in each category and the director observing 5 and 6, respectively. Most frequently, the director marked a tally when she overheard teacher and parent comments about the child, such as "Alyssa, I put your drawing on my refrigerator, and my husband said your skyscrapers reminded him of growing up in Chicago." That comment pleased Alyssa and added to her happy transition to school, and Bessie suggests the T-CEH and P-CEH category descriptions be amended to include comments about the child. The two observers also decide to eliminate the *other* categories (thus they now use sign systems for the teacher and parent sets of categories); observers can note helpful strategies under the comments section. Their revised category descriptions for T-CEH and P-CEH are as follows:

- *T-CEH*—Parent comments about the child, room, activities, or other children; encourages the child to begin an activity; or helps the child to do so.
- *P-CEH*—Parent comments about the child, room, activities, or other children; encourages the child to put belongings in cubby and begin an activity; or helps the child to do so.

Using the revised instrument, Bessie and the director observe together the next morning and accomplish a 96% agreement. Bessie is ready to observe Winona's classroom.

Collect Data

A reasonable amount of data is collected to provide a fair sample of the behaviors being studied. Observers plan when during the classroom schedule to observe and how much data to collect. A clear observational question and a concise recording form facilitate data collection.

Classroom Example

Bessie arranges for the director to cover her class for 15 minutes for the next five mornings so that she can observe the arrival of Winona's children. She wants to paint a thorough and well-balanced picture of the separation and transition processes. The data for the five days are compiled in Figure 12.3.

Analyze and Present the Data

The collected data may be analyzed through various procedures, and computer programs offer a multitude of shortcuts to this process. Observers select data analysis procedures that will provide information relevant to the observational question and present the data in a clear format. Then the observers will be able to interpret what the data mean for real children and teachers in real classrooms. An assortment of data analysis and presentation procedures is given below; not all of these procedures need to be used in any one observational study.

Frequencies

Frequencies allow observers to answer questions about how often behaviors, events, or strategies occurred (e.g., How often do children quarrel during outside time? How often do children use materials for classification during free-play time? How often do children participate in circle time?). To compute frequencies on a grid, (horizontal) row tallies or (vertical) column tallies are simply added. Computing frequencies is a productive way to begin studying the data.

Parent–Child Separations

Center/Age level: High Street Child Care/3-Year-Olds

Dates:	9/28–30, 10/1–2	Time:	8:45–9:00 A.M.
Observer:	Bessie	Teacher:	Winona
		Children:	10 children

Event: Parent–child separation—the process of children separating from their parents upon arrival at school.

Codes: See reverse side.

Instructions. Mark one tally in the appropriate box for each teacher strategy, parent strategy, and child separation observed. Mark only one tally per box for each session.

Strategy and Separation / Child	Teacher Strategies				Parent Strategies			Child Separations	
	T-G	T-CEH	T-P	T-D	P-W	P-CEH	P-D	C-SS	C-US
Alyssa	/	//	//		卌		卌	/	////
Connor	//	/	/	/	///	//	////	//	///
Kailey	///			卌	////		卌	/	////
Kayl	//	/			/			///	//
Parker	/	///	///	//	////	//	卌	卌	
Elaine	卌	///	卌	///	卌	卌	卌	卌	
Rosemary	////		///	/	///	//	////	////	/
George	//	//			//	///	///		卌
Noel	///		/		/			///	//
Tak	卌	///	///		卌	//		//	///

28

Comments·

Figure 12.3. Data: parent–child separations.

Classroom Example Bessie can easily determine how frequently each teacher and parent strategy was used per session and how frequently children successfully and unsuccessfully transitioned to school by computing the column totals. Remember that each box may be tallied only once per day, so each column total can have a maximum of 50 tallies; for example, if Winona greeted each child every day for five days (10 × 5), Bessie would have marked 50 tallies in the T-G column.

Practice Activity 12.1
Counting Frequencies of Observations

Working with the data presented in Figure 12.3, count the column frequencies. You may write the totals directly on the recording form.

Example: T-G total: 1 + 2 + 3 + 2 + 1 + 5 + 4 + 2 + 3 + 5 = 28

Percentages

Frequencies show the sheer magnitude of observed behaviors, but unlike percentages, frequencies do not lend themselves to easy comparisons. Observing that primary grade children make 53 visits to the science center over the course of a week does not produce useful information in isolation; computing the percentages of children's visits to all of the classroom areas, however, begins to describe how the science center is used in the context of children's available choices. Percentages help put the data in perspective.

Classroom Example Bessie can easily compute the percentages of teacher and parent strategies used as well as the proportions of successful and unsuccessful separations. Percentages will quickly convey the overall picture.

Practice Activity 12.2
Computing Percentages

Using the column totals, compute the percentages of Winona's use of each strategy. For example, to compute the percentage of times Winona greeted the children, divide the column total (28) by the possible greetings (50) and multiply by 100. Now you see that over the course of 5 days with 10 children, Winona greeted them 56% of the time and, conversely, did not greet them 44% of the time. Record your calculations in the chart on the top of the next page.

Percentages of Teacher's Separation Strategy Use

Strategy	Frequency	Percentage
T-G	28	56 (28 ÷ 50 × 100)
T-CEH		
T-P		
T-D		

Next, again using the column totals, compute the percentages of the parents' uses of strategies to help their children successfully separate and transition to school. In the example given, you see that over the week, parents demonstrated warmth to their children 66% of the time.

Percentages of Parents' Separation Strategy Use

Strategy	Frequency	Percentage
P-W	33	66 (33 ÷ 50 × 100)
P-CEH		
P-D		

Finally, using the last two column totals, compute the percentages of children's successful and unsuccessful separations from their parents.

Percentages of Children's Successful and Unsuccessful Separations

Transition	Frequency	Percentage
C-SS	26	
C-US		

Practice Activity 12.3
Computing More Percentages

Bessie also wants a clear picture of Winona's *relative* use of the teacher separation strategies to guide helpful follow-through plans. She adds up all of Winona's strategies using the column totals (28 + 15 + 18 + 12 = 73) and then computes the percentage of each strategy used. Complete the following computations in the chart below; then do the same for parents' strategies. Note that your percentages will add up to 100% with these calculations.

Percentages of Teacher Strategies

Strategy	Frequency	Percentage
T-G	28	38 (28 ÷ 73 × 100)
T-CEH		
T-P		
T-D		

Percentages of Parent Strategies

Strategy	Frequency	Percentage
P-W	33	41 (33 ÷ 80 × 100)
P-CEH		
P-D		

Tables and Graphs

Tables and graphs present data visually. Tables promote the clear presentation of information. Graphs represent a relation or relations in two dimensions (Kerlinger, 1986) and also serve to highlight important results often embedded in the data on recording sheets. A few options are reviewed below.

Classroom Example   Bessie wants Winona to understand how infrequently teachers and parents used strategies to help children separate from their parents (the percentages you computed in Practice Activity 12.2). Bessie wants to present both sets of data together (she could have prepared two separate tables) so Winona will readily see that both she and the parents have room for improvement. She prepares the table in Figure 12.4.

Given the observed data, Bessie wants to illustrate the relative proportion of strategies on which Winona and the parents relied. Pie charts display percentages of data in sections of a circle. In Figure 12.5 on page 288, Bessie presents Winona's and the parents' relative use of the strategies observed (you computed these percentages in Practice Activity 12.3).

Conclusion

The preceding methods of data analysis and presentation represent options for the observer. All need not be used, and additional methods might be helpful to some observers. For example, the analysis of some data may be enhanced by computing means (averages) or plotting changes in behaviors over time on a graph. Remember that the primary goals of data analysis and presentation are to use the data to answer the observational question and to present the information in clear, visual formats.

Interpret the Data

Uninterpreted data are of no use. After the data are collected, data interpretation is the next step in the process of designing and using an observational instrument.

Percentages of Teacher and Parent Use of Separation Strategies		
Teacher/Parents Strategy	Teacher	Parents
T-Greets	56	
T-Comments, encourages, helps	33	
T-Establishes physical proximity	36	
T-Acknowledges parent's departure	24	
P-Expresses warmth		60
P-Comments, encourages, helps		32
P-Acknowledges own departure		62

Figure 12.4.   Percentages presented in a table.

Classroom Example

Bessie and Winona sit down together with a block of time and Figures 12.3, 12.4, and 12.5 in front of them. Bessie carefully describes the categories on the instrument and reviews their definitions on the reverse side. She explains that each box could receive only one tally per day and uses Alyssa as an example of the data collected:

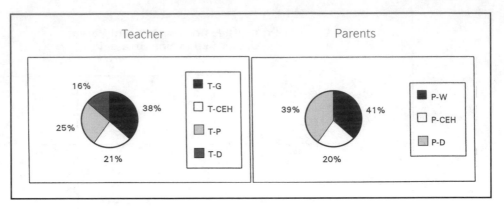

Figure 12.5. Percentages of teacher's and parents' relative use of separation strategies. Data presentation in pie charts.

- "Let's look at all of Alyssa's boxes. One tally in the T-G box means you greeted her one day out of five."
- "You commented about Alyssa, the room, the activities, or the other children; encouraged Alyssa to begin an activity; or helped her to do so on 2 days."
- "You established physical proximity after Alyssa's arrival on 2 days as well."
- "You never, however, acknowledged Alyssa's mom's departure."
- "Alyssa's mom expressed warmth and said good-bye to Alyssa all 5 days."
- "The mom, however, never used a P-CEH strategy."
- "Each day the mom acknowledged her own departure to Alyssa either verbally or physically."
- "Alyssa only made one successful transition to school during the week I observed."

Already Winona begins to make notes of strategies she and the mom can try to ease Alyssa's transition to school. Using Figures 12.3, 12.4, and 12.5, Bessie and Winona draw additional specific conclusions. Do the same in Practice Activity 12.4.

Practice Activity 12.4 _____
Interpreting the Data

- Study the raw data in Figure 12.3, and state two conclusions about the separation processes of individual children.

Example: Elaine received the most teacher and parent helpful strategies and successfully transitioned to school each day.

1.

2.

- Study the percentages in Figure 12.4, and state two conclusions about Winona's and the parents' uses of separation strategies.

Example: Winona greeted children 56% of the time.

Example: Parents acknowledged their own departures to their children 62% of the time.

1.

2.

- Study the percentages in Figure 12.5, and state two conclusions about Winona's and the parents' relative uses of helpful strategies.

Example: Winona's uses of helpful strategies were fairly even (38%, 21%, 25%, and 16%).

1.

2.

Consider Our Ethical Responsibilities to Colleagues

NAEYC Ideal I-2.2

"To acknowledge and build upon strengths and competencies as we support families in their task of nurturing children" (Feeney & Kipnis, 1992, p. 6).

Read on to see how Winona and Bessie write a parent newsletter article to fulfill this ethical responsibility.

Formulate Follow-Through Plans

Observation in the early childhood classroom provides information about children, teachers, the environment, and sometimes parents to evaluate current development and practices and to plan appropriate activities and adjustments. The detailing of follow-through plans is the culmination of the observational process.

Observations of parent–child separations in the early childhood classroom can lead to supportive follow-through plans.

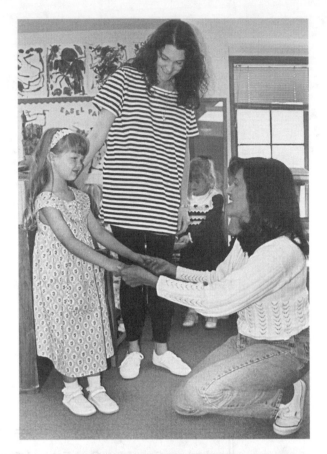

Classroom Example

Bessie's warm and supportive discussion of her observation ends with attention to the "What next?" question. Knowing that observation is often the best teacher, Bessie arranges to have Winona observe a morning class with her, using the same observational instrument. She selects a class known for its smooth separations; Winona will gain clear demonstrations of the teacher's and parents' helpful strategies in action. This is the first follow-through plan implemented. Read additional examples below, and add your own in Practice Activity 12.5.

Practice Activity 12.5
Detailing Follow-Through Plans

Use the interpretations from Practice Activity 12.4 to stimulate ideas for effective follow-through plans for Winona.

Example: Winona will put a notecard of the teacher strategies she wants to implement in her pocket for quick reminders and easy access.

Example: Bessie and Winona will jointly write a brief article for the parent newsletter about child–parent separations at school. They will encourage parents to view separation as a transition, not an event, and to consciously try the following strategies from Bessie's observational instrument.

- Express warmth to the child verbally and/or by physical contact (e.g., hold a hand).
- Comment about the child, room, activities, or other children; encourage the child to begin an activity; or help the child to do so.
- Acknowledge own departure verbally (e.g., say good-bye) or physically (e.g., give a farewell hug and kiss).

1.

2.

Action Project 12.1
Designing and Using an Observational Instrument

Replicate the steps of designing an observational instrument as discussed in this chapter and exemplified by Bessie and Winona. Design a checklist, rating scale, tally event sampling instrument, or time sampling instrument to answer a specific question about children or classroom processes. Pilot test the completed instrument, and establish inter-rater reliability. Collect data in a classroom or classrooms (whichever is appropriate) to gain the experience of analyzing and interpreting real data. Finally, put the data to practical use and formulate follow-through plans. Be sure to refer to and follow all 11 steps presented in this chapter.

Points to Remember

Skilled observers have the freedom to select an observational question of personal interest and possible importance to a classroom in which they work. They have the tools and skills necessary to follow a question from the construction of an observational instrument through the creation of follow-through plans based on real data. The steps of this process, as detailed in this chapter, are as follows:

1. Select an appropriate topic, and formulate an observational question.
2. Select an appropriate method of observation. If using the tally event sampling or time sampling method, define the event.
3. Research the topic in libraries and classrooms.
4. Identify clear, distinct categories.
5. Design a recording form.
6. Pilot test the instrument. Revise, if necessary, and pilot test again.
7. Establish inter-rater reliability.
8. Collect data.
9. Analyze and present the data.
10. Interpret the data.
11. Formulate follow-through plans.

Take a Moment to Reflect

The 3-year-olds in Winona's classroom are new to school. They are leaving the familiarity of their home environments for the unknown experiences of school. Hopefully these experiences will be interesting, fun, challenging, supportive, and rewarding on many levels. For the first few weeks, however, the processes of separating from parents may dominate many children's feelings about school. Try to empathize with their experiences by reflecting on the following:

1. Recall a first experience in your own life. Perhaps you may not remember your first day of school, but you probably remember your introduction to a group experience during childhood (swimming lessons, scouts, camp, team sports). Articulate your initial feelings of discomfort or wariness.

2. Describe your eventual adjustment to the preceding group experience. Was it generally positive or negative? What factors were critical to your successful or unsuccessful adjustment? What suggestions would you now give to the adults responsible for children beginning new experiences?

CHAPTER 13

Selecting Methods to Observe, Plan, and Enrich the Physical Environment

I n a college class on observation, Kirin, a student, designs an observational instrument around a topic near and dear to her heart. As an aide in a preschool classroom, she encounters relentless problems in trying to get children's attention at the end of free-choice time. She wonders if the children don't respect her because she is an aide or if she works with an exceptionally difficult group. In any case, they seem oblivious to her attempts to get their attention. Before Kirin gets much of a start on her project, the head teacher rearranges the classroom and the transition problems disappear! Is this a miracle, or might some classroom problems be solved by observing, evaluating, and changing the physical environment rather than by studying children's and teachers' behaviors in isolation?

Do teachers gain children's attention more easily in some room arrangements than in others? What are the potential attention-getting problems in a classroom with a 5-foot-tall room divider in the writing area and the book nook behind the piano? How could the placement of children's interest centers help or hinder the process? What impact does the physical environment actually have on teachers' ability to get the children's attention in a modern complex classroom? Some teachers endure unnecessary problems because they overlook the effect the physical environment has on teaching and learning. Once again, we gaze through the looking glass, but this time, the focus is on the setting itself.

This chapter, like Chapters 2 and 3, deviates from the format of the other chapters. The goal is to supply a knowledge base for environmental observation, an often overlooked, but important subject. The first half of the chapter explores the major elements that produce an effective learning environment, both indoors and outdoors. The latter part of the chapter examines observational strategies used to assess the functional design of the physical setting. With a sound basis in observation, the teacher can assess how well the environmental elements support the educational process. If changes are warranted, the teacher can use the results of the observational data to make instructional decisions.

Indoor Environments

Recall a place in which you felt right at home the first moment you set foot inside. Perhaps it was a cafe or restaurant, a friend's family room, your grandma's porch, a library corner, or a ski lodge. What did it look like? What made you feel so welcome?

Now think for a moment of indoor places in which you did not feel comfortable—places that were cold, alienating, or unwelcoming. What did the uncomfortable rooms look like? What did those places have in common? Pause and identify specific factors that contributed to a sense of disfavor or uneasiness.

Our first reaction to a physical environment is emotional. Although the initial impression may be influenced by the purpose of the visit, the function of the facility, or the people within the space, the welcome feeling is fundamentally associated with the physical setting itself. All environments have the potential to enhance and support comfort levels.

Let's move the investigation into the early childhood classroom. Figure 13.1 illustrates portions of two different room arrangements for a specific preschool classroom. Take a moment to examine them. What observations can be made about these learning environments? What are your first impressions?

Now look more closely. Do the rooms welcome children's play? What can be said about the choice and location of interest centers, boundaries, traffic flow, visual stimulation, accessibility of materials, equipment choice, and storage? Imagine a young child and then a teacher working and communicating in these two different arrangements.

The room arrangement in the top photograph in Figure 13.1 appears confusing and lacks an overall organizational plan utilizing area boundaries. Visualize this room with energetic children actively engaged in free play. Could a child move easily from one area to another? Suppose two children were role-playing, dressed up in high heels and swishy dresses, cuddling their baby dolls wrapped in blankets. Imagine them clomping off to the grocery store. Using this scenario, these children might be wondering about the following question. Where could the market be? If the children could find an unoccupied area, could they get there without interfering with block builders, puzzle assemblers, or book readers?

Take a look at the visual stimuli in the top photograph in Figure 13.1. Young children working in this setting may be overstimulated by the wall clutter. If the photograph had been reproduced in color, you would see that the color scheme contributes to overstimulation by using bright and vibrant reds, blues, and yellows. Examine the textures and surfaces. Where is the softness?

On the other hand, the bottom photograph in Figure 13.1 represents the same room rearranged to create a physical environment supported by research findings—designed to enhance learning, provide comfort, and increase the usability of space. Study the clear flow of the traffic pattern, the distinct separation of quiet and noisy areas, and the strategic placement of dividers. Take another glance. What can be said about the display of children's work, accessibility of materials, and additional touches of texture? If the teachers in this classroom were able to repaint, they would have chosen a light shade of peach. Room accents would have been in pastel green, thus giving a balance of warm and cool colors.

Compare the rooms presented in Figure 13.1. Is there a difference in coziness and emotional warmth? What growth opportunities for children are promoted by these two room arrangements? What evidence is there that the room at the bottom of Figure 13.1 was planned according to developmental goals—to encourage children's autonomy, initiative, competence, exploration, discovery, cooperation, and interactions with others?

A well-planned environment is an effective teaching strategy. Many potential problems can be eliminated by room design. Consider possible arrangements that reflect the following management concerns: capturing children's attention, providing smooth transitions, increasing the possibility of cooperative play, decreasing opportunities for potential quarrels, and minimizing wandering.

As Poysner (1983) advised us, "The physical environment of the classroom is a web of micro-variables, which are highly interrelated and in many instances interdependent. Each factor of the classroom environment can and should be examined

Figure 13.1. Two photographs of the same preschool classroom. *Top,* limited room arrangement; *bottom,* effective room arrangement.

independently" (p. 36). This chapter discusses three key indoor factors in detail: room arrangement, lighting, and visual appeal.

Room Arrangement

Classrooms come in an assortment of sizes and shapes, and seldom are two arranged exactly alike; classroom organization has no prescribed formula. Instead, certain elements necessitate special consideration. This section of the chapter emphasizes room arrangement: relations to program goals, layout, traffic patterns, and material selection and equipment location.

    Unless teachers are fortunate enough to build their own schools, options in room arrangements are initially restricted by the fixed space—the direction the room faces, configuration of the room and the placement of the electrical outlets, plumbing, floor coverings, windows, doors, and built-in shelves and closets.

Relation to Program Goals   As we explore the implications of program goals on room arrangement, recall the top photograph in Figure 13.1. Do you think the teacher in this classroom coordinated the design of the room arrangement with developmental principles and program goals? An incongruity occurs when the program plan and the classroom environment are in conflict. In contrast, room arrangements backed by developmental principles and congruent with school goals result in conducive learning conditions. Figure 13.2 gives an extensive list of program goals accompanied by implications for preschool classroom planning. While

---

Preschool Program Goals Implications for Classroom Arrangements

To support children's active learning through exploration and interaction with other children, adults, and concrete materials, thus strengthening children's construction of knowledge	Diverse materials are available, organized, labeled, and accessible to children.
	There are places and spaces to work alone or with others.
	Dramatic play centers are present. Varied and abundant props are changed on the basis of the children's interests.
	The arrangement allows for overflow and opportunities for conversations.
	Every interest center provides materials to stimulate cognitive development.
To create a sense of security and promote trust	The door to the classroom opens into a cozy welcoming area that reflects children's interests.
	Materials for children's use are arranged on low, open shelves.

Figure 13.2. Foundations of preschool room arrangements.

	Interest center boundaries are well-defined. The paths leading to the centers are unobstructed and easy to view.
	Safe plants and fabrics with soft textures are present.
	Wall colors are a balance of warm and cool colors.
	Room decorations reflect the children's work and are carefully selected to avoid an environment that is overstimulating.
To enhance children's autonomy	Furniture is child-size. Drinking fountains, sinks, and toilets are child-height.
	Cubbies are labeled with names and pictures.
	Classroom areas are well-defined and labeled with words and pictures.
	Materials are accessible for the children's choice. Empty tables or work spaces are available for child-planned activities using self-chosen materials.
To foster children's natural curiosity	Traffic flow takes children past centers of possible interest.
	Center content changes to reflect the children's emerging interests.
To encourage initiative-taking (children explore and act on their own ideas)	Materials can be manipulated and re-formed. Materials and props are open-ended, varied, abundant, organized, and accessible to the children.
	There is space to safely arrange and rearrange materials.
To recognize each child's importance and uniqueness	Bulletin boards and room decorations are at the children's eye level. Wall decorations involve the children and display their work.
To allow children to develop at their own individual rates	Individual labeled cubbies are provided.
	Various materials and centers based on the children's developmental needs, cultural heritages, interests, and town/city/rural orientation are available.
To allow children to be physically active	Adequate space is supplied in all areas and traffic paths.

Figure 13.2.   *(Continued)*.

To support literacy development through the child's own experiences	Print-rich environment is supplied. Listening, writing, and reading centers; experience stories; dictated stories; poetry charts; typewriters; and computers are visible. Housekeeping includes cookbooks, note pads and pencils, telephone books, etc.
	Centers have enough space for children to converse easily with each other.
To enhance children's creativity and appreciation of fine art	Art, music, writing, and dramatic play materials are readily available and accessible.
	Pictures of artists, musicians, authors, and actors/actresses are displayed at child's eye level and frequently changed.

Figure 13.2.   (*Continued*).

reading through the list, think about what additions, deletions, expansions, or revisions would be necessary for primary grade classrooms (e.g., *Program goal*—To assist children in understanding the meaning, as well as the mechanics of math. *Implication for classroom arrangements*—Variety of math manipulatives available at math center and on the children's resource self). If composing the K–3 list, you may want to refer to the Taylor and Vlastos (1988) guidelines for classroom design.

Within the field of early childhood, there are many variations in programs. Not all have the same developmental goals. All programs, however, are enhanced when the underlying principles and stated goals work together with the room arrangement in mutual support. In the next exercise try your hand at identifying program goals and the corresponding implications for classroom arrangements.

Action Project 13.1
Program Goals and Classroom Implications

Choose two different types of schools from the list below:

Private half-day preschool   Campus laboratory schools
Parent cooperative preschool   Employer-related preschool
Head Start   All-day child care
Family day care   Montessori
Private primary (K–3)   Public primary (K–3)
A school with a High/Scope curriculum
A school with a Waldorf curriculum
A school with a Reggio Emilio approach

Arrange visits to your two selections. Obtain a copy of each school's goals; perhaps an introductory brochure provides this information. Observe one class at each site for approximately ½ to 1 hour, and watch for environmental implications of the stated goals. Using the information from your observation, fill in the following form by stating two goals for each school and the corresponding implications.

Example:

School: Growing and Learning: Center for Early Childhood Development
Program type: Parent cooperative preschool

Goal	**Implications for Classroom Arrangements**
1. To provide an anti-bias curriculum	Pictures, books, and materials on walls or shelves abundantly reflect diversity, are free of stereotypes, and are authentic representations of the cultures they depict.
	Dramatic play areas reflect a variety of sex-role options.

School:
Program type:

Goals	**Implications for Classroom Arrangements**
1.	
2.	

School:
Program type:

Goals	**Implications for Classroom Arrangements**
1.	
2.	

Layout   "Establishing well-defined interest areas is one concrete way to foster children's capacities for initiative, autonomy, and social relationships" (Hohmann & Weikart, 1995, p. 115). Using the interest center approach, Greenman (1988) identified three plans for room layouts: the *maze* (defined areas are separate and placed throughout the room—sides, corners, and middle area), the *perimeter strategy* (areas are placed around the outside with the central space left open for traffic access and overflow from centers), and the *central activity area strategy* (areas are grouped together in the center of the room with open space on the outer edges). One layout is not superior to another, and indeed many teachers design their own classroom layouts using modifications of these plans. A well-designed layout, however, will reflect the program goals and maximize the use of classroom space.

After the general layout has been chosen, the designation of specific centers within the classroom should follow "some guiding principle or principles, such as importance, frequency of use, functional relationships, or sequence of use" (McCormick & Ilgen, 1980, p. 355). Examples associated with the principle of functional relationships are shown in the following list.

- Noisy areas are adjacent (e.g., blocks and housekeeping).

- Quiet areas are adjacent (e.g., independent reading and computers or manipulatives).

- Areas that flow into one another are adjacent (e.g., reading and science or writing and independent reading).

- Areas that need access to the sink or electrical outlets are adjacent (e.g., art and science or music and science).

Traffic Patterns   Traffic patterns, which are planned concurrently with the location of areas, also affect the room arrangement design. "No matter what the strategy, clear pathways are essential" (Greenman, 1988, p. 142). While looking at the top photograph in Figure 13.1, you thought about potential mobility problems. The skillful teacher plans traffic patterns that minimize interference in interest centers and leave all doorways unobstructed.

> Children need to know where they are going, how to get through a space, and the quickest way to an activity area. Hard-to-reach areas receive less use; paths that cut through an area interfere with "work in progress" and create distractions; and narrow pathways cause congestion. Therefore, create a network of pathways that connect activity areas. This network should also limit the access to areas; for instance, one entrance to an area. There should be no dead ends. . . . Define the edges of pathways with furniture and changes in floor covering. (Vergeront, 1987, p. 5)

Kudos go to teachers who map out the traffic flow between centers or desk areas and during cleanup and transitions. The final test, however, comes when the teacher bends down to see whether the planned traffic routes and spatial organization are visible from the child's eye (Graves, 1993).

As with any other component of the room arrangement, traffic paths need to be observed periodically and then analyzed for workability. Listening to children and teachers' verbalizations of problems may give clues related to needed traffic pattern adjustments.

> When caregivers hear comments such as "She knocked over my building," or "Tell those feet to walk," or "Where is . . . ?" or when all the children are in only one part of the room, it is time to reevaluate the environment. If those feet need to be told to walk, there is too much open space and the children are running. New traffic patterns need to be established by repositioning storage cabinets. (Fisher, 1995, p. 37)

Material Selection and Equipment Location   Also adding to the room arrangement design are the selection and placement of materials within an area. The knowledgeable practitioner selects classroom materials that reflect the program goals, developmental appropriateness, and assessed individual needs and interests. For example, one study (Petrakos & Howe, 1996) found that materials and equipment choice in the dramatic play area affected children's opportunities to enter into solitary or interactive play.

Additionally teachers carefully select equitable representations of gender, culture, ethnic backgrounds, and abilities. "What isn't seen can be as powerful a contributor to attitudes as what is seen" (Derman-Sparks & the A.B.C. Task Force, 1989, p. 11). To build positive identity and self-esteem, special emphasis is given to classroom materials and equipment that represent the specific classroom populations.

> It also contributes to the feeling of homeyness and comfort when the ethnic and cultural backgrounds of children are matter-of-factly represented in the physical environment of the school. The inclusion of multiethnic pictures, books, and artifacts will contribute to the children's overall feelings of being valued for their own cultural richness. (Hendrick, 1994, p. 96)

Effective room arrangements take into consideration shelving and storage for materials. Children can exercise initiative and creativity when materials are labeled clearly, organized systematically, and accessed easily. Some pieces of equipment and furniture can double as natural dividers or boundaries when thoughtfully placed (see Figure 13.1).

Researchers (DeLong et al., 1991) offered another dimension to consider in material location as they compared children's attention span and levels of play in relation to small and large spaces. The data indicated that in smaller places preschool children "enter complex forms of play more quickly, engage in complex play segments of longer duration and tend to spend a slightly greater percentage of their overall play time in complex play" (p. 8). For classrooms that are large and open, this study has clear suggestions. Smaller defined spaces can be created by the use of small rugs within an area; many Montessori schools effectively use this principle. Dividers and different colored floor areas create smaller spaces within an often overwhelming large setting.

In addition to providing small places within larger spaces, room arrangements offer private spaces for children to be alone during emotional regrouping or to take a break from groups and the stimulation of active rooms. Some children arrive at school not quite awake and need a private wake-up place. Other children benefit from a few chosen moments away from groups, just as adults do. Private spaces include areas just for one; a cardboard barrel with a cutaway door and a decorated interior just big enough for a single child is a welcomed addition to all-day child care settings. Niches under a desk or up in a small loft can serve the same purpose. A special designated private space can be a child's retreat where no one else can enter, not even the teacher.

Effective room arrangement reflects numerous components. It requires the teacher to articulate sound program goals and philosophy. Then the following ele-

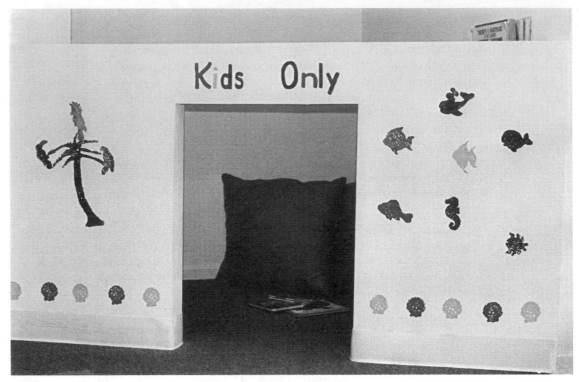

Well-planned room arrangements invite children into small, defined spaces.

ments can be thoughtfully woven into the classroom design: layout, traffic patterns, and material selection and equipment location.

Lighting

"Lighting? That's not a teacher matter," early childhood educators may say. "Lighting is an architect's job; it's determined before teachers first walk into the classroom." This may be the case, but what if research revealed that lighting affects the learning process? Would it then become an educator's issue? Let's investigate how the amount and types of lighting influence the early childhood classroom.

If all the lights in houses or offices were uniform, giving off the same amount of light no matter what room the occupant was in, visual comfort would not be met. In homes, focused bright lights are used on desks and night stands for doing paperwork and reading, whereas a more diffused light can be placed on ceilings. How effectively is lighting used as a tool in the early childhood classroom? Are the lights bright in the areas requiring close-up work, such as the art, manipulative, and language areas? Or are they the same throughout—even in areas where less intensity is required (e.g., cubby, coat storage, or lunch area)?

In the past, school lighting systems supplied invariable bright light. The lighting was basically the same throughout the entire school. As lighting becomes appreciated as a teaching tool, educators are looking to research to challenge this approach; two important facts have been disclosed. First, the amount of lighting needed for children's and teachers' comfortable vision depends on the number of windows, the size of the room, and the color of and reflection from the walls, tops of tables, floors, ceilings, and mirrors (Greenman, 1988; Walter, 1996). Second, eye fatigue is reduced when light levels are responsive to the activities within the room and the action required by the activities (Ruud, 1978).

Design of the Times: Day Care (the report of the National Task Force on Day Care Interior Design, 1992) noted several environmental recommendations; two apply to lighting. "Storytelling in a lower lighting level can settle children down. It also signals to them that a new activity is about to occur and renews their attention" (p. 52). The Task Force also recommended varying the lights—for example, adding soft spotlights to specific areas.

Lighting choice can also contribute to a feeling of homeyness. Try adding a lamp in the check-in area, entrance hall, or director/principal's office to embrace a sense of warmth. Use "wall-mounted sconces or indirect cove lighting" (Walter, 1996, p. 44) to meet varied classroom lighting needs, such as in the reading corner. What about installing dimmer switches for varying the intensity of overhead lighting?

Now let's turn our attention to some practical information on types of classroom lighting. Three kinds of lighting are traditionally used in classrooms: natural, incandescent, and fluorescent. Most classrooms are designed with windows to let in natural light. Some elementary classrooms, however, have no windows, and all early childhood classrooms use some artificial light (incandescent and fluorescent) even in sunny climates.

An alternate source of artificial light has been developed and is now available for home, school, and work use. It's called full-spectrum lighting, "yielding the closest solar match in commercially available light, [and] is perhaps the 'state of the art' in present-day lighting technology" (Liberman, 1991, p. 55). Full-spectrum lighting can best be understood by comparing lighting sources using the *color rendering index* (CRI). This evaluative measure "was developed to describe how well colors are rendered by artificial light sources compared with natural light" (Mahnke, 1996, p. 122). According to the specifications of the International Commission on Illumination, outdoor sunlight has a perfect CRI of 100, fluorescent full-spectrum light 90 and above, fluorescent cool-white light 62, fluorescent warm-white light 56, and incandescent light about 40.

At the date of this publication, experiments comparing the effects of the various light sources conclude that lighting with high CRI and trace amounts of ultraviolet (UV) light provides increased visual acuity, less fatigue, improved academic performance, increased attendance, and decreased hyperactivity (Grangaard, 1993; Hathaway, 1995; Hathaway, Hargreaves, Thompson, & Novitsky, 1992; Küller &

Lindsten, 1992; Papa-Lewis & Cornell, 1987; Yizhong, 1984). Imagine assisting the learning process by simply changing the light bulb!

One teacher at Banks Street College Family Center (Schreiber, 1996), reported that she "often left the center with headaches and feelings of fatigue" (p. 11). When she installed full-spectrum lighting in her classroom, the headaches and fatigue disappeared.

Ultraviolet light (which is present in full-spectrum lighting and sunlight) plays a key role in visual acuity, but because ordinary window glass filters out ultraviolet light (Mahnke, 1996), all classrooms, even those with large windows, could benefit from full-spectrum lighting. The increased sharpness of black-and-white images in natural and full-spectrum lighting (Duro-Test, 1988) has important implications. Print, after all, is black and white. Perhaps full-spectrum light may assist literacy development. Educators can begin by adding full-spectrum lighting to specific rooms or changing the already existing fluorescents to full-spectrum lights.

The early childhood educator can help facilitate positive learning conditions by observing children's vision needs, providing sufficient but not excessive lighting, planning lighting systems with variation, and using full-spectrum lighting.

Visual Appeal

> A school's values are made explicit in the visual "face" that is put forward for the public view. When you enter a school the first sensory impact you may receive is the smell of the disinfectant used to cleanse the halls, but the one that remains longer in memory is the visual information you receive. (Fredette, 1994, p. 236)

When children and teachers enter a classroom and spend a great deal of time in it, the visual face of the environment should provide a feeling of balance and comfort so that children can grow in all areas of development. Venolia (1988) suggested that individuals should be "both relaxed and stimulated, reassured and invited to expand" (p. 7). To satisfy that request, the indoor environment must have an organized and wisely planned room arrangement, sufficient and appropriate lighting, and pleasing visual appeal. This section has already discussed the first two aspects—room arrangement and lighting. We now turn our attention to the concept of visual appeal.

Certainly, every classroom is different and deserves to be examined on an individual basis. This section is meant to serve as an information base from which the reader can apply general knowledge to specific situations. It is broken down into four parts: color, visual clutter, unity and complexity, and emotional warmth and texture.

Color   "Man responds to form with his intellect and to color with his emotions; he can be said to survive by form and to live by color" (Sharp, 1974, p. 123). Many have studied the psychological effects of color on people and their behavior (Birren, 1978; Grangaard, 1993; Hamid & Newport, 1989; Levy, 1984; Torrice & Logrippo, 1989; Wohlfarth, 1981). Architects, educators, hospital administrators, surgeons, optometrists, beauticians, industrialists, and military personnel have applied these findings about color effects to their respective occupations. Scores of fascinating studies have been done on this topic; Hathaway (1982) reviewed several and summarized their results as follows:

- Color can alter perception of temperature, room size, weight, and the passage of time.
- Color can influence work speed, moods, pulse rate, blood pressure, muscle reactions, and psychomotor performance.
- Colors affect our emotions; cool colors (blues and greens) initially relax whereas warm colors (reds and oranges) initially stimulate.

Wohlfarth (1981), found that by changing the standard color and lighting in a classroom of severely handicapped children to that of a psychodynamically prescribed environment (using a coordinated color scheme and full-spectrum lighting), the children exhibited fewer aggressive behaviors, a significant drop in blood pressure, and a decrease in nonattentive behaviors—indicating that children were more on task in the planned environment.

Based on applied color psychology (Mahnke, 1996), Figure 13.3 enables teachers to begin to apply color associations to early childhood classroom environments.

Color adds dimensionality to young children's space. It gives them a point of spatial reference as does shape. Mahnke (1996) reported that "color is the major factor in establishing a desired room experience. It contributes heavily to the 'emotional loading' a space exhibits" (p. 130). The main classroom color choice is the interior color scheme. Many classrooms boast primary colors, assuming that these vivid colors are pleasing to spirited young children. However, Birren (1972) warned, that, "when the colors chosen are too bright, the combinations too dramatic, the effect may be wholly out of place, and the observer may actually be distracted from his tasks or made uncomfortable in his environment" (p. 256). Instead, designers and color consultants for young children's classrooms prefer to complement youngsters' extroverted nature by using "light salmon, soft, warm yellow, pale yellow-orange, coral, and peach" for walls (Mahnke, 1996, p. 183); accents are in either green or blue shades (calming colors). The balance of both warm and cool colors equalizes the emotional climate and avoids a specific mood. Ideally, the classroom colors blend well together and with the room rather than stand out on their own, grabbing the children's attention when they first enter the room. Birren (1972) also warned about neutral white shades for walls.

> Despite the fact that some lighting engineers may freely recommend white and off-white colors for working environments (to gain as much light as possible per watt consumed) the bright environment is quite objectionable. White walls may close the pupil opening, making seeing difficult, and set up annoying distractions. For the sake of 5 or 10 percent increase in lighting efficiency, there may be a drop of 25 percent or more in human efficiency. (pp. 246–247)

Choosing the exact color scheme for the classroom is not a task to be entered into lightly. Besides consideration for the balance of warm and cool colors, several

Color	Effect	Implications for Classroom
Red	Draws attention, can alarm	Large, red butcher paper on table under new materials or new activity
	Suggests strength/importance	Background or letter color on a parent board or notice when a communicable disease or other information needs highlighting
		Background for emergency rules
	Stimulates activity	Motor development equipment, bean bags, and balls
Orange	Stimulates activity	Motor development equipment
	Cheers	Light tints on interior walls
Yellow	Emits light, luminous	The bathroom door or frame around it, yellow line on floor leading to bathroom in young preschoolers' classrooms
		Baskets for completed work in K–3 grades
	Cheers	Warm soft tints on interior walls
Green	Reduces muscle tension, reflects nature/growth, refreshes, calms	Water table, play dough Science area accents Room accent color Inside color of a "private space"
Blue	Reduces weight perception (if pale in color)	Baskets for picking up blocks, bean bags
	Reduces time perception	Napping cots
	Calms/comforts	Water table, play dough Rug or cushions in reading corner Inside color of a "private space" Room accent color
Brown	Suggests stability	Natural wood used in high climbing equipment or lofts

Figure 13.3. Color effects and their classroom implications.

other factors help to determine the intensity of color choices. Some of the influences in color selection listed by Walter (1996) are existing equipment colors and architectural features, lighting (including variation in sunlight throughout the day), backdrop colors outside the windows, color reflectance, and room size.

The influence of color in children's environments is just beginning to receive research attention. Watch for new information in this area. When reading on the subject of the psychological effects of color, however, be sure to check the author's sources. Some books and articles are not based on research and cannot support their color claims.

Visual Clutter   Think about visits to early childhood classrooms. Many have several different colors throughout each room as well as numerous items decorating the walls or hanging from the ceiling, sometimes in disarray. Grangaard (1993) alerted us that "elementary classrooms have become places to display innumerable, 'cute' decorations because we believe this is what will make children comfortable and stimulated" (p. 101). When some parents or administrators first walk into a classroom that is overly decorated and filled with bright colors, they often reply, "Isn't this a happy room." This may be the initial reaction, but teachers and children must live in these visually impacted environments for many hours each day.

Together, disharmonious colors and numerous, unorganized wall displays can overstimulate and give a circus appearance. Moreover, if teachers laminate the materials displayed on walls, glare results and irritates vision clarity. Thus a case of visual clutter is created.

One study (Tegano, Moran III, DeLong, Brickey, & Ramassini, 1996) compared the length of time children spent in play when two walls were covered with either a large geometric pattern or a small geometric pattern. The study concluded that as children felt smaller within their environment (sensation created by a large geometric wall pattern as opposed to a small pattern), they spent less time in play. The question raised by this study is this: Could excessive wall displays not only overstimulate but also decrease children's play duration?

Choosing what to display and where to place selected items is an important consideration when the intent is to avoid visual clutter. As with the pictures in our homes, school wall decorations are best when treated as accessories that help give the message of ownership to the children. Most classrooms, particularly preschool centers, choose children's art work for wall displays. The sections about creative development in Chapters 2 and 3 made the point that ownership is felt when a child's art is original to the child and not a reproduction of the teacher's model. The realization of this point is reflected in the following wall-decoration example. After cutting out look-alike art patterns for hours on end, one teacher-in-training came to the conclusion, "When I become a teacher, I now know that if I want penguins that look alike for a bulletin board I will buy wallpaper!"

Having chosen wall items appropriately, framing children's work in colors that coordinate with the room scheme helps to unify the overall design and give a calming effect. The wise teacher also places wall displays of children's work or important learning concepts (e.g., alphabet letters or numbers) at the child's eye level. Visual appeal is enhanced when the arrangement of the wall items is ordered in a specific pattern.

Unity and Complexity   "Unity involves various components and parts fitting together into a coherent unit. Complexity involves more variation. Extreme unity (monotony or sensory deprivation) can lead to understimulation, and extreme complexity to overstimulation (Mahnke, 1996, p. 23). For example, in the early childhood classroom, using one color throughout (walls, carpet, shelving, window treatments) would be unifying but boring. Using too many colors throughout would be distracting and fatiguing. Healthy environments strive for harmony through balance.

Unity with variety can be achieved through the use of an appropriate color scheme. For example, walls may be painted different shades of the same color (Colby, 1990). On a lesser scale, mounting pictures in the same size and shape of frames, but using different colors coordinating with the over-all color scheme, can also add to the desired effect. Another example is the use of labeling for classroom materials. By using the same size and color of cards for labels in the various centers unity is accomplished. Changing the way the item is pictured on the label beside the word (e.g., cutout catalog picture, sketch, outline of the item, the item itself) creates variety. Some teachers have augmented harmony as well as autonomy by using colored plastic trays to store materials, color coding each area (e.g., all art materials classified by item and kept in green trays). The trick here is to keep the color choices within the classroom color scheme; otherwise the variety of colored trays can contribute to visual clutter.

There is no exact formula for the amount of environmental stimulation that children need (Walter, 1996). Each classroom must be continuously examined to monitor changes. The goal for interior spaces for children is to reflect safety and comfort and foster development. This goal becomes increasingly important when planning for children who have been drug exposed or those who have attention deficit disorder.

Warmth and Texture   Recall the discussion early on in this chapter about comfortable and uncomfortable places. Did you identify two of the essential comfort qualities as softness and variation in textures? In early childhood classrooms, a simple look around the room can check for applications of softness and variations in texture.

Children applaud softness; it seems to go hand-in-hand with security. Visualize children plopping down on a lap, petting the classroom bunny, or taking their blankets to nap.

> A soft, responsive, physical environment reaches out to children. It helps children feel more secure, enabling them to venture out and explore the world, much like homes provide adults the haven from which they can face an often difficult and heartless world. (Greenman, 1988, p. 74)

In classrooms equipped with colorful, easy-care, durable plastic furniture, softness and texture may be added by introducing a few small rugs, bean bag chairs, oversize floor pillows, cushions for the seats or fabric slipcovers on the backs of the plastic chairs paired with tables, and fire retardant valances to windows. (Of course, selections are compatible with the classroom color scheme.)

Ceilings appear lower and rooms become cozier when dado borders are applied.

Plants of various sizes can add softness and texture within the early child hood classroom; "the presence of plants can also modulate our indoor atmosphere, influencing temperatures, humidity, and air quality" (Venolia, 1988, p. 130). Many teachers not only integrate plants in the science area but also place them around the room, as we would do in our homes. The use of plants brings living things indoors, enhances the feeling of coziness and homeyness, and adds an opportunity to experience responsibility. Extreme caution must be exercised when selecting plants for the classroom; some have poisonous leaves, bulbs, or other parts.

In discussions of classroom warmth, an important consideration is children's height in relationship to the ceiling. One effective way to visually lower the ceiling proportionately to the children's level is to use dados (a decorative wallpaper or paint border) that coordinates with the classroom color scheme. "The best way to determine placement of a dado is to estimate the average height of the children oc-

These pastel-colored canvas banners serve two purposes—to reduce the noise with three quarter height walls and to enhance the visual appeal of the learning space.

cupying the room. The dado should then be placed one adult-hand's measure above that height" (Center Management Staff, 1990, p. 14).

Another idea in providing psychological warmth and security in the classroom setting is offered by Janina, a primary teacher. While doing home visits, she observes and listens attentively. She watches to identify what the child favors in her or his home that can be added to the classroom. This is a golden opportunity to say to the child, "You are special," and to make the child feel more secure. Perhaps she adds a book about the child's new pet or some long sheets of computer paper that the child loves to draw on at home. These simple ideas help create a magnetic ambiance.

"Where noise is a problem, minimize hard, nonporous surfaces such as plaster, glass, concrete, and sheet plastics that reflect sound" (Venolia, 1988, p. 94). Choosing soft, dense materials (e.g., carpet, large area rugs, fabrics on the walls, upholstery, quilts used as wall hangings) can add to comfort levels by helping to reduce the noise level. This is significant in many classrooms that have an institutional design.

Outdoor Environments

More than ever before, the early childhood outdoor play yard of today is of paramount importance for the healthy development of children (Senda, 1992). At home, parents are often concerned about their children's safety if they are allowed to play outdoors unsupervised. Many children living in cities have small yards or no yards and unsafe parks. In addition, many children are lured into spending their free time inside by an endless supply of computer games, videos and television programs. With this in mind, Greenman (1993) warned that we are becoming an "indoor culture" (p. 36). Children's time on school playgrounds is therefore highly prized.

This section of the chapter emphasizes the value of outdoor school environments by examining the developmental benefits, the design factors, the teacher's role, and the material and equipment selection. As you read on, keep in mind these wise words: "the best playgrounds are never finished. Rather, they are constantly changing as new challenges replace old ones and as play equipment and material are used in fresh combinations" (Frost, 1992, p. 102).

Developmental Benefits

"Children demonstrate different abilities in the outdoor setting than they do inside. They may show themselves, for example, to be skilled climbers and balancers, or imaginative large-scale builders" (Hohmann & Weikart, 1995, p. 144). The big difference between indoor and outdoor environments is the amount of opportunities, equipment, and planned experiences for children's gross motor development. Motor activities are emphasized in the outdoor environment because of the greater area per child. "For playgrounds to incorporate active motor play, 100 square feet per child is a reasonable playground minimum" (Greenman, 1988, p. 187). In contrast, recommended minimum space indoors is "35 square feet of usable playroom floor space per child" (National Academy of Early Childhood Programs, 1991b, p. 43).

Outdoor play yards are usually furnished with permanent structures and pieces of moveable equipment that promote large motor development. Preschools and kindergartens generally offer swings, climbers, a sandbox, a hard surface for tricycle riding, an empty table or two, and perhaps a slide. Grades 1 through 3 often have climbers, bars, slides, swings, and open spaces for group games in place of riding toys.

Play spaces outside can also be designed to provide opportunities for emotional, social, and cognitive development (Eriksen 1985; Frost, 1992). Picture what a play yard looks like as a group of youngsters move from the indoors to the outdoors. See them gleefully spread out, choosing a variety of activities; some choose to play on permanent equipment or ride those ever popular tricycles whereas others choose open-ended materials or new activities that have been thoughtfully set up by the teacher. In these activities, children are learning to problem-solve, communicate ideas to one another, improve small motor skills and eye–hand coordination, trust their own ideas, play cooperatively, use their imaginations, expand their vocabularies, recognize similarities and differences, form friendships, and overcome fears; the list goes on and on.

Outdoor play spaces can offer developmental benefits that are difficult to facilitate in the indoor environment. In grades 1 through 3, "it is difficult, for example, in most classrooms to evaluate how a child spontaneously interacts with other children. On the playground, with its natural and free environment, the child as explorer and social being becomes more visible." (Brett, Moore, & Provenzo, 1993, p. 164). If nature is incorporated into the setting, a relaxing ambiance invites children to slow down the indoor play tempo and take time to wonder, make discoveries about insects and other living things, and have lazy daydreams. Activities that relieve stress, such as fingerpainting, water play, and woodworking can be given larger work spaces and are easy to clean up outside.

The key to maximizing the full range of developmental benefits is providing a variety of equipment, materials, activities, and experiences within a natural setting that are age and individually appropriate.

Outdoor Design Factors

Whether the teacher is embarking on the adventure of designing a new outdoor environment, expanding or renovating an existing yard, or simply observing to evaluate the present condition of the outdoor setting, there are several factors to consider. The basic list that follows is built on this following framework: All play yard designs are developed within the shape and size of a given plot of land. Each space has its own unique features, and generally all yard designs have monetary limitations.

- Outdoor arrangements welcome children. Landscaping, such as hills for rolling and dirt or sand for digging, enhances the developmental processes. Surfaces are varied in texture, shape, and height. Some choices are wood, concrete, sand, grass, dirt, rubber, fabric, brick, or stones.

- Microclimates are created using vegetation and added structures. Children can play in "sunny and shady spots, breezy spaces, still spaces" (Greenman, 1993, p. 40).

- Nature is woven throughout the play space. Incorporating trees, plants, and flowers on playgrounds extends the scope of play; provides shade or winter sunlight (deciduous trees); illustrates the cycle of seasons; assists in surface runoff and erosion control; furnishes a variety of shape and form for area or entire playground enclosures; contributes sensory variety through plants that differ in texture, color, size, and smell; and supplies gentle indoor–outdoor transitions gradually exposing the child to a change in light levels (Moore, Goltsman, & Iacofano, 1992). A Swedish study (Lindholm, 1995) found that children between the ages of 6 and 12 participated in more activities in playgrounds that had natural areas than in playgrounds that lacked natural areas.

- The entire outside area is fenced for safety (with secure gates) but allows children to see out.

- Boundaries (e.g., change in ground covering, landscape elevation, use of plants or shrubs) within the designated plot of land define specific areas or play zones.

- Traffic patterns are clear, safe, and direct. Bike paths do not cross pedestrian paths.

- All play zones are easily supervised; no blind spots exist.

- Play zones provide for a variety of physical activity—open spaces for mastering gross motor skills or child-initiated activities and protected quiet spaces for resting, dreaming, or watching. Play zones also provide for a variety of interactions. Spaces are designed for playing in small groups, in pairs, or alone.

- A small "parking lot" near the bike path is designated for returning large wheel toys (e.g., tricycles, wagons, scooters) when the rider is finished so that vehicles are not left on the path, creating an unsafe condition.

- A variety of sturdy, size-appropriate equipment is provided to accommodate gross motor play activities (e.g., climbing structures, swings), constructive play activities (e.g., woodworking tools, sand), dramatic play activities (e.g., playhouse and props), and group games (e.g., balls, jump rope, follow-the-leader, ring toss) (Frost, 1992).

- Impermanent activities are selected based on children's developmental needs and interests, space, staff, and weather conditions. They are teacher planned and set up on a daily basis (e.g., small plastic buckets of water and large paintbrushes for wall or sidewalk painting, a blanket under a shade tree and a basket of manipulatives or books brought from the inside, an obstacle course).

- An abundance of equipment and materials is available for different developmental levels. Examples are sandbox and water table tools for emptying, filling, and pouring as well as tools that can be used for representing. On the primary grade playground, climbing bars of varying heights can be available.

- Materials, equipment, and experiences in the various play zones offer the children gradual and continuous challenges (Henniger, 1994b).

- All equipment is kept in safe condition; cushioned materials are provided under swings and climbing structures. Sand is kept clean. A locked storage facility secures moveable equipment when school is not in session.

Teacher's Role

"Teachers, administrators and others generally consider playgrounds and the activities that occur there less important than indoor spaces in the lives of young children" (Henniger, 1994a, p. 87). Moreover, some teachers perceive their roles indoors very differently from their roles outdoors. These teachers spend their planning time focused on indoor activities. When they are outside, they act only as safety supervisors. To support a child's developmental growth both indoors and outdoors, informed teachers view the outdoor physical setting as an extension of the indoor setting and act accordingly (Esbensen, 1987). Weekly planning for the play yard is commensurate with indoor planning.

> Teachers have an important role in the success or failure of any playground program. Their principle task is to prepare the environment for play, observe what happens in that environment, and then decide what action needs to be taken either to modify the environment or interact with the children. (Brett et al., 1993, p. 157)

Once the planning and setup is complete and the children are actively engaged in outdoor play, the teacher's number one responsibility is the children's safety. Many schools report that most playground accidents are the result of inappropriate supervision. When play yards are designed so that children are challenged and can take healthy risks, teachers must give the children space to explore while anticipating possible mishaps, always seeing the big picture.

With one eye out for safety, teachers also use outdoor time to make anecdotal observations, have one-on-one conversations with children, assist children in successfully entering play groups, support conflict resolution, and facilitate and extend play through adding materials, asking questions, and joining in play when appropriate.

Outdoor Materials and Equipment Selection

When choosing outdoor equipment and materials, Kritchevsky and Prescott with Walling (1977) suggested considering both the variety and the complexity of the play units. They define variety as "the number of different kinds of units" (p. 12) and complexity as "the extent to which they [play units] contain potential for active manipulation and alteration by children" (p. 11). Think about these two points and inspect the two playgrounds pictured in Figure 13.4.

Figure 13.4 presents photographs of outdoor play arenas not yet set up for a particular day. Before bringing out additional activities or equipment, teachers informally assess the play space by considering the following:

- Equipment or space provisions for children to develop and practice the motor skills of running, hopping, jumping, climbing, balancing, throwing, and catching.
- A variety of climbing equipment (e.g., ropes, ladders, platforms, poles, or nets) and variations of specific kinds of equipment (e.g., tire swings, rope swings, or swings with seats).
- Different levels of difficulty offered through materials and equipment that can be used in simple and complex ways.
- Enough equipment so children won't have long waits for turns. (Long waits rob children of the very purpose of outdoor time.)

Figure 13.4. Playgrounds. *Top,* preschool; *bottom,* primary grade.

When evaluating a play yard, also appraise the open-endedness of the materials. Outdoor yards that supply only simple equipment often entice children to seek out the prized equipment (e.g., tricycles) on a preschool play yard. Several children will race to see who gets them first, and unless the teacher intervenes, a few children may spend the entire outside time cruising bike paths on shiny pedaled vehicles. In this case, the environment limits the child's chance at well-rounded motor development and sets the stage for much quarreling.

In contrast, if the materials are open-ended and always accessible for children's use, they will design their own complex units. Available materials that can be moved, manipulated, and changed feed developmental needs. Material flexibility and availability, however, make some teachers very nervous. They worry about safety as the children enthusiastically drag materials around and build creations. Certainly, watchful supervision and occasional advisement is necessary as children solve problems and create. Greenman (1988), however, cautioned that on playgrounds offering only simple play units, "children will add risk and daring in order to cope with boredom. They will jump off inappropriate equipment like slide ladders, play chicken, and test the limits of people and things" (p. 188).

Practice Activity 13.1
Outdoor Developmental Opportunities

List additional equipment (fixed or portable) that could be added to these outdoor yards in Figure 13.4, and state a brief justification. Think about furthering children's development of gross motor, imagination, creativity, communication, and investigative skills.

Example: In the preschool yard: Tire swing—provides variety and promotes the development of coordination, strength and communication.

Garden—promotes the understanding of the growth cycle, provides "an excellent setting for integrating children with and without disabilities" (Moore et al., 1992, p. 142).

1.

2.

3.

4.

This section would not be complete without a discussion of the drinking fountain. Some states have licensing regulations requiring child care centers to have drinking water readily available to young children. Permitting each child to get drinks as needed is preferred to asking the child to wait and then making one long line for drinks before the children go inside (recall information on impulse control in Chapter 2). Allowing children free access encourages autonomy and independence as well as good health practices.

Observing the Physical Environment

Up to this point, the details of the major elements of the physical environment (indoors and outdoors) have been examined. The importance of various factors in promoting positive learning conditions has been discussed. Now the focus of the chapter shifts to the use of observational strategies in the physical environment.

"From observation, teachers can learn whether more time, space, or play materials are needed, whether certain materials are beyond a child's ability, or if the play situation is not sufficiently stimulating" (Brett et al., 1993, p. 163). Checklists, rating scales, tally event sampling, and time samplings are the observational methods most commonly used for environmental assessments. In previous chapters you have read about these methods and have already had some practice assessing environments (e.g., autonomy in Chapter 7). Using your experiences and the information in this chapter, think for a moment about possible topics for observation in the physical environment and appropriate methods to use in assessment; then proceed to Practice Activity 13.2. Be aware that checklists and rating scales look directly at environmental items whereas tally and time samplings look indirectly at environments, assessing how people use the environment.

Practice Activity 13.2
Environmental Observation Topics

This activity has three parts. First, list four possible topics that early childhood teachers could observe either outside or inside. Second, after each topic form a specific observational question. Third, suggest an observational method that could be used to collect information systematically to answer the question.

Topic	Question	Method
Example:		
Traffic paths	Which traffic paths are used most often, and are they congested or free flowing?	Tally event or time sampling
1.		
2.		
3.		
4.		

Classroom Example

Consider Our Ethical Responsibilities to Our Co-Workers

NAEYC Ideal I-3A.2

"To share resources and information with co-workers" (Feeney & Kipnis, 1992, p. 8).

Read on to see how the college students and the Cypress School teachers fulfill this ethical responsibility.

An early childhood art professor enlisted her college students in a variety of class projects. One project, in conjunction with a local school, was to construct a checklist of art materials and make recommendations to the school staff for yearly art supply orders and requests for donations.

Five students eagerly chose this project option. The college students responsibly constructed an art checklist utilizing the guidelines in Chapter 6 and the knowledge gained in their college creative art class. As they selected items to put on the list, they were mindful to choose items that were not so small that the youngest children in the school could swallow them or put them in their ears or noses. Realizing that material choice is often restricted by limited budgets, they included ideas that could be obtained free-of-charge. Figure 13.5 is the students' form and the results of their art inventory.

Art Materials Inventory

School/Grade: Cypress School/Preschool–Third Grade

Date: 5/15   Time: 4:00 P.M.

Observers: Star, Lalaynia, Clark,   Child/Age: N/A
Mihoko, Buffy

Instructions: Check the box before the items that the school has in sufficient supply.

Background Materials:
☑ Construction paper
☑ Poster board/cardboard
☐ Butcher paper
☑ Finger paint paper
☑ Watercolor paper
☑ Newsprint paper

Items For Fastening:
☑ Glue and paste
☑ Hole punch and yarn
☑ Tape/scotch or masking — *Just for teacher's use*
☐ Gummed labels or stickers
☐ Pipe cleaners or thin wire
☑ Large plastic needles/thin yarn
☑ Clear ConTact

Figure 13.5. Inventory checklist.

☑ Fabric
❏ Aluminum foil
❏ Paper plates
☑ Clear ConTact
☑ Tissue paper
☑ Tagboard
❏ Computer paper*
❏ Lined paper
❏ Magazines*

Drawing and Writing Materials:
☑ Crayons
☑ Pencils/colored pencils
☑ Tempera paints
☑ Watercolors
☑ Fat chalks
☑ Markers
❏ Shaving cream
☑ Finger paints

Tools for Detaching:
☑ Scissors (left- and right-handed) *only*

Collage Box Items:
☑ Fabric pieces*
☑ Paper scraps*
☑ Wallpaper samples*
☑ Corrugated cardboard scraps*
❏ Lace and leather scraps*
☑ Ribbons, yarn, and used gift wrappings* *only*
❏ Dried flowers*
❏ Carpet/padding scraps*
☑ Sawdust*
☑ Assorted donations!*

Tools For Painting:
☑ 3/4- and 1-inch paintbrushes
☑ Watercolor brushes
❏ Toothbrushes
☑ Dabbers (Cotton wrapped in fabric and attached to tongue depressor with rubber bands)
☑ Cotton swabs
☑ Feather dusters/feathers
☑ Small cars
☑ Roll-on deodorant bottles with pop-off lids*
☑ Golf balls*

Three-Dimensional Items:
❏ Craft sticks
❏ Gummed paper strips
❏ Clay and plasticine
❏ Wood scraps*
☑ Styrofoam pieces (all sizes)*
❏ Nature items (branches, pinecones, etc.)*
☑ Play dough
❏ Cardboard cylinder tubes (all sizes)*
❏ Small cardboard boxes*
❏ Cotton balls
❏ Braid and fabric trims*
❏ Wooden or plastic spools (all sizes)*
❏ Broom straws/drinking straws*
❏ Bottle caps*
❏ Wood shavings*
❏ Rocks*
❏ Empty yogurt containers, berry baskets*

Tools For Printing:
☑ Gadgets*
☑ Sponges*
☑ Items of different shapes*
❏ Blocks with weather stripping designs

Other:
☑ Easels
☑ Smocks
☑ Drying area or rack

*Donated or free materials

Comments: *Organizing the supply cupboard by the categories presented above would expedite restocking. Check the usability of markers. No skin-tone crayons, markers, or paints are available.*

Figure 13.5. *(Continued).*

Observational data assist teachers in selecting materials and planning activities.

The Cypress School staff felt fortunate to have the input from the college students. The teachers however, were surprised to see that they had not considered three-dimensional supplies prior to the inventory check using a designed list. Coincidentally, the school had a few materials in the three-dimensional area; the teachers were acutely embarrassed to admit they had overlooked the importance of obtaining and offering three-dimensional materials for the development of spatial relations and increased opportunities for creative expression. The teachers had never had an organized inventory appraisal form. In fact, they had never used systematic observation to look at the physical environment. Instead they had used the "Mother Hubbard" approach: look in and see what is or isn't left. The teachers were grateful to have a checklist that would ensure a well-rounded collection of art materials that contribute to a comprehensive developmental program.

Action Project 13.2
Outdoor Environment Assessment

Assess the outside yard of a preschool or kindergarten using Section I of the *Playground Rating System* (Frost, 1992, pp. 107–108) that follows. Utilizing your observation and the information in this chapter on outdoor environments, make suggestions for improvement. State your rationale for suggestions. (Note: In Chapter 7, three types of rating scale designs were discussed. This rating scale provides another possible configuration.)

Outdoor Rating Scale

Center or School/Age level or Grade:
Date: Time:
Observer: Teachers:
                                        Children:

Instructions: Rate each item on a scale from 0 to 5. Possible high score
                on Section I is 100 points.

Playground Rating System (Ages 3–8)

Section I.   What does the playground contain?

Rate each item for degree of existence and function on a scale of 0–5 (0 = not existent; 1 = some elements exist but are not functional; 2 = poor; 3 = average; 4 = good; 5 = all elements exist, excellent [function]).

_____ 1. A hard-surfaced area with space for games and a network of paths for wheeled toys.

_____ 2. Sand and sand equipment.

_____ 3. Dramatic play structures (play house, car or boat with complementary equipment, such as adjacent sand and water and housekeeping equipment).

_____ 4. A superstructure with room for many children at a time and with a variety of challenges and exercise options (entries, exits and levels).

_____ 5. Mound(s) of earth for climbing and digging.

_____ 6. Trees and natural areas for shade, nature study, and play.

_____ 7. Zoning to provide continuous challenge; linkage of areas, functional physical boundaries, vertical and horizontal treatment (hills and valleys).

_____ 8. Water play areas, with fountains, pools and sprinklers.

_____ 9. Construction area with junk materials such as tires, crates, planks, boards, bricks and nails; tools should be provided and demolition and construction allowed.

_____ 10. An old (or built) vehicle, airplane, boat, car that has been made safe, but not stripped of its play value (should be changed or relocated after a period of time to renew interest).

_____ 11. Equipment for active play: a slide with a large platform at the top (slide may be built into side of a hill); swings that can be used safely in a variety of ways (soft material for seats); climbing trees (mature dead trees that are horizontally positioned); climbing nets.

_____ 12. A large soft area (grass, bark mulch, etc.) for organized games.

_____ 13. Small semi-private spaces at the child's own scale: tunnels, niches, playhouses, hiding places.

_____ 14. Fences, gates, walls and windows that provide security for young children and are adaptable for learning/play.

_____ 15. A garden and flowers located so that they are protected from play, but with easy access for the child to tend them. Gardening tools are available.

_____ 16. Provisions for the housing of pets. Pets and supplies are available.

_____ 17. A transitional space from outdoors to indoors. This could be a covered play area immediately adjoining the playroom which will protect the children from the sun and rain and extend indoor activities to the outside.

_____ 18. Adequate protected storage for outdoor play equipment, tools for construction and garden areas, and maintenance tools. Storage can be separate: wheel toys stored near the wheeled vehicle track; sand equipment near the sand enclosure; tools near the construction area. Storage can be in separate structures next to the building or fence. Storage should aid in children's picking-up and putting equipment away at the end of each play period.

_____ 19. Easy access from outdoor play areas to coats, toilets, and drinking fountains. Shaded areas and benches for adults and children to sit within the outdoor play area.

_____ 20. Tables and support materials for group activities (art, reading, etc.)

Source: From Complete Playground Rating System in *Play and Playscapes,* by Joe L. Frost, 1992, Albany, New York: Delmar. Reprinted by permission of Joe L. Frost.

Suggestions: *Rationale:*

1.

2.

3.

4.

Points to Remember

The physical environment may enhance or hinder the learning process. Significant factors to consider, observe, and assess in the indoor classroom setting are room arrangement, lighting, and visual appeal. Important outdoor elements are developmental benefits, design factors, the teacher's role, and equipment and materials selection.

Diligent environmental planning, based on developmental principles and class goals, is necessary for both the outdoor and indoor settings. Various observational methods can assist the teacher in evaluating the physical components. On the basis of data obtained through observations, the teacher can change or rearrange equipment, materials, and centers to best serve the growing needs and interests of children in the classroom.

Take a Moment to Reflect

Picture in your mind a real place you go or would like to go when you want to study or do paper work that requires concentration. Visualize the conditions that surround your choice. Try to be as specific as possible. In addition to the location, analyze the climate. Give attention to colors, lighting and windows, floor coverings, room arrangement, wall decorations, furniture, temperature, and sounds. After you have a clear image of your favorite learning environment ask two or three other people to visualize and describe their preferred place. Compare your findings. Then reflect on the following questions.

1. How are these learning environments alike and different?
2. Reflect on an ideal, imaginary place you would create for studying or doing paper work that requires concentration. Based on that picture, what additions, deletions, or changes would you recommend for your real place?

Observing Clearly

Τhe journey of *Through the Looking Glass* ends in Part IV, with one chapter to summarize and integrate the previous 13. Your job is to review the observational keys you have learned along the way: the *why, what, how,* and *communication* keys. Chapter 14 aids in this process by presenting a comparison of the observational methods you have studied that includes their subjects, purposes, data produced, and suggested frequency of use. You then gain experience in selecting an appropriate observational method to study a given classroom question in a practice activity. You should leave *Through the Looking Glass* with a firm understanding of the benefits of observation in the early childhood classroom and a personal commitment to engage in sound observational practices to enrich your own professional life and the development of children whose lives you touch.

CHAPTER 14

Through the Looking Glass

T.G.I.F.—Friday already, and three good friends and fellow recent graduates with degrees in early childhood education share a monthly dinner. Maliha is teaching young 5-year-olds in a classroom on an elementary school campus. Clay has remained with his beloved parent participation program and is now a teacher, rather than an aide, in the 3- and 4-year-old classroom. Heather is reeling from the exhaustion and exhilaration of adjusting to teaching first grade after doing her student teaching in a university laboratory school.

The three friends catch up, and inevitably the conversation turns to their classrooms and the people who bring them to life. Maliha describes a child who is angry and resentful that she is not in kindergarten with her next-door neighbor and the ABC narrative event sampling results that helped Maliha identify which activities and interactions with other children support the child's self-esteem. Clay relates the uncomfortable entry of a new child with limited English and the exciting plans that resulted from a timely parent conference. Heather shares her feelings of jubilation that her aide now engages in activities with children ever since they agreed to video-tape him in the classroom and then view the results together. Think about these remarkable teachers and the role that observation plays in their success.

Marian Wright Edelman (1992), a tireless advocate for children, seemed to know Maliha, Clay, and Heather as she wrote: "Focus on what you have, not what you don't have; on what you can do rather than what you cannot do" (p. 102). These teachers bring their knowledge of child development, appropriate curriculum, and observation to a full embrace of their teaching responsibilities. They know in their hearts and minds that their teaching matters to each child in their classrooms. Edelman urges us all to have confidence that we can make a difference. Let this message ring true for the educators of young children who practice observation in their classrooms. Let each teacher strive to be remarkable for all the Annies and Songs and Blancas of the world.

So we come to the end of this book and rely on the final chapter to complete and summarize the journey begun in Chapter 1. Our passage followed the introduction of highlights of development during the preschool and primary grade years, methods for observing the development of individual children, and guidelines for organizing portfolios and planning effective parent conferences. The route then turned to methods for observing children and teachers at work in early childhood classrooms and included the processes of selecting and designing observational instruments and enriching environments through observation. As you now stand before the observational looking glass, appreciate your sharp and developed vision.

- Your study of developmental growth indicators and observational methods has strengthened your knowledge of *what* to observe in the early childhood classroom and *how* to observe.

Method	Subjects	Purpose	Data Produced	Frequency of Use
Running records	Individual children	Observe and document developmental growth; gain overall picture	Qualitative	As necessary
Anecdotes	Individual children	Document developmental growth and significant incidents	Qualitative	Daily
Checklists	Individual children or teachers, programs, and environments	Assess presence or absence of specific characteristics; assess changes over time	Qualitative*	Periodically
Rating scales	Individual children or teachers, programs, and environments	Assess strengths of specific characteristics; assess changes over time	Qualitative*	Periodically
ABC narrative event sampling	Individual children	Observe specific problems and developmental growth in context	Qualitative	As necessary
Tally event sampling	Individual children or teachers and groups; programs and environments indirectly	Study frequencies of predetermined events	Quantitative	As necessary
Time sampling	Individual children or teachers and groups; programs and environments indirectly	Study frequencies of events within predetermined time sampling units	Quantitative	As necessary

* This book discussed only the qualitative analysis of checklist and rating scale data. Occasionally, you might see quantitative data produced and analyzed when using checklists and rating scales.

Figure 14.1. Comparison of observational methods for early childhood classrooms.

- You understand that observational methods are varied and require specific procedures; choice is driven by the purpose of your inquiry. All methods are equally applicable for preschool and primary grade use.
- Your observations of children, teachers, interactions, programs, and environments are recorded as objectively as possible.
- You are prepared to select a portfolio system and plan parent conferences that enrich home/school partnerships.
- Your proficient applications of the various methods introduced in this book have resulted in satisfying results.
- You understand the processes of designing instruments and analyzing and presenting data that allow teachers to find the answers to specific observational questions.
- Above all, your practice in applications has prepared you to plan for each child's unique growth based on sound observations.

Your well-earned observational skills offer a broad perspective, not readily available to the untrained eye, of children, teachers, and the early childhood classroom. You now enter preschools or primary grade classrooms armed with the ability to recognize and meet each child's individual developmental needs by applying observational methods and planning appropriately. You are able to examine specific classroom questions and concerns using instruments that you designed. Experience will offer additional practice to further refine and mature your observational skills. Here is an account of a teacher's similar transition:

> In thinking about what my own experience can contribute to ideas about deepening a teacher's understanding about children and teaching, I would probably point to the gradual shift of emphasis from What and how do I teach? to What can I learn about teaching from children? Watching children learn, studying them, documenting what we see and hear, and becoming researchers in our own classrooms gives us the raw materials from which to evolve our own ways of teaching. (Martin, 1994, p. 195)

The greater part of the journey in this book provided an in-depth study of seven different observational methods within the framework of child development (Chapters 4–8, 10, and 11). Now is the time to cement together an overall view of observation in the early childhood classroom by clearly comparing the distinctive features of each method. Figure 14.1 provides the mortar, and Practice Activity 14.1 some practice.

Practice Activity 14.1
Selecting Observational Methods

Read the following scenarios from early childhood classrooms. Write down an appropriate observational method for responding to each.

Scenario: A preschool teacher, Beverly, realizes she thinks about some children in her classroom more than others and worries that she does not support their growth equally.

She asks the director to plan an observation to answer the question, "How frequently does Beverly interact with each child during a preschool session?"

Method:

Scenario: A child has just arrived in Costa's child care program in the middle of the year and is having difficulty adjusting. Costa wants to begin observing his adjustment.

Method:

Scenario: An early childhood education student, Lida, would like to begin learning about classroom management techniques. She plans to observe several different classrooms to answer the question, "How do teachers deal with children's conflicts?"

Method:

The Teachers Commitment to Observation

The ability to understand children through observation might be compared to the ability to judge fine art. We all respond to art—positively, negatively, indifferently—but the person with experience and training can better assess the aesthetic value of a work of art. Similarly, we all form impressions of children, but for the inexperienced observer, the impression may be inaccurate, biased, or limited in scope. (Phinney, 1982, pp. 23–24).

To best serve the education of all children in a classroom, the teacher demonstrates an active commitment to observation. The wheels of observation do not turn alone. They require the leadership of a teacher willing to plan observations of each child, the program, and the environment. Observation is a continuous process; to successfully integrate observation into the classroom, the teacher builds time into the daily schedule.

Although based on the teacher's commitment and leadership, observation need not be a solitary activity. Teachers will find support by sharing efforts with directors, principals, colleagues, aides, parents, child study teams, and college students. Burdens of scheduling and time allocations are eased by involving the energies of others. The rewards of observation justify the commitment and follow-through of remarkable teachers.

The Benefits of Observation in the Early Childhood Classroom

The benefits of observation in preschool and primary grade classrooms are plentiful and have been noted throughout this book. Observation serves individual children by providing their teachers with information to chart their developmental

The benefits of observation
return to individual children.

growth, plan appropriate activities to support continued growth, uncover the roots
of problems, and prepare useful feedback to their parents. Multiple observational
methods offer the teacher a realistic view of the whole child. Observation renews
the energies of teachers who can monitor their own effectiveness and make productive adjustments. Observation helps teachers evaluate programs and environments to improve the quality of education offered children.

In closing, the benefits of observation return to children. All children have individual strengths and emerging interests and aspirations. The headwaters that
nourish a vital commitment to a life's work might hardly be noticed during early
childhood but, nonetheless, may contribute to later choices. Corey, a young gradu-
ate student in Spanish literature, traces his interest in the subject to his experience
in a bilingual kindergarten program. Early childhood is a time for initial exploring
and experimenting with possible areas of enjoyment and interest. Look beyond the
young child for a moment. A complex society such as ours requires the diverse talents of its citizens to function and progress; fostering and supporting individual
abilities thus serves society as well as the individual.

How can early childhood educators advance the development of each child?
You know:

- By understanding each child as an individual within the context of a family and
culture.

And how can these educators learn about each child? You know so well:

- By watching, listening to, and recording what each child does and says.
- By using the information gathered to plan developmentally appropriate experiences and to adjust the program and environment.
- By using a record-keeping system and designing portfolios that bear witness to individuality and then by sharing treasures and concerns with parents.
- By observing through the looking glass with affection, competence, and commitment.

May your vision always be clear as you observe through the looking glass in an early childhood classroom.

Take a Moment to Reflect

Over the past 15 years, new advances in microcomputer technology have made assessment and data collection less time-consuming, simpler, more sensitive, and more useful in classroom environments. These microcomputer systems, traditionally geared for researchers, are becoming more user-friendly and have important applications for assisting educators in assessment and data summation. (Johnson, Brady, & Larson, 1996, p. 254)

As you look toward the future, reflect on the following:

1. Data may be collected using a small hand-held remote control that transmits information to a nearby computer. Speculate on the differences between being an observer in an early childhood classroom with a clipboard and pencil and being an observer with a hand-held remote control easily carried in a pocket.

2. Observers can currently rely on computer programs to collect data using the ABC narrative event sampling, tally event sampling, and time sampling methods. Reflect on your own initial reactions to technology. Think about your own responses to change in general. While studying this book, for example, what were some of your responses to suggested changes in your observation practices? What positive results did you experience when you tried an unfamiliar teaching strategy or observational method? Change is not always easy and comfortable. Reflect on processes that ease transitions toward professional growth and expertise.

The National Association for the Education of Young Children Code of Ethical Conduct

PREAMBLE

NAEYC recognizes that many daily decisions required of those who work with young children are of a moral and ethical nature. The NAEYC Code of Ethical Conduct offers guidelines for responsible behavior and sets forth a common basis for resolving the principal ethical dilemmas encountered in early childhood education. The primary focus is on daily practice with children and their families in programs for children from birth to 8 years of age: preschools, child care centers, family day care homes, kindergartens, and primary classrooms. Many of the provisions also apply to specialists who do not work directly with children, including program administrators, parent educators, college professors, and child care licensing specialists.

Standards of ethical behavior in early childhood education are based on commitment to core values that are deeply rooted in the history of our field. We have committed ourselves to

Appreciating childhood as a unique and valuable stage of the human life cycle

Basing our work with children on knowledge of child development

Appreciating and supporting the close ties between the child and family

Recognizing that children are best understood in the context of family, culture, and society

Respecting the dignity, worth, and uniqueness of each individual (child, family member, and colleague)

Helping children and adults achieve their full potential in the context of relationships that are based on trust, respect, and positive regard

Source: This Code of Ethical Conduct and Statement of Commitment was prepared under the auspices of the Ethics Commission of the National Association for the Education of Young Children by Stephanie Feeney and Kenneth Kipnis. The Commission members were Stephanie Feeney (Chairperson), Bettye Caldwell, Sally Cartwright, Carrie Cheek, Josué Cruz, Jr., Anne G. Dorsey, Dorothy M. Hill, Lilian G. Katz, Pamm Mattick, Shirley A.; Norris, and Sue Spayth Riley. Copyright © 1992 by the National Association for the Education of Young Children. (Feeney & Kipnis, 1992, pp. 3–12).

The Code sets forth a conception of our professional responsibilities in four sections, each addressing an arena of professional relationships: (1) children, (2) families, (3) colleagues, and (4) community and society. Each section includes an introduction to the primary responsibilities of the early childhood practitioner in that arena, a set of ideals pointing in the direction of exemplary professional practice, and a set of principles defining practices that are required, prohibited, and permitted.

The ideals reflect the aspirations of practitioners. The principles are intended to guide conduct and assist practitioners in resolving ethical dilemmas encountered in the field. There is not necessarily a corresponding principle for each ideal. Both ideals and principles are intended to direct practitioners to those questions which, when responsibly answered, will provide the basis for conscientious decision making. While the Code provides specific direction for addressing some ethical dilemmas, many others will require the practitioner to combine the guidance of the Code with sound professional judgment.

The ideals and principles in this Code present a shared conception of professional responsibility that affirms our commitment to the core values of our field. The Code publicly acknowledges the responsibilities that we in the field have assumed and in so doing supports ethical behavior in our work. Practitioners who face ethical dilemmas are urged to seek guidance in the applicable parts of this Code and in the spirit that informs the whole.

SECTION I: ETHICAL RESPONSIBILITIES TO CHILDREN

Childhood is a unique and valuable stage in the life cycle. Our paramount responsibility is to provide safe, healthy, nurturing, and responsive settings for children. We are committed to supporting children's development by cherishing individual differences, by helping them learn to live and work cooperatively, and by promoting their self-esteem.

Ideals:

I-1.1   To be familiar with the knowledge base of early childhood education and to keep current through continuing education and in-service training.

I-1.2   To base program practices upon current knowledge in the field of child development and related disciplines and upon particular knowledge of each child.

I-1.3   To recognize and respect the uniqueness and the potential of each child.

I-1.4   To appreciate the special vulnerability of children.

I-1.5   To create and maintain safe and healthy settings that foster children's social, emotional, intellectual, and physical development and that respect their dignity and their contributions.

I-1.6   To support the right of children with special needs to participate, consistent with their ability, in regular early childhood programs.

Principles:

P-1.1   Above all, we shall not harm children. We shall not participate in practices that are disrespectful, degrading, dangerous, exploitative, intimidating, psychologically damaging, or physically harmful to children. *This principle has precedence over all others in this Code.*

P-1.2   We shall not participate in practices that discriminate against children by denying benefits, giving special advantages, or excluding them from programs or activities on the basis of their race, religion, sex, national origin, or the status, behavior, or beliefs of their parents. (This principle does not apply to programs that have a lawful mandate to provide services to a particular population of children.)

P-1.3 We shall involve all of those with relevant knowledge (including staff and parents) in decisions concerning a child.

P-1.4 When, after appropriate efforts have been made with a child and the family, the child still does not appear to be benefitting from a program, we shall communicate our concern to the family in a positive way and offer them assistance in finding a more suitable setting.

P-1.5 We shall be familiar with the symptoms of child abuse and neglect and know and follow community procedures and state laws that protect children against abuse and neglect.

P-1.6 When we have evidence of child abuse or neglect, we shall report the evidence to the appropriate community agency and follow up to ensure that appropriate action has been taken. When possible, parents will be informed that the referral has been made.

P-1.7 When another person tells us of their suspicion that a child is being abused or neglected but we lack evidence, we shall assist that person in taking appropriate action to protect the child.

P-1.8 When a child protective agency fails to provide adequate protection for abused or neglected children, we acknowledge a collective ethical responsibility to work toward improvement of these services.

P-1.9 When we become aware of a practice or situation that endangers the health or safety of children, but has not been previously known to do so, we have an ethical responsibility to inform those who can remedy the situation and who can keep other children from being similarly endangered.

SECTION II: ETHICAL RESPONSIBILITIES TO FAMILIES

Families are of primary importance in children's development. (The term *family* may include others, besides parents, who are responsibly involved with the child.) Because the family and the early childhood educator have a common interest in the child's welfare, we acknowledge a primary responsibility to bring about collaboration between the home and school in ways that enhance the child's development.

Ideals:

I-2.1 To develop relationships of mutual trust with the families we serve.

I-2.2 To acknowledge and build upon strengths and competencies as we support families in their task of nurturing children.

I-2.3 To respect the dignity of each family and its culture, customs, and beliefs.

I-2.4 To respect families' childrearing values and their right to make decisions for their children.

I-2.5 To interpret each child's progress to parents within the framework of a developmental perspective and to help families understand and appreciate the value of developmentally appropriate early childhood programs.

I-2.6 To help family members improve their understanding of their children and to enhance their skills as parents.

I-2.7 To participate in building support networks for families by providing them with opportunities to interact with program staff and families.

Principles:

P-2.1 We shall not deny family members access to their child's classroom or program setting.

P-2.2 We shall inform families of program philosophy, policies, and personnel qualifications, and explain why we teach as we do.

P-2.3 We shall inform families of and, when appropriate, involve them in policy decisions.

P-2.4 We shall inform families of and, when appropriate, involve them in significant decisions affecting their child.

P-2.5 We shall inform the family of accidents involving their child, of risks such as exposures to contagious disease that may result in infection, and of events that might result in psychological damage.

P-2.6 We shall not permit or participate in research that could in any way hinder the education or development of the children in our programs. Families shall be fully informed of any proposed research projects involving their children and shall have the opportunity to give or withhold consent.

P-2.7 We shall not engage in or support exploitation of families. We shall not use our relationship with a family for private advantage or personal gain, or enter into relationships with family members that might impair our effectiveness in working with children.

P-2.8 We shall develop written policies for the protection of confidentiality and the disclosure of children's records. The policy documents shall be made available to all program personnel and families. Disclosure of children's records beyond family members, program personnel, and consultants having an obligation of confidentiality shall require familial consent (except in cases of abuse or neglect).

P-2.9 We shall maintain confidentiality and shall respect the family's right to privacy, refraining from disclosure of confidential information and intrusion into family life. However, when we are concerned about a child's welfare, it is permissible to reveal confidential information to agencies and individuals who may be able to act in the child's interest.

P-2.10 In cases where family members are in conflict we shall work openly, sharing our observations of the child, to help all parties involved make informed decisions. We shall refrain from becoming an advocate for one party.

P-2.11 We shall be familiar with and appropriately use community resources and professional services that support families. After a referral has been made, we shall follow up to ensure that services have been adequately provided.

SECTION III: ETHICAL RESPONSIBILITIES TO COLLEAGUES

In a caring, cooperative work place human dignity is respected, professional satisfaction is promoted, and positive relationships are modeled. Our primary responsibility in this area is to establish and maintain settings and relationships that support productive work and meet professional needs.

A—Responsibilities to Co-workers

Ideals:

I-3A.1 To establish and maintain relationships of trust and cooperation with co-workers.

I-3A.2 To share resources and information with co-workers.

I-3A.3 To support co-workers in meeting their professional needs and in their professional development.

I-3A.4 To accord co-workers due recognition of professional achievement.

Principles:

P-3A.1   When we have concern about the professional behavior of a co-worker, we shall first let that person know of our concern and attempt to resolve the matter collegially.

P-3A.2   We shall exercise care in expressing views regarding the personal attributes or professional conduct of co-workers. Statements should be based on firsthand knowledge and relevant to the interests of children and programs.

B—Responsibilities to Employers

Ideals:

I-3B.1   To assist the program in providing the highest quality of service.

I-3B.2   To maintain loyalty to the program and uphold its reputation.

Principles:

P-3B.1   When we do not agree with program policies, we shall first attempt to effect change through constructive action within the organization.

P-3B-2.   We shall speak or act on behalf of an organization only when authorized. We shall take care to note when we are speaking for the organization and when we are expressing a personal judgment.

C—Responsibilities to Employees

Ideals:

I-3C.1   To promote policies and working conditions that foster competence, well-being, and self-esteem in staff members.

I-3C.2   To create a climate of trust and candor that will enable staff to speak and act in the best interests of children, families, and the field of early childhood education.

I-3C.3   To strive to secure an adequate livelihood for those who work with or on behalf of young children.

Principles:

P-3C.1   In decisions concerning children and programs, we shall appropriately utilize the training, experience, and expertise of staff members.

P-3C.2   We shall provide staff members with working conditions that permit them to carry out their responsibilities, timely and non-threatening evaluation procedures, written grievance procedures, constructive feedback, and opportunities for continuing professional development and advancement.

P-3C.3   We shall develop and maintain comprehensive written personnel policies that define program standards and, when applicable, that specify the extent to which employees are accountable for their conduct outside the work place. These policies shall be given to new staff members and shall be available for review by all staff members.

P-3C.4   Employees who do not meet program standards shall be informed of areas of concern and, when possible, assisted in improving their performance.

P-3C.5   Employees who are dismissed shall be informed of the reasons for their termination. When a dismissal is for cause, justification must be based on evidence of inadequate or inappropriate behavior that is accurately documented, current, and available for the employee to review.

P-3C.6   In making evaluations and recommendations, judgments shall be based on fact and relevant to the interests of children and programs.

P-3C.7   Hiring and promotion shall be based solely on a person's record of accomplishment and ability to carry out the responsibilities of the position.

P-3C.8   In hiring, promotion, and provision of training, we shall not participate in any form of discrimination based on race, religion, sex, national origin, handicap, age, or sexual preference. We shall be familiar with laws and regulations that pertain to employment discrimination.

SECTION IV: ETHICAL RESPONSIBILITIES TO COMMUNITY AND SOCIETY

Early childhood programs operate within a context of an immediate community made up of families and other institutions concerned with children's welfare. Our responsibilities to the community are to provide programs that meet its needs and to cooperate with agencies and professions that share responsibility for children. Because the larger society has a measure of responsibility for the welfare and protection of children, and because of our specialized expertise in child development, we acknowledge an obligation to serve as a voice for children everywhere.

Ideals:

I-4.1   To provide the community with high-quality, culturally sensitive programs and services.

I-4.2   To promote cooperation among agencies and professions concerned with the welfare of young children, their families, and their teachers.

I-4.3   To work, through education, research, and advocacy, toward an environmentally safe world in which all children are adequately fed, sheltered, and nurtured.

I-4.4   To work, through education, research, and advocacy, toward a society in which all young children have access to quality programs.

I-4.5   To promote knowledge and understanding of young children and their needs. To work toward greater social acknowledgment of children's rights and greater social acceptance of responsibility for their well-being.

I-4.6   To support policies and laws that promote the well-being of children and families. To oppose those that impair their well-being. To cooperate with other individuals and groups in these efforts.

I-4.7   To further the professional development of the field of early childhood education and to strengthen its commitment to realizing its core values as reflected in this Code.

Principles:

P-4.1   We shall communicate openly and truthfully about the nature and extent of services that we provide.

P-4.2   We shall not accept or continue to work in positions for which we are personally unsuited or professionally unqualified. We shall not offer services that we do not have the competence, qualifications, or resources to provide.

P-4.3   We shall be objective and accurate in reporting the knowledge upon which we base our program practices.

P-4.4   We shall cooperate with other professionals who work with children and their families.

P-4.5   We shall not hire or recommend for employment any person who is unsuited for a position with respect to competence, qualifications, or character.

P-4.6   We shall report the unethical or incompetent behavior of a colleague to a supervisor when informal resolution is not effective.

P-4.7   We shall be familiar with laws and regulations that serve to protect the children in our programs.

P-4.8   We shall not participate in practices which are in violation of laws and regulations that protect the children in our programs.

P-4.9   When we have evidence that an early childhood program is violating laws or regulations protecting children, we shall report it to persons responsible for the program. If compliance is not accomplished within a reasonable time, we will report the violation to appropriate authorities who can be expected to remedy the situation.

P-4.10   When we have evidence that an agency or a professional charged with providing services to children, families, or teachers is failing to meet its obligations, we acknowledge a collective ethical responsibility to report the problem to appropriate authorities or to the public.

P-4.11   When a program violates or requires its employees to violate this Code, it is permissible, after fair assessment of the evidence, to disclose the identity of that program.

Statement of Commitment

As an individual who works with young children, I commit myself to furthering the values of early childhood education as they are reflected in the NAEYC Code of Ethical Conduct.

To the best of my ability I will

Ensure that programs for young children are based on current knowledge of child development and early childhood education.

Respect and support families in their task of nurturing children.

Respect colleagues in early childhood education and support them in maintaining the NAEYC Code of Ethical Conduct.

Serve as an advocate for children, their families, and their teachers in community and society.

Maintain high standards of professional conduct.

Recognize how personal values, opinions, and biases can affect professional judgment.

Be open to new ideas and be willing to learn from the suggestions of others.

Continue to learn, grow, and contribute as a professional.

Honor the ideals and principles of the NAEYC Code of Ethical Conduct.

The Statement of Commitment expresses those basic personal commitments that individuals must make in order to align themselves with the profession's responsibilities as set forth in the NAEYC Code of Ethical Conduct.

Growth Indicators

PRESCHOOL PHYSICAL DEVELOPMENT

Growth Indicators of Gross Motor Skills
> Increasing competency in running
> Increasing competency in jumping
> Increasing competency in hopping
> Increasing competency in galloping
> Increasing competency in skipping
> Increasing competency in climbing
> Increasing competency in balancing
> Increasing competency in catching
> Increasing competency in throwing
> Increasing competency in kicking

Growth Indicators of Fine Motor Skills
> Increasing ability to grasp and control small objects
> Increasing ability to fasten and unfasten
> Increasing ability to insert and remove small pieces
> Increasing ability to string and lace
> Increasing ability to cut with scissors

PRIMARY GRADE PHYSICAL DEVELOPMENT

Growth Indicators of Gross Motor Skills
> Increases strength of legs and arms
> Increases speed
> Increases coordination
> Increases agility
> Increases endurance
> Increases specialized skills in sports

Growth Indicators of Fine Motor Skills
> Increases ability to skillfully use writing tool, scissors, and small objects
> Increases ability to arrange numbers and letters uniformly
> Increases eye–hand coordination

PRESCHOOL COGNITIVE DEVELOPMENT

Growth Indicators of Representational Abilities
> Forms mental images

Imitates
Uses language
Pretends
Role-plays
Represents in two dimensions
Represents in three dimensions
Decodes others' representations

Growth Indicators of Language
Advances, but does not complete, understanding of grammar
Progresses in articulation, but limitations remain
Expands vocabulary
Constructs increasingly complex sentences (structure and length)
Converses with increasing competence with adults and peers

Growth Indicators of Reasoning
Often reasons and problem-solves thoughtfully
Often reasons on the basis of perceptions (not logic)
Thinks in concrete or tangible terms

Growth Indicators of Theory of Mind
Understands that thinking is an internal, mental process
Understands that others have their own emotional, social, and cognitive points of view
Demonstrates limited interpretations of others' points of view

Growth Indicators of Classification
Explores diverse attributes of objects
Recognizes similarities and differences
Sorts objects with increasing sophistication

Growth Indicators of Seriation
Makes comparisons
Seriates a limited number of objects

Growth Indicators of Number Development
Compares quantities of small sets
Learns number names
Understands numbers as representations of quantities
Counts limited number of objects with one-to-one correspondence

Growth Indicators of Memory
Remembers by recognizing
Remembers by recalling
Demonstrates individual knowledge

PRIMARY GRADE COGNITIVE DEVELOPMENT

Growth Indicators of Representational Thought
Expands complexity of preschool growth indicators
- Forms mental images
- Imitates
- Uses language
- Pretends

- Role-plays
- Represents in two dimensions
- Represents in three dimensions
- Decodes others' representations

Decodes and uses abstract symbols (letters and numbers)

Growth Indicators of Language
Expands vocabulary
Understands there can be literal and figurative meanings of words
Discerns subtle differences among words
Uses and understands many grammatical rules and exceptions
Becomes a proficient communicator with adults and peers
Constructs increasingly complex sentences (structure and length)

Growth Indicators of Logical Thought
Often reasons flexibly and logically about tangible problems
Continues to demonstrate concrete thinking

Growth Indicators of Metacognitive Knowledge
Demonstrates increasing knowledge about people as cognitive processors
Demonstrates increasing knowledge about cognitive requirements of tasks
Demonstrates increasing knowledge about cognitive strategies

Growth Indicators of Classification
Sorts and re-sorts objects flexibly and usually by concrete attributes
Compares whole class with its parts with increasing accuracy

Growth Indicators of Number Development
Counts increasingly large sets of objects
Understands cardinality
Develops measurement strategies
Adds and subtracts objects and numbers

Growth Indicators of Memory
Increasingly uses memory strategies spontaneously and deliberately
Exhibits early development of metamemory, including knowledge about people as re-memberers, varying task difficulty, and appropriate memory strategies

PRESCHOOL PSYCHOSOCIAL DEVELOPMENT

Growth Indicators of Expanding Relationships with Adults and Peers
Demonstrates strong attachment to parents and family
Establishes emotional bonds to nonfamilial people
Forms friendships
Exhibits concern and empathy

Growth Indicators of Self-Concept
Understands that the self has physical and psychological attributes
Aware of private, thinking self
Overestimates own abilities
Correctly identifies own gender
Often rigidly applies gender roles

Growth Indicators of Play
- Explores materials on own
- Expands social interactions
- Engages in dramatic play
- Engages in physical play

Growth Indicators of Fears
- Fears of real objects, people, and experiences
- Fears of the unknown or the imagined

Growth Indicators of Changing Aggressions
- Instrumental aggression
- Hostile aggression
- Increasing reliance on communication to settle disputes

Growth Indicators of Impulse Control
- Usually acts before considering consequences
- Has difficulty waiting
- Makes choices at own developmental level
- Benefits from joint activities with adults

PRIMARY GRADE PSYCHOSOCIAL DEVELOPMENT

Growth Indicators of Self-concept and Self-Esteem
- Includes psychological assessment, uncommon characteristics, active abilities as well as concrete characteristics in descriptions of self and others
- Considers group ties as part of self-definition
- Does not rigidly adhere to all stereotyped gender roles
- Becomes aware that gender roles are societal customs
- Searches out areas of interest that contribute to self-esteem
- Gains more accurate understanding of strengths and weaknesses

Growth Indicators of Play
- Participates in cooperative play
- Participates in and makes up games with rules

Growth Indicators of Relationships with Peers
- Increasingly focuses friendships on loyalty and intimacy as well as on mutual interests
- Usually prefers same-gender playmates
- Is aware of and sometimes vulnerable to peer-group influences

Growth Indicators of Prosocial Moral Reasoning
- Increasingly evaluates the intent of the actor
- Increasingly takes into account the relevant issues of a moral situation
- Demonstrates perspective-taking skills in many, but not all, situations
- Expands prosocial behavior

PRESCHOOL CREATIVE DEVELOPMENT

Growth Indicators of Creativity
- Expands mental flexibility
- Expands sensitivity
- Expands imagination
- Expands risk taking

Expands resourcefulness
Expands expressive experiences and skills using creative materials

Growth Indicators of Drawing
Preschool
Early primary

Growth Indicators of Block Play
Stage 1   Child carries blocks around, not used for construction
Stage 2   Child makes mostly rows, either horizontal (on the floor) or vertical (stacked)
Stage 3   Child makes bridges
Stage 4   Child makes enclosures
Stage 5   Child makes elaborate designs using pattern and balance
Stage 6   Child names structures related to their functions
Stage 7   Child reproduces or symbolizes familiar structures with buildings

PRIMARY GRADE CREATIVITY

Growth Indicators of Creativity
Expands representations, moving from single idea to interrelated ideas
Expresses individual strengths
Expands flexibility
Expands sensitivity
Expands imagination
Expands risk taking
Expands resourcefulness
Expands expressive experiences and skills using creative materials

Growth Indicators of Drawing
Early primary
Middle primary

Glossary

ABC narrative event sampling An observational method used to explore the antecedents and consequences of individual children's behaviors within their naturally occurring contexts. Four columns on the recording sheet are labeled *Time, Antecedent Event, Behavior,* and *Consequence.*

Anecdotal record An observational method used to summarize a single developmental incident after it occurs. The summary recounts *who, what, how,* and sometimes *when* and/or *where.* This method documents incidents involving individual children.

Anti-bias curriculum A proactive approach including materials, experiences, teacher attitudes, and interventions that works toward freeing children of prejudice and stereotypes regarding gender roles, race, culture, handicaps, and social class. It empowers children to like themselves and to respect and appreciate diversity

Assessment An appraisal based on observations or other measurements.

Authentic assessment Observation done in a natural setting (e.g., the child's gross motor skills are observed while the child is engaged in outdoor play as opposed to requesting the child to perform a skill in isolation).

Autonomy An ability to act independently.

Axiom Principle recognized as truth.

Cardinality The understanding that the last number counted in a set represents its total number of objects.

Category rating scale A specific type of rating scale design used to appraise selected characteristics; the observer assesses each item that is presented in gradations by choosing one of the possible designations listed under each item.

Category system An approach used when selecting the types of items to be observed (e.g., in tally event or time sampling). In this approach all categories must be mutually exclusive; each category must be distinct and separate from the others, and the categories must be exhaustive.

Cephalocaudal The physical growth pattern characterized by development from head to tail.

Checklist An observational method containing a register of items which, if present, the observer marks off on a predesigned instrument. This method is used to assess the current characteristics of a child, teacher, curriculum, or environment; to track changes in these characteristics over time; and to support program planning.

Classification The sorting of objects into classes and subclasses according to similarities and differences.

Closed question An interrogative that has a single correct answer.

Cognitive development The changing and expanding intellectual processes of human beings.

Collaborative apprenticeship The process of peer teaching.

Conference form The written framework for reporting a child's development and arriving at joint parent/teacher goals.

Conservation The concept that something remains the same if nothing is added or taken away (includes conservation of number, length, mass, volume, area, and volume displacement).

Cooperative learning group   An assigned number of children given a task to complete together.

Creativity   The process of self-expression as it relates to unique ideas in art, music, movement, drama, and thinking. According to theorists, expressing is creative if it is new to the individual; others may have expressed the same or similar ideas independently.

CRI   The color rendering index is a measure used to compare artificial light sources with natural light; the higher the number, the closer the artificial light shows colors as they would look under natural light. CRI is reported as a percentage.

Cultural diversity   A variety of ethnic and social groups.

Developmentally appropriate   Results from knowledge about "human development and learning, individual characteristics and experiences, and social and cultural contexts" (Bredekamp & Copple, 1997, p. 9).

Divergent thinking   Cognitively being open to new alternatives, exploring possibilities, and evaluating information from many perspectives.

Educational practitioner   A trained adult who teaches in a setting for learning.

Environment (physical, indoors)   Refers in general to the room arrangement (layout, traffic patterns, and material selection and equipment location); lighting; and visual appeal (color, visual clutter, unity and complexity, and warmth and texture).

Error of central tendency   The inclination for an observer to rate in the middle when using an odd number of descriptors.

Event   An identified behavior or incident.

Fast mapping   A vocabulary-building process through which children add new words to their mental maps of interconnected categories. Initially, children frequently construct limited or erroneous understandings of new words.

Fine motor development   The maturing of small muscles (e.g., fingers).

Fluorescent lighting   An artificial light source in a glass tube that gives off light through the interaction of mercury vapor and electrons.

Full-spectrum lighting   A fluorescent lighting source that has a range of colors similar to that of sunlight.

Gender identity   Knowing one's own gender.

Graphic rating scale   A specific type of rating scale design used to appraise selected characteristics; the observer assigns each item a value on a given horizontal or vertical continuum.

Grid   The graphed box formed by the intersection of horizontal rows of categories with vertical columns of categories.

Gross motor development   The maturing of large muscles (e.g., upper arms).

Growth indicators   The markers of development that denote and describe advancement. They are generally the focus for observations.

Halo effect   The susceptibility of an observer to be influenced by preconceived ideas or impressions.

Hand dominance   Preference for the use of the left or the right hand for single-handed tasks.

Help-yourself art shelf   An organized, categorized, and designated low cabinet filled with materials for creating. Children may independently use these materials at their own discretion during free-choice times.

Hostile aggression   Aggression in which the intent is to hurt or dominate another.

Impulse control   Self-control of actions and emotions.

Incandescent lighting   An artificial light source in a vacuum bulb.

Inclusive education   An approach embracing children's special needs within the classroom and demonstrating commitment to the values of acceptance, belonging, and community.

Individual Education Plan (IEP)   A team-written instructional program designed for a specific special needs child and based on the child's unique needs, interests, impairment, and abilities. The team usually includes a diagnostic specialist, the teacher, the parent(s), other specified professionals, and the child (if appropriate).

Individual Family Services Plan (IFSP)   A multidisciplinary team-written program for the optimum development of a specific handicapped infant, toddler, or preschool child. The program includes support, instruction, and counseling for the family and a comprehensive program for the child.

Instrument   (See observational instrument.)

Instrumental aggression   Aggression in which the intent is not to hurt but to gain possession of an object, territory, or privilege.

Integrated curriculum approach   A program design that incorporates all subjects or disciplines around a central topic or theme.

Interest centers   Areas of the room set up around an organizational feature (e.g., housekeeping, manipulatives, blocks).

Inter-rater reliability   The degree of agreement (expressed in a percentage or decimal) between observers when they observe the same setting at the same time using the same instrument.

Invariance   See conservation (of number).

Journalistic approach   A technique used to select the contents of anecdotes; the observer records *who, what, how,* and sometimes *when,* and/or *where* of an incident.

Maturation   The process of physical development involving the central nervous system.

Metacognition   Knowledge about thinking, including knowledge about cognitive tasks, cognitive strategies, and people as thinkers.

Metamemory   Knowledge about memory including knowledge about people as rememberers, varying difficulty of memory tasks, and appropriate memory strategies.

Motor development   The maturing of small and large muscles (fine and gross motor development, respectively); this maturing is characterized by fluid movements.

Numerical rating scale   A specific type of rating scale design used to appraise selected characteristics; the observer assesses each characteristic by choosing one of the given number values for each item.

Observation   Watching and recording significant behaviors, characteristics, situations, events, or surroundings.

Observational instrument   The predesigned form on which an observer records the data for checklists, rating scales, and tally event and time sampling. The instrument includes a heading, space for data, and other pertinent information (e.g., instructions, definitions, codes, comments).

Observational question   An educational problem or concern to be studied that is stated as an interrogatory.

Observational records   Entries of accounts that have been witnessed and noted.

Observer bias   A prejudice or judgment based on the feelings or impressions of one who is assessing or recording.

One-to-one correspondence   The ability to count objects in sequence, labeling each object with the correct number.

Open question   An interrogative that has many possible answers and allows the respondent an opportunity to expand and explain.

Operationally defined   A description based on the function of the item.

Overt   Observable and apparent.

Parent conference   An arranged meeting between a teacher and family member(s) for the purpose of establishing a partnership in the child's education to discuss progress and support the child's development.

Pilot testing   The process of trying out an observational instrument to assess its workability.

Portfolio   A collection of observational records and work samples for one child, usually kept for a period of one year.

Power words   Child-spoken profanity or words that stretch the acceptable limits within a school environment.

Practitioner　(See educational practitioner.)

Preschool　Planned learning experiences in a developmental environment for children ages 2 to 5 years old. Usually scheduled for 2½ hours in the morning or afternoon.

Primary grade　Kindergarten through third grade.

Private spaces　Designed areas in a classroom big enough for a single child and used as a child-chosen retreat.

Process approach to creativity　A belief that creativity is the result of possessing abilities and having conditions that allow for practice and improvement.

Prosocial behavior　Behavior that reflects a concern for others.

Proximodistal　Physical growth pattern characterized by development from the center of the body to the outside.

Psychosocial development　The changes in human beings involving self-understanding, emotions, personality, and social relationships.

Qualitative data　Information that yields narrative results.

Quantitative data　Information that yields numerical results.

Rating scale　An observational method in which the observer, using a predesigned instrument, selects a value for each of the listed characteristics. This method is used to evaluate specific characteristics of a child, teacher, curriculum, or environment and to monitor changes over time.

Recall memory　Remembering without a cue being present.

Recognition memory　Remembering by recognizing something familiar.

Recording form　A document used to collect observational data (e.g., running records or ABC narrative event sampling).

Record-keeping system　An organizational method used for systematically storing observations.

Representational thought　The cognitive ability to allow a mental symbol, word, or object to stand for something else (e.g., a child's drawing may represent a house).

Running record　An observational method used to explore the development of individual children; the observer writes a detailed, factual, sequential narrative of events in progress and adds a brief summary conclusion at the end.

Sampling behaviors or events　The process of collecting a subset of data to represent the behaviors or events under investigation.

Scaffolding　A metaphor to describe the necessary assistance for children's learning within the zone of proximal development that is responsive to their individual developmental levels.

Self-concept　The psychological construct of the self, nourished by expanding cognitive and social maturity.

Self-esteem　The evaluative component of the sense of self, deriving from the warmth, acceptance, and respectful treatment given a child and from the child's success in selected areas of interest.

Sensory table　A large container or a specially designed piece of equipment used for mixing, pouring, feeling, and experiencing various textured items (e.g., water, sand, or Styrofoam bits).

Seriation　Arranging objects in order along one characteristic (e.g., arranging four pieces of sandpaper from smooth to rough).

Sign system　An approach used when selecting the types of items to be observed (e.g., in tally event or time sampling). In this approach all categories must be mutually exclusive, but they do not need to be exhausive.

Systematized　Organized in an orderly fashion.

Tally event sampling　An observational method used to systematically record the frequency of occurrence for an identified behavior or situation within a designated period. This method collects quantitative data about children, teachers, or interactions on a predesigned instrument.

Technological records　Media for maintaining data other than paper and pencil (e.g. videotape, computer disk).

Thematic units A curriculum approach that integrates all content areas by organizing instructional objectives, materials, and activities around a specific topic or theme.

Theory of mind An expanding understanding of human mental processes, one's own and others' mental states, mental activities, perceptions, and emotions.

Three-dimensional materials Items that have depth (e.g., cylinders, wood blocks).

Time sampling An observational method used to methodically investigate behaviors that occur in rapid succession. Predetermined units of time and a recording grid guide the observer's collection of quantitative data on a predesigned instrument dealing with children, teachers, and interactions.

Traffic patterns The pathways used to get from one area to another. They can be inside or outside.

Trait approach to creativity A belief that creativity is innate and unfolds in a natural fashion.

Vignette A short story or scenario.

Visual acuity Clarity of sight.

Visual appeal (classroom) Pleasing and comfortable to the eyes.

Zone of proximal development The hypothetical, dynamic distance between the level of children's independent functioning and the level of their functioning with the help of adults or more competent peers.

References

Alkin, M. C., with Linden, M., Noel, J., & Ray, K. (Eds.). (1992). *Encycolopedia of educational research* (6th ed.). New York: Macmillan

Amabile, T. M. (1989). *Growing up creative: Nurturing a lifetime of creativity.* New York: Crown Publishers.

Bailey, S. (1996). Shortchanging girls and boys. *Educational Leadership, 53,* 75–79.

Bandura, A., Barbaranelli, C., Caprara, G. V., & Pastorelli, C. (1996). Multifacted impact of self-efficacy beliefs on academic functioning. *Child Development, 67,* 1206–1222.

Baratta-Lorton, M. (1995). *Mathematics their way.* Menlo Park, CA: Addison-Wesley.

Beaty, J. J. (1994). *Observing development of the young child* (3rd ed.). New York: Macmillan.

Bell, D., & Low, R. M. (1977). *Observing and recording children's behavior.* Richland, WA: Performance Associates.

Bem, S. (1989). Genital knowledge and gender constancy in preschool children. *Child Development, 60,* 649–662.

Benelli, C., & Yongue, B. (1995). Supporting young children's motor skill development. *Childhood Education, 71,* 217–220.

Benjamin, A. C. (1994). Observations in early childhood classrooms: Advice from the field. *Young Children, 49,* 14–19.

Berger, E. H. (1995). *Parents as partners in education: Families and schools working together* (4th ed.). Englewood Cliffs, NJ: Prentice–Hall.

Berger, K. S., & Thompson, R. A. (1995). *The developing person through childhood and adolescence* (4th ed.). New York: Worth.

Berk, L. E., & Winsler, A. (1995). *Scaffolding children's learning: Vygotsky and early childhood education.* Washington, DC: National Association for the Education of Young Children.

Billman, J., & Sherman, J. (1996). *Observation and participation in early childhood settings.* Needham Heights, MA: Allyn & Bacon.

Birren, F. (1972). *Color psychology and color therapy.* New York: University Books.

Birren, F. (1978). *Color and human response.* New York: Van Nostrand Reinhold.

Bloom, B. S. (Ed.). (1985). *Developing talent in young people.* New York: Ballantine Books.

Boehm, A. E. (1992). Glossary of assessment terms. In L. R. Williams & D. P. Fromberg (Eds.), *Encyclopedia of early childhood education* (pp. 218–293). New York: Garland.

Boehm, A. E., & Weinberg, R. A. (1997). *The classroom observer: Developing observation skills in early childhood settings* (3rd ed.). New York: Teachers College Press.

Borg, W. R., & Gall, M. D. (1989). *Educational research: An introduction* (5th ed.). White Plains, NY: Longman.

Brause, R. S., & Mayher, J. S. (1991). Collecting and analyzing classroom data in theory and in practice. In R. S. Brause & J. S. Mayher (Eds.), *Search and re-search: What the inquiring teacher needs to know* (pp. 131–156). Bristol, PA: Falmer Press.

Brazelton, T. B. (1992). *Touchpoints.* Reading, MA: Addison–Wesley.

Bredekamp, S. (1992). What is "developmentally appropriate" and why is it important? *Journal of Physical Education, Recreation, and Dance, 63,* 31–32.

Bredekamp, S., & Copple, C. (Eds.). (1997). *Developmentally appropriate practice in early childhood pro-*

grams (Rev. ed.). Washington, DC: National Association for the Education of Young Children.

Bredekamp, S., & Rosegrant, T. (1992). Reaching potentials: Introduction. In S. Bredekamp & T. Rosegrant (Eds.), *Reaching potentials: Appropriate curriculum and assessment for young children, Vol. 1* (pp. 2–27). Washington, DC: National Association for the Education of Young Children.

Brett, A., Moore, R., & Provenzo, E. Jr. (1993). *The complete playground book*. Syracuse, NY: Syracuse University Press.

Brown, J. R., Donelan-McCall, N., & Dunn, J. (1996). Why talk about mental states? The significance of children's conversations with friends, siblings, and mothers. *Child Development, 67,* 836–849.

Brown, J. R., & Dunn, J. (1996). Continuities in emotion understanding from three to six years. *Child Development, 67,* 789–802.

Buell, L. H. (1984). *Understanding the refugee Vietnamese*. San Diego: Los Amigos Research Associates.

Burton, A. W. (1992). The development of movement skills. *Early Report, 19,* 3–4.

Burts, D. C., Hart, C. H., Charlesworth, R., Fleege, P. O., Mosley, J., & Thomasson, R. H. (1992). Observed activities and stress behaviors of children in developmentally appropriate and inappropriate kindergarten classrooms. *Early Childhood Research Quarterly, 7,* 1–17.

Calkins, L. (1994). *The art of teaching writing* (New ed.). Portsmouth, NH: Heinemann Educational Books.

Carlo, G., Koller, S., Eisenberg, N., DaSilva, M., & Frohlich, C. B. (1996). A cross-national study on the relations among prosocial moral reasoning, gender role orientations, and prosocial behaviors. *Developmental Psychology, 32,* 231–240.

Carlson, K., & Cunningham, J. L. (1990). Effect of pencil diameter on the graphomotor skill of preschoolers. *Early Childhood Research Quarterly, 5,* 279–293.

Cazden, C. B. (1988). *Classroom discourse*. Portsmouth, NH: Heinemann Educational Books.

Center Management Staff. (1990). Design: Keep the kids in mind. *Center Management,* September/October, pp. 10, 12, 14–15.

Cherry, C. (1990). *Creative art for the developing child* (2nd ed.). San Bernadino, CA: David S. Lake.

Chi, M. H. T. (1978). Knowledge structures and memory development. In. R. S. Siegler (Ed.), *Children's thinking: What develops?* (pp. 73–96). Hillsdale, NJ: Erlbaum.

Clark, J. E., & Phillips, S. J. (1985). A developmental sequence of the standing long jump. In J. E. Clark & J. H. Humphrey (Eds.), *Motor development: Current selected research* (pp. 73–85). Princeton, NJ: Princeton Book Company.

Clinton, H. R. (1995). *It takes a village and other lessons children teach us*. New York: Simon & Schuster.

Colby, B. (1990). *Color and light: Influences and impact*. Glendale, CA: Author.

Coopersmith, S. (1967). *The antecedents of self-esteem*. San Francisco: W. H. Freeman.

Corbin, C. B. (1980). A *textbook of motor development*. Dubuque, IA: William. C. Brown.

Cozby, P. C. (1997). *Methods in behavioral research* (6th ed.). Mountain View, CA: Mayfield.

Cratty, B. J. (1986). *Perceptual and motor development in infants and children* (3rd ed.). Englewood Cliffs, NJ: Prentice–Hall.

Cropley, A. J. (1992). *More ways than one: Fostering creativity*. Norwood, NJ: Ablex.

Crosswhite, L. (1995). *A guide to a shared reading experience*. Jacksonville, IL: Perma-bound.

Crosswhite, L., & Rossman, M. (1995). *Teaching real reading through real books*. Glendale, AR: Rossman Publishing House.

Davis, G. A., & Rimm, S. B. (1989). *Education of the gifted and talented* (2nd ed.). Englewood Cliffs, NJ: Prentice-Hall.

DeLong, A. J., Tegano, D. W., Moran, J. D. III, Brickey, J., Morrow, D., & Houser, T. L. (1991). Effects of spatial scale on cognitive play in preschool children. *ASID Report,* July/August, 8–9.

Derman-Sparks, L. (1994). Empowering children to create a caring culture in a world of differences. *Childhood Education, 70,* 66–71.

Derman-Sparks, L., & the A.B.C. Task Force (1989). *Anti-bias curriculum: Tools for empowering young children*. Washington, DC: National Association for the Education of Young Children.

Diffily, D., & Fleege, P. O. (1992). *Portfolio assessment: Practical training in evaluating the progress of kindergarten and primary grade children in individualized portfolio formats.* Houston, TX: Texas Association for the Education of Young Children. (ERIC Document Reproduction Services No. ED 354082).

Diffily, D., & Fleege, P. O. (1993). *Sociodramatic play: Assessment through portfolio.* Fort Worth, TX: Alice Carlson Applied Learning Center (ERIC Document Reproduction Service No. ED 354079).

Dixon, G. T., & Chalmers, F. G. (1990). The expressive arts in education. *Childhood Education, 67,* 12–17.

Dooley, D. (1990). *Social research methods* (2nd ed.). Englewood Cliffs, NJ: Prentice-Hall.

Dunn, J., Brown, J. R., & Maguire, M. (1995). The development of children's moral sensibility: Individual differences and emotional understanding. *Developmental Psychology, 31,* 649–659.

DuRandt, R. (1985). Ball catching proficiency among 4-, 6-, and 8-year-old girls. In J. E. Clark & J. H. Humphrey (Eds.), *Motor development: Current selected research* (pp. 35–43). Princeton, NJ: Princeton Book Company.

Duro-Test. (1988). *A guide for simulating natural light in interior environments to maximize the quality of working life.* Fairfield, NJ: Author.

Eccles, J. S., Wigfield, A., Harold, R. D., & Blumenfeld, P. (1993). Age and gender differences in children's self- and task perceptions during elementary school. *Child Development, 64,* 830–847.

Edelman, M. W. (1992, May). Letter to my sons. *Parents,* pp. 98–102.

Edwards, C., Gandini, L., & Forman, G. (Eds.) (1993). *The hundred languages of children: The reggio emilia approach to early childhood education.* Norwood, NJ: Ablex.

Elkind, D. (1988). *The hurried child* (rev. ed.), Reading, MA: Addison-Wesley.

Elkind, D. (1994). *Ties that stress: The new family imbalance.* Cambridge, MA: Harvard University Press.

Engle, B. S. (1995). *Considering children's art: Why and how to value their works.* Washington DC: National Association for the Education of Young Children.

Erikson, A. (1985). *Playground design: Outdoor environments for learning and development.* New York: Van Nostrand Reinhold.

Esbensen, S. B. (1987). *An outdoor classroom.* Ypsilanti, MI: High/Scope Press.

Evertson, C. M., & Green, J. L. (1986). Observation as inquiry and method. In M. C. Wittrock (Ed.), *Handbook of research on teaching* (3rd ed.) (pp. 162–213). New York: Macmillan.

Feeney, S., Christensen, D., & Moravcik, E. (1996). *Who am I in the lives of young children?: An introduction to teaching young children* (5th ed.). Englewood Cliffs: NJ: Prentice-Hall.

Feeney, S., & Kipnis, K. (1992). *Code of ethical conduct & statement of commitment.* (pp. 3–12). Washington, DC: National Association for the Education of Young Children. Copyright NAEYC. Reprinted by permission.

Feldman, D. H. (1980). *Beyond universals in cognitive development.* Norwood, NJ: Ablex.

Feldman, D. H., Csikszentmihalyi, M., & Gardner, H. (1994). *Changing the world: A framework for the study of creativity.* Westport, CT: Greenwood.

Fisher, S. (1995). The child and the learning environment. *Early Childhood News, 7,* 4–37.

Flavell, J. H., Green, F. L., & Flavell, E. R. (1995). Young children's knowledge about thinking. *Monographs of the Society for Research in Child Development, 60*(1, Serial No. 243).

Flavell, J. H., Miller, P. H., & Miller, S. A. (1993). *Cognitive development* (3rd ed.). Englewood Cliffs, NJ: Prentice-Hall.

Follmi, O. (1989, December). Journey to knowledge. *Life, 12,* 109–116.

Framer, J. F. (1994). Defining competence as readiness to learn. In S. G. Goffin & D. E. Day (Eds.), *New perspectives in early childhood teacher education: Bringing practitioners into the debate* (pp. 29–36). New York: Teachers College Press.

Fredette, B. W. (1994). Use of visuals in schools. In D. M. Moore & F. M. Dwyer (Eds.), *Visual literacy: A spectrum of visual learning* (pp. 235–256). Englewood Cliffs, NJ: Education Technology Publications.

Freeman, Y., & Freeman, D. (1991). Portfolio assessment: An exciting view. *Bilingual Education Office Outreach, 2,* 7.

Frost, J. L. (1992) *Play and playscapes.* New York: Delmar.

Gallahue, D. L. (1989). *Understanding motor development: Infants, children, adolescents* (2nd ed.). Indianapolis, IN: Benchmark.

Gallahue, D. L. (1993). *Developmental physical education for today's children* (2nd. ed.). Dubuque, IA: William C. Brown and Benchmark.

Gardner, H. (1980). *Artful scribbles: The significance of children's drawings.* New York: Basic Books.

Geary, D. C. (1994). *Children's mathematical development.* Washington, DC: American Psychological Association.

Gelfer, J. I., & Perkins, P. G. (1996). A model for portfolio assessment in early childhood education programs. *Early Childhood Education Journal, 24,* 5–10.

Genishi, C. (1982). Observational research methods for early childhood education. In B. Spodek (Ed.), *Handbook of research in early childhood education* (pp. 564–591). New York: Free Press.

Genishi, C., McCarrier, A., & Nussbaum, N. R. (1988). Research currents: Dialogue as a context for teaching and learning. *Language Arts, 65,* 182–191.

Getty Center for Education in the Arts. (1985). *Beyond creativity: The place for art in America's schools.* Los Angeles, CA: The J. Paul Getty Trust.

Ginsburg, H., & Opper, S. (1988). *Piaget's theory of intellectual development* (3rd ed.). Englewood Cliffs, NJ: Prentice-Hall.

Goetz, E. M. (1989). The teaching of creativity to the preschool child. In J. A. Glover, R. R. Ronning, & C. R. Reynold (Eds.), *Handbook of creativity* (pp. 411–428). New York: Plenum.

Goleman, D. (1995). *Emotional intelligence.* New York: Bantum.

Golinkoff, R. M., Hirsh-Pasek, K., Bailey, L. M., & Wenger, N. R. (1992). Young children and adults use lexical principles to learn new nouns. *Developmental Psychology, 28,* 99–108.

Gordon, A. M., & Williams-Browne, K. (1995). *Beginnings and beyond* (4th ed.). Albany, NY: Delmar.

Grangaard, E. (1993). *Effects of color and light on selected elementary students.* Doctoral dissertation.

Las Vegas, NV: University of Nevada-Las Vegas. (ERIC Documents Reproduction Service No. ED 383445)

Graves, B. E. (1993). *School ways: The planning and design of America's schools.* New York: McGraw-Hill.

Greenman, J. (1988). *Caring spaces, learning places: Children's environments that work.* Redmond, WA: Exchange Press.

Greenman, J. (1993). It ain't easy being green. *Child Care Information Exchange, 91,* 36–40.

Gunderson, L. (1989). *A whole language primer.* Ontario, Canada: Scholastic TAB.

Hamid, N. P., & Newport, A. G. (1989). Colour of reading material and performance decrement. *Perceptual and Motor Skills, 74,* 689–690.

Harms, T., Jacobs, E. V., & White, D. R. (1996). *School-age environment rating scale.* New York: Teachers College Press.

Hartup, W. W. (1992). Peer relations in early and middle childhood. In V. B. Van Hasselt & M. Hersen (Eds.), *Handbook of social development: A lifespan perspective* (pp. 257–281). New York: Plenum.

Hartup, W. W., Laursen, B., Stewart, M. I., & Eastenson, A. (1988). Conflict and the friendship relations of young children. *Child Development, 59,* 1590–1600.

Hathaway, W. E. (1982, September). *Lights, window, color: Elements of the school environment.* Paper presented at the Council of Educational Facility Planners 59th annual conference, Columbus, OH.

Hathaway, W. E. (1995). Effects of school lighting on physical development and school performance. *Journal of Educational Research, 88,* 228–241.

Hathaway, W. E., Hargreaves, J. A., Thompson, G. W., & Novitsky, D. (1992). *A study into the effects of light on children of elementary school age—a case of daylight robbery.* Unpublished paper. Planning and Information Services Division, Edmonton, Alberta, Canada.

Heidemann, S., & Hewitt, D. (1992). *Pathways to play.* St. Paul, MN: Redleaf Press.

Hendrick, J. (1994). *Total learning: Developmental curriculum for the young child* (4th ed.). New York: Macmillan.

Hendrick, J. (1996). *The whole child* (6th ed.). Englewood Cliffs, NJ: Prentice-Hall.

Henniger, M. L. (1994a). Enriching the outdoor play experience. *Childhood Education, 70,* 87–90.

Henniger, M. L. (1994b). Planning for outdoor play. *Young Children, 49,* 10–15.

Herberholz, B., & Hanson, L. (1995). *Early childhood art* (5th ed.). Dubuque, IA: William C. Brown.

High/Scope Educational Research Foundation. (1992a). *High Scope child observation record for ages 2½–6.* Ypsilanti, MI: High/Scope Press.

High/Scope Educational Research Foundation. (1992b). *Teacher's manual of the COR.* Ypsilanti, MI: High/Scope Press.

Hintze, J. M., & Shapiro, E. S. (1995). Best practices in the systematic observations of classroom behavior. In A. Thomas & J. Grimes (Eds.), *Best practices in school psychology-III* (pp. 651–660). Washington, DC: The National Association of School Psychologists.

Hirsch, E. S. (Ed.). (1996). *The block book* (3rd. ed.). Washington, DC: National Association for the Education of Young Children.

Hoffman, S., Kantner, L., Cobert, C., & Sims, W. (1991). Nurturing the expressive arts. *Childhood Education, 68,* 23–26.

Hohmann, M. & Weikart, D. P. (1995). *Educating young children: Active learning practices for preschool and child care programs.* Ypsilanti, MI: High/Scope Press.

Hopkins, D. (1993). *A teacher's guide to classroom research* (2nd ed.). Bristol, PA: Open University Press.

Houghton Mifflin. (1989). *Houghton Mifflin literary readers; Selection plans and instructional support* (Book 1, Teacher's Guide). Boston: Houghton Mifflin.

Johnson, H., Brady, S. J., & Larson, E. (1996). A microcomputer-based system to faciliatate direct observation data collection and assessment in inclusive settings. *Journal of Computing in Childhood Education, 7,* 253–269.

Kalverboer, A. F., Hopkins, B., & Geuze, R. (Eds.). (1993). *Motor development in early and later childhood: Longitudinal approaches.* New York: Press Syndicate of the University of Cambridge.

Kapel, D. E., Gifford, C. S., & Kapel, M. B. (1991). *American educators' encyclopedia.* New York: Greenwood Press.

Kaplan, P. S. (1994). *A child's odyssey: Child and adolescent development* (3rd ed.). St. Paul, MN: West.

Kellogg, R. (1970). *Analyzing children's art.* Palo Alto, CA: Mayfield.

Kerlinger, F. N. (1986). *Foundations of behavioral research* (3rd ed.). New York: Holt, Rinehart & Winston.

Kerr, R. (1985). Fitts' law and motor control in children. In J. E. Clark & J. H. Humphrey (Eds.), *Motor development: Current selected research.* (pp. 45–53) Princeton, NJ: Princeton Book Company.

Kettman, S. (1994). *Family friendly childcare.* Waco, TX: WRS Publishing.

Kochanska, G., Padavich, D. L., & Koenig, A. (1996). Children's narratives about hypothetical moral dilemmas and objective measures of their conscience: Mutual relations and socialization antecedents. *Child Development, 67,* 1420–1436.

Konner, M. (1991). *Childhood.* Boston: Little, Brown.

Kreutzer, M. A., Leonard, C., & Flavell, J. H. (1975). An interview study of children's knowledge about memory. *Monographs of the Society for Research in Child Development, 40*(1, Serial No. 159).

Kritchevsky, S., Prescott, E., with Walling, L. (1977). *Planning environments for young children: Physical space.* Washington, DC: National Association for the Education of Young Children.

Küller, R., & Lindsten, C. (1992). Health and behavior of children in classrooms with and without windows. *Journal of Environmental Psychology, 12,* 305–317.

Ladd, G. W., & Coleman, C. C. (1993). Young children's peer relationships: Forms, features, and functions. In B. Spodek (Ed.), *Handbook of research on the education of young children* (pp. 57–76). New York: Macmillan.

Ladd, G. W., Kochenderfer, B. J., & Coleman, C. C. (1996). Friendship quality as a predictor of young children's early school adjustment. *Child Development, 67,* 1103–1118.

Lawler, S. D. (1991). *Parent–teacher conferencing in early childhood education.* Washington, DC: National Education Association of the United States.

Leavitt, R. L., & Eheart, B. K. (1991). Assessment in early childhood programs. *Young children, 46,* 4–9.

Levy, B. I. (1984). Research into the psychological meaning of color. *American Journal of Art Therapy, 23,* 58–62.

Liberman, J. (1991). *Light: Medicine of the future.* Sante Fe, NM: Bear & Company.

Linderman, M. G. (1990). *Art in the elementary school: Drawing, painting, & creating for the classroom* (4th ed.). Dubuque, IA: William C. Brown.

Lindholm, G. (1995). Schoolyards: The significance of place properties to outdoor activities in schools. *Environment and Behavior, 27,* 259–293.

Lobel, T. E., & Menashri, J. (1993). Relations of conceptions of gender-role transgressions and gender constancy to gender-typed preferences. *Developmental Psychology, 29,* 150–155.

Lovett, S. B., & Flavell, J. H. (1990). Understanding and remembering: Children's knowledge about the differential effects of strategy and task variables on comprehension and memorization. *Child Development, 61,* 1842–1858.

Lowenfeld, V., & Brittain, W. L. (1987). *Creative and mental growth* (8th ed.). New York: Macmillan.

Lyon, T. D., & Flavell, J. H. (1994). Young children's understanding of "remember" and "forget." *Child Development, 65,* 1357–1371.

Maccoby, E. E. (1980). *Social development.* New York: Harcourt Brace Jovanovich.

Maccoby, E. E. (1990). Gender and relationships: A developmental account. *American Psychologist, 45,* 513–520.

Maccoby, E. E. (1992). The role of parents in the socialization of children: An historical overview. *Developmental Psychology, 28,* 1006–1017.

Mahnke, F. H. (1996). *Color, environment, and human response.* New York: Van Nostrand Reinhold.

Mann, J., Ten Have, T., Plunkett, J. W., & Meisels, S. J. (1991). Time sampling: A methodological critique. *Child Development, 62,* 227–241.

Martin, A. (1994). Deepening teacher competence through skills of observation. In S. G. Goffin & D. E. Day (Eds.), *New perspectives in early childhood teacher education: Bringing practitioners into the debate* (pp. 95–108). New York: Teachers College Press.

Maslow, A. H. (1970). *Motivation and personality* (2nd ed.). New York: Harper & Row.

Mayesky, M. (1995). *Creative activities for young children* (5th ed.). Albany, NY: Delmar.

McAfee, O., & Leong, D. (1994). *Assessing and guiding young children's development and learning.* Needham Heights, MA: Allyn & Bacon.

McCormick, E. J., & Ilgen, D. (1980). *Industrial psychology.* Englewood Cliffs, NJ: Prentice-Hall.

McCutcheon, G. (1981). On the interpretation of classroom observations. *Educational Researcher, 10,* 5–10.

McKernan, J. (1991). *Curriculum action research.* New York: St. Martin's Press.

Medinnus, G. (1976). *Child study and observation guide.* New York: John Wiley.

Medley, D. M., & Mitzel, H. E. (1963). Measuring classroom behavior by systematic observation. In N. L. Gage (Ed.), *Handbook of research on teaching* (pp. 247–328). Chicago: Rand McNally.

Meisels, S. (1993). Remaking classroom assessment with the work sampling system. *Young Children, 48,* 34–40.

Mindes, G., Ireton, H., & Mardell-Czudnowski, C. (1996). *Assessing young children.* Albany, New York: Delmar.

Moore, R. C., Goltsman, S. M., & Iacofano, D. S. (Eds.). (1992). *Play for all guidelines: Planning, design, and management of outdoor play setting for all children* (2nd ed.). Berkeley, CA: Communications.

Morrison, G. S. (1995). *Early childhood education today* (6th ed.). Englewood, NJ: Prentice-Hall.

National Academy of Early Childhood Programs. (1991a). *Guide to accreditation* (Rev. ed). Washington, DC: National Association for the Education of Young Children.

National Academy of Early Childhood Programs. (1991b). *Accreditation criteria and procedures of the national academy of early childhood programs* (Rev. ed.). Washington, DC: National Association for the Education of Young Children.

National Association for the Education of Young Children and the National Association of Early Childhood Specialists in State Departments of Education. (1991). Guidelines for appropriate curriculum content and assessment in programs serving children age 3 through 8: A joint position statement. *Young Children, 46,* 21–38.

National Task Force on Day Care Interior Design. (1992). *Design of the times: Day care.* Seattle, WA: Dan B. Spinelli.

Page, R. M., Frey, J., Talbert, R., & Falk, C. (1992). Children's feelings of loneliness and social dissatisfaction: Relationship to measures of physical fitness and activity. *Journal of Teaching in Physical Education, 11,* 211–219.

Papa-Lewis, R., & Cornell, C. (1987). Selecting the best lighting for your school facility. *School Business Affairs, 53,* 32–35.

Parten, M. B. (1932). Social participation among pre-school children. *Journal of Abnormal and Social Psychology, 27,* 243–269.

Paton. S. (1995). *Cry, the beloved country.* New York: Scribner.

Payne, V. G., & Isaacs, L. D. (1987). *Human motor development: A lifespan approach.* Mountain View, CA: Mayfield Publishing.

Pellegrini, A. D., & Boyd, B. (1993). The role of play in early childhood development and education: Issues in definition and function. In B. Spodek (Ed.), *Handbook of research on the education of young children* (pp. 105–121). New York: Macmillan.

Perner, J., Ruffman, T., & Leekam, S. (1994). Theory of mind is contagious: You catch it from your sibs. *Child Development, 65,* 1228–1238.

Petrakos, H. & Howe, N. (1996). The influences of the physical design of the dramatic play center on children's play. *Early Childhood Research Quarterly, 11,* 63–77.

Phinney, J. S. (1982). Observing children: Ideas for teachers. *Young Children, 37,* 16–24.

Piaget, J., & Inhelder, B. (1969). *The psychology of the child.* New York: Basic Books.

Poest, C. A., Williams, J. R., Witt, D. D., & Atwood, M. (1990). Challenge me to move: Large muscle development in young children. *Young Children, 45,* 4–9.

Poysner, L. R. (1983). *An examination of the classroom physical environment.* Unpublished research paper. Indiana University, South Bend, IN.

Rhodes, L., & Nathenson-Mejia, S. (1992). Anecdotal records: A powerful tool for ongoing literacy assessment. *Reading Teacher, 45,* 502–509.

Rody, M. (1995). A visit to Reggio Emilia. *Early Childhood News, 7,* 14–16.

Rudd, A. (1978). What to look for in classroom lighting. *American School and University, 51,* 45, 48.

Sax, G. (1989). *Principles of educational and psychological measurement and evaluation* (3rd ed.). Belmont, CA: Wadsworth.

Scherer, M. (1996). On our changing family values: A conversation with David Elkind. *Educational Leadership, 53,* 4–9.

Schickedanz, J. A., Schickedanz, D. I., Hansen, K., & Forsyth, P. D. (1993). *Understanding children.* Mountain View, CA: Mayfield.

Schirrmacher, R. (1993). *Art and creative development for young children* (2nd ed.). Albany, NY: Delmar.

Schneider, W., & Pressley, M. (1989). *Memory development between 2 and 20.* New York: Springer-Verlag.

Schreiber, M. E. (1996). Lighting alternatives: Considerations for child care centers. *Young Children, 51,* 11–13.

Schwartz, S., & Pollishuke, M. (1991). *Creating the child-centered classroom.* Katonah, NY: Richard C. Owen.

Schweinhart, L., & McNair, J. (1991). The NEW child observation record. *High-Scope ReSource,* pp. 4–9.

Senda, M. (1992). *Design of children's play environments.* New York: McGraw-Hill.

Serbin, L. A., Powlishta, K. K., & Gulko, J. (1993). The development of sex typing in middle childhood. *Monographs of the Society for Research in Child Development, 53*(2, Serial No. 232).

Shaffer, D. R. (1993). *Developmental psychology: Childhood and adolescence* (3rd ed.). Pacific Grove, CA: Brooks/Cole.

Sharpe, D. T. (1974). *The psychology of color and design.* Chicago: Nelson-Hall.

Silverman, I. W., & Ragusa, D. M. (1990). Child and maternal correlates of impulse control in 24-month-old children. *Genetic, Social, and General Psychology Monographs, 116,* 435–473.

Smith, L., Kuhs, T. M., & Ryan, J. M. (1993). *Assessment of student learning in early childhood education.* Columbia, SC: South Carolina Center for Excellence in the Assessment of Student Learning. (ERIC Document Reproduction Service No. ED 358163).

Sovik, N. (1993). Development of children's writing performance: Some educational implications. In A. F. Kalverboer, B. Hopkins, & R. Geuze (Eds.), *Motor development in early and later childhood: Longitudinal approaches* (pp. 229–246). New York: Cambridge University Press.

Stallings, J. A., & Mohlmar, G. G. (1990). Observation techniques. In H. J. Walberg, & G. D. Haertel (Eds.), *The international encyclopedia of educational evaluation* (pp. 639–643). Elmsford, NY: Pergamon.

Stipek, D., Feiler, R., Daniels, D., & Milburn, S. (1995). Effects of differential instructional approaches on young children's achievement and motivation. *Child Development, 66,* 209–223.

Stipek, D., Recchia, S., & McClintic, S. (1992). Self-evaluation in children. *Monographs of the Society for Research in Child Development, 57*(1, Serial No. 226).

Stoddart, T., & Turiel, E. (1985). Children's concepts of cross-gender activities. *Child Development, 56,* 1241–1252.

Taylor, A. P., & Vlastos, G. (1988). *Guidelines for classroom designs.* Corrales, NM: School Zone.

Taylor, B. J. (1995). *A child goes forth: A curriculum guide for preschool children* (8th ed.). Englewood Cliffs, NJ: Prentice-Hall.

Tegano, D. W., Moran, J. D. III, DeLong, A. J., Brickey, J., & Ramassini, K. K. Designing classroom spaces: Making the most of time. *Early Childhood Education Journal, 23,* 35–141.

Torrance, E. P. (1976). Education and creativity. In A. Rothenberg & C. R. Hausman (Eds.), *The creativity question* (pp. 217–227). Durham, NC: Duke University Press.

Torrice, A. F., & Logrippo, R. (1989). *In my room: Designing for and with children.* New York: Ballantine.

Tull, C. Q. (1994). Preserving commitment to teaching and learning. In S. G. Goffin, & D. E. Day (Eds.), *New perspectives in early childhood teacher education: Bringing practitioners into the debate* (pp. 108–119). New York: Teachers College Press.

Veale, A., & Piscitella, B. (1988). *Observation and record keeping in early childhood programs.* Watson,

Australia: Australian Early Childhood Association Resource Booklet No. 1. (ERIC Document Reproduction Service No. ED 373925)

Venolia, C. (1988). *Healing environments.* Berkley, CA: Celestial Arts.

Vergeront, J. (1987). *Places and spaces for preschool and primary (indoors).* Washington, DC: National Association for the Education of Young Children.

Vygotsky, L. S. (1987). *Thinking and speech* (N. Minick, Trans.). New York: Plenum.

Walter, M. B., (1996). *The beneficial use of color and light in child care environments.* Unpublished thesis. San Diego, CA: International Association of Color Consultants.

Watson, D. L., Omark, D. R., Grouell, S. L., & Heller, B. (1981). *Nondiscriminatory assessment: Volume I—practitioner's guide.* San Diego, CA: Los Amigos Research Associates.

Way, L. (1997). Fall conference form. Laguna Niguel, CA: Pacific Preschool.

Wellman, H. M., & Hickling, A. K. (1994). The mind's "I": Children's conception of the mind as an active agent. *Child Development, 65,* 1564–1580.

Wellman, H. M., Hollander, M., & Schult, C. A. (1996). Young children's understanding of thought bubbles and thoughts. *Child Development, 67,* 768–788.

Werner, E. E., & Smith, R. S. (1982). *Vulnerable but invincible: A study of resilient children.* New York: McGraw-Hill.

Wheeler, P., & Haertel, G. D. (1993). *Resource handbook on performance assessment and measurement.* Berkeley, CA: Owl Press.

Witt, J., Heffer, R., & Pheiffer, J. (1990). Structured rating scales: A review of self-report and informant rating processes, procedures, and issues. In C. R. Reynolds & R. W. Kamphaus (Eds.), *Handbook of psychological and educational assessment of children: Personality, behavior, and contest* (pp. 364–394). New York: Guilford.

Wohlfarth, K. (1981). *The effects of color/light changes on severely handicapped children.* Unpublished paper, University of Edmonton, Alberta, Canada: Alberta Education.

Wolfgang, C. H., & Wolfgang, M. E. (1992). *School for young children: Developmentally appropriate practices.* Needham Height, MA: Allyn & Bacon.

Worthham, S. C. (1995). *Measurement and evaluation in early childhood education* (2nd ed.). Englewood Cliffs, NJ: Prentice-Hall.

Wright C., & Fresler, L. (1987). Nurturing creative potential: A model early childhood program. *The Creative Child and Adult Quarterly, 12,* 152–161.

Wright, H. (1960). Observational child study. In P. Mussen (Ed.), *Handbook of research methods in child development* (pp. 71–139). New York: John Wiley.

Yizhong, Z. (1984). Effects of color rendering properties of light sources on visual acuity. *Acta Psychologic Sinica, 16,* 193–203.

York, S. (1991). *Roots and wings: Affirming culture in early childhood programs.* St. Paul, MN: Redleaf Press.

Youngblade, L. M., & Dunn, J. (1995). Individual differences in young children's pretend play with mother and sibling: Links to relationships and understanding of other people's feelings and beliefs. *Child Development, 66,* 1472–1492.

Zahn-Waxler, C., & Smith, K. D. (1992). The development of prosocial behavior. In V. B. Van Hasselt & M. Hersen (Eds.), *Handbook of social development: A lifespan perspective* (pp. 229–256). New York: Plenum.

Index